The Whirling Circles
of Ba Gua Zhang

The Whirling Circles
of Ba Gua Zhang

The Art and Legends of the Eight Trigram Palm

FRANK ALLEN AND TINA CHUNNA ZHANG

BLUE SNAKE BOOKS
BERKELEY, CALIFORNIA

Published by Blue Snake Books
Blue Snake Books books are distributed by
North Atlantic Books
P.O. Box 12327
Berkeley, California 94712

Cover photo by Zhang Weiwei
Cover and book design by Susan Quasha
Printed in the United States of America

The Whirling Circles of Ba Gua Zhang: The Art and Legends of the Eight Trigram Palm is sponsored by the Society for the Study of Native Arts and Sciences, a nonprofit educational corporation whose goals are to develop an educational and crosscultural perspective linking various scientific, social, and artistic fields; to nurture a holistic view of arts, sciences, humanities, and healing; and to publish and distribute literature on the relationship of mind, body, and nature.

PLEASE NOTE: The creators and publishers of this book disclaim any liabilities for loss in connection with following any of the practices, exercises, and advice contained herein. To reduce the chance of injury or any other harm, the reader should consult a professional before undertaking this or any other martial arts, movement, meditative arts, health, or exercise program. The instructions and advice printed in this book are not in any way intended as a substitute for medical, mental, or emotional counseling with a licensed physician or healthcare provider.

Library of Congress Cataloging-in-Publication Data
Allen, Frank.
  The whirling circles of ba gua zhang : the art and legends of the eight
trigram palm / by Frank Allen and Tina Chunna Zhang.
      p. cm.
  Summary: "Relates the history & legends of ba gua zhang, has detailed
basic training, step-by-step practice of both open-hand and weapons forms,
new translations of ba gua zhang classics, and an explanation of circle
walking as a moving exploration of the I Ching"—Provided by publisher.
  ISBN-13: 978-1-58394-189-8 (trade paper)
  ISBN-10: 1-58394-189-4 (trade paper)
  1. Hand-to-hand fighting, Oriental. I. Zhang, Tina Chunna. II. Title.
GV1112.A44 2007
796.815—dc22
                                    2007008184

2 3 4 5 6 7 8 9 UNITED 12 11 10 09 08

Contents

In January, 2007 Frank Allen and Tina Zhang did the Bai Shi Ceremony with and became the formal disciples of cheng style Ba Gua Zhang Grandmaster Liu Jing Ru.

Foreword

Ba gua zhang, a graceful and profound Chinese martial art, has always had a special place in my heart. Its energy, healing abilities, and fighting concepts and techniques are deeply rooted in the Chinese classical philosophy of change, the study and understanding of which has bettered all aspects of my life.

Growing up in Beijing, I experienced kung fu and Chinese folk dancing throughout my youth, which laid the foundation for a lifelong interest in the principles of these arts. The impressive movements of ba gua zhang and the names of its champions, Master Liu Jing Ru and Ge Chun Yan, were always admired by my young heart. But nothing excited and inspired me more than starting ba gua zhang training with Master Frank Allen, who has a true mastery of the art, fully understands all the aspects of the art, and has never stopped learning from other respected masters (making annual winter trips to Beijing for training). His Daoist philosophy, professional manner, endless patience, and "have fun" attitude elevate his teachings far above simple physical training. His deep, detailed, invaluable teaching advanced my knowledge of ba gua zhang quickly, and he helped me pursue my desire to pass on the art by becoming an instructor.

Many students and practitioners have benefited from Frank's 30-plus years of daily practice in ba gua zhang, tai ji quan, and xing yi quan; his dedication and discipline constantly raise the level of his knowledge and skills. He invests large amounts of physical and mental energy into training his students and openly shares his knowledge with them. More importantly, he truly cares about his students and always encourages them to pass on the art to others. It's not surprising that he has so many students around the globe who become dedicated practitioners, fighters, and qualified teachers of ba gua zhang. Through his hard work and that of all other teachers and ba gua zhang practitioners, the art's popularity has greatly increased worldwide.

Ba gua zhang is an art of change; it's about accepting change—which is what life is about—and learning how to deal with it an effective and positive manner. If there is no change, you are not practicing the art of ba gua zhang; if there is no change, you are not living actively. Learning how to handle the changes in our life and make those transitions easier is a valuable skill for anyone to have. I personally prefer a simple approach to life, but life is never a simple thing, and change is always on the way. If you're not afraid of it, change actually makes life more valuable—and a more interesting experience. I love ba gua zhang and its regard for the basics of life, in which nothing is permanent except change. I have learned a lot from practicing the principles of this life art, which enables us to find a way to accept the impermanence in our lives and grow from it; to develop the skill of adjusting to change in a smooth way; and to form positive thoughts in new situations, living a new life with full energy.

The fighting methods of ba gua zhang are equally as great as its other aspects; they are also based on the principles of change. The efficiency of ba gua zhang's palm strikes, along with its internal spiraling power, the uniqueness of its footwork, its employment of the soft and hard aspects of martial techniques, and its distinction as the only Chinese martial art based on circle walking, all brought this relatively young art special consideration among the practitioners of tai ji quan and xing yi quan. The three arts together are recognized as the Chinese internal martial arts. All three are based on internal methods and train internal power, though their forms differ in appearance. All three represent the basic philosophies and sciences of human life in the Chinese tradition. Tai ji quan brings *yin* and *yang* into reality; ba gua zhang makes the eight natural energies connect to human life; xing yi quan perfectly explains the cycles of the five elements.

The art of ba gua zhang, through its nearly two-hundred-year history, has proven its great fitness and internal health benefits; many serious practitioners enjoy long and healthy lives both mentally and physically. The positive medical and therapeutic values of practicing ba gua zhang, made me wonder about its origins and development, its secrets and its essentials. This brought me back to Beijing, China, which is the birthplace of ba gua zhang and still a main gathering place for the best masters of the art. I spent the past six years making eight trips to Beijing to track down the origins and traditions of the art, mostly those of the Cheng Style of ba gua. I met with the masters of ba gua zhang that I could find and contact in Beijing, refining my own practice as I learned from them. (I enjoy absorbing knowledge and guidance from many different masters of ba gua zhang, and I find uncovering the similarities and differences in the art from teacher to teacher a fascinating and worthwhile pursuit. After all, none of those masters would have their great skills without having learned from multiple teachers.) In addition to meeting with the Beijing masters, I was very inspired by my visit to the tomb of ba gua zhang's founder, Dong Hai Chuan. There are many other masters' tombs nearby, making it a very special place—it's as if the famous ba gua zhang masters of the past are still "gathering" together in Beijing.

Dong Hai Chuan was a superior martial artist working in the Emperor's Palace. He was the first person to teach ba gua zhang, and he trained his students according to their specific backgrounds. Because each of his students had already mastered another style of martial arts before they studied ba gua zhang, the art of ba gua zhang branched off into many different styles, each one influenced by the previous martial arts style of its founder. Through the genius work of the second generation of masters, ba gua zhang developed into a high-level internal martial art. Its training methods and fighting techniques have continuously been used by palace guards, soldiers, and martial arts enthusiasts throughout China.

The most popular styles practiced today are Cheng Style, Yin Style, and Liang Style. These styles accurately represent the original shape of the art; however, in the old days, Chinese martial artists were very conservative about teaching their techniques, because these techniques were used to defend their lives and their families and they obviously did not want others to have too much knowledge about their fighting capabilities. Also, most martial artists could not read or write, so the "secrets" of each art were only passed by oral transmission from the master to his disciples, and the arts were practiced privately. Luckily, some of the scholar disciples recorded these valuable principles in writing and, of course, secretly taught them among their inner circle of students.

These behind-closed-doors training methods stayed underground until the third generation of ba gua zhang masters unveiled them in "The Ba Gua Zhang Classics," which presented the thirty-six songs and the forty-eight methods that form the foundation of the art. These are lyrically formatted instructions that Dong Hai Chuan passed on to his disciples orally and the work is the sole classical piece in ba gua zhang study. I have spent countless hours over the years studying and discussing these classics with ba gua zhang masters in Beijing, and it is very interesting and encouraging to know that the classical principles of all styles of ba gua zhang are based on this one work. I have tried to the best of my knowledge and understanding to translate these classics into English in this book. It is my wish to give readers the opportunity to get a taste of the original instructions of ba gua zhang practice.

My passion for the art of ba gua zhang, my memories of all the masters who devoted their lives to developing and spreading the art, and my respect for those who carry on the art and teach it to new generations have inspired me to create this book. I hope it will give readers a starting point from which to develop an interest in ba gua zhang—an interest that will certainly develop into a lifelong practice. I also hope that every practitioner who embarks on this great path finds both happiness and superior health.

—TINA CHUNNA ZHANG

Tina practices ba gua zhang in Tian Tan Park, Beijing.

1

The Origins of Ba Gua Zhang: A Blend of History and Legend

"Legends are apt, however, to be as right in substance as they are wrong in detail."

—RICHARD HENRY TAWNEY

It Began with a Banquet

The palace courtyard was buzzing. The emperor's nephew, Prince Su Wang, had hired a new martial arts instructor for his household and was giving a banquet to commemorate the occasion. The crowd was excited to see the skills of this new martial arts expert and to taste the culinary delights of the prince's kitchen. As the afternoon began, the Muslim Master of the Springy Leg Style, who was named Sha, enthralled the crowd with the speed and strength of his straight-line punches and kicks and impressed them with the quickness of his linear footwork. As they discussed the skills that the new boxing master of Su Wang's household had displayed, the guests eagerly awaited the impending feast.

As the guests settled in for the feast, however, the head chef realized that he had a major problem. He had prepared his most delectable delicacies for the prince's personal table, but now that it was time to serve them, he found that the courtyard pathways to the prince's table were jammed with overenthusiastic guests, and his waiters were unable to reach the prince's table. Compounding the problem was the fact that these dishes had to be served quickly—they were only delicacies for

Prince Su Wang

1

a short amount of time after which they were garbage, and to serve garbage to the emperor's nephew was a quick way to lose one's head. Just as the chef was becoming frantic, the eunuch who handled the lowliest of the kitchen duties announced from the back of the kitchen that he could serve the meal. Normally, the head chef wouldn't allow such a man near his delicacies (or the prince's table), but he had no choice but to take what little opportunity he had been presented with to get the meal served on time—and thereby keep his head firmly attached to his shoulders.

The chef shuddered as the eunuch grabbed a large serving platter in each hand and ran into the courtyard. The large eunuch then leaped up onto the courtyard wall, and while balancing a steaming platter on each of his outstretched palms, ran around the wall until he reached the prince's table. The head of the prince's kitchen closed his eyes when he saw the eunuch actually jump down from the wall onto the prince's table. When he opened them a slit to peek out and see what had happened, he spied the eunuch serving the delicacies to the guests by quickly, lightly, and deftly stepping along the table while handing food to the waiting diners using a seemingly endless variety of twisting and spiraling movements. With each successive visit to the prince's table, there was more food and less space on the table and yet the big eunuch never seemed to slow down and his feet never even nudged a plate, cup, or platter, much less knocked one over. This elegant footwork was augmented by an ever more flamboyant array of twisting and coiling upper-body movements. The prince and his dining guests were thrilled by their waiter's skills and the head chef was overjoyed by the turn of events.

That the skill of this eunuch waiter held martial value did not go unnoticed by Prince Su Wang. When the meal was finished and the remnants of the feast had been cleared away, the prince called upon the eunuch to demonstrate his martial skills for the prince and his guests. The eunuch stepped to the center of the courtyard and began to walk in spiraling and circling patterns at an ever-increasing rate of speed. As he did so, his hands and arms traced coiling and circling, thrusting and cutting, and soaring and floating designs in the air. His legs and torso seemed to never stop twisting this way and then suddenly coiling that way, even when he would drop down into the lowest of stances, shoot a foot high above his head, or stand on a single leg with his other leg held high and bent like the leg of a resting crane. They were movements no one had ever seen before and yet their inherent martial value was undeniable and easily discernable to the trained eye.

Two of the best-trained eyes in the courtyard that day belonged to the new household martial arts instructor, Sha. His were perhaps the only eyes that were not pleased by what they saw. Sha feared that he would be required to share the position of household boxing instructor with the eunuch, and he certainly had no intention of giving up any of his newfound wealth. As the eunuch's demonstration came to an end, the Muslim boxer decided to defend his household position right there and then and challenged the eunuch to fight him on the spot. It turned out to be the worst decision of Sha's life: His first lightning-fast attacks somehow only struck air, as the eunuch seemed to miraculously always be behind him no matter which way Sha turned. Things then went from bad to worse as Sha found not only his punches and kicks in the air but his entire body, too. Of course, being in the air wasn't the problem. The problem occurred when Sha's body slammed into the courtyard after being lifted higher over the eunuch's head and effortlessly tossed a few feet. After taking a few of these embarrassing flights and enduring their pulverizing landings, Sha's entire body ached and his head throbbed. But he was soon relieved of his pain when a huge palm slammed into the side of his head, sending him into blissful unconsciousness. When he awoke, Sha was out of a job, and the eunuch Dong Hai Chuan had become the one and only martial arts instructor for the household of Prince Su Wang.

Of course, Sha did not intend to let this loss of revenue, prestige, and pride go unavenged, so he enlisted the aid of his wife, who was the proud owner of a brace of Western pistols and considered herself an expert in her chosen weapons. Late that night, they crept into Prince Su Wang's compound to the quarters that would have been their new home. They peered into the window and saw the eunuch asleep on the bed. Sha's wife positioned herself at the window and pointed her pistols at the shape on the bed, while her husband quietly slipped through the door of the room and moved toward the bed. In one hand, he held a dagger with a curved blade and a razorlike edge. As Sha paused above the bed with his dagger at the ready, the shape on the bed suddenly exploded upwards in a blur, and Sha flew against the left wall of the

Dong Hai Chuan, the founder of ba gua zhang

room as his blade skittered across the floor to the right. Before Sha's wife could take aim at any definite shape in the room, she felt her forearms clamped in viselike grips as she was hauled through the window and into the room. Her pistols dropped from her now numb hands, and she was unceremoniously tossed on top of her groaning husband's writhing body. The Shas were not complete idiots, so they immediately rolled over onto their hands and knees and began to bang their heads against the floor while begging Dong Hai Chuan to forgive them and accept them as students. Dong knew that these two needed to be closely watched, but he also believed that they might make better allies than enemies, so he pardoned them and accepted them as his students. The Shas proved the sincerity of their apology and their awe of the eunuch by becoming loyal and hard-working students.

The Story of Dong Hai Chuan

Stories and legends abound as to where Dong Hai Chuan came from and how he came to be a eunuch in the kitchen of the emperor's nephew. One of the most popular versions tells of a young thief who was proficient both as a burglar and a highwayman, which gave him both town and country work. Eventually, like most young thieves, he found that he wasn't quite as proficient as he thought, and he was forced to hide in a desolate mountain range to escape capture and execution. Unfamiliar with this new terrain, the young thief found himself lost and hungry, facing death from exposure. Fortunately, a Daoist hermit who lived in a nearby cave stumbled upon the young thief before it was too late. The hermit took the thief to his cave where he nursed the young man back to health.

When the thief was healthy, the hermit taught him a Daoist circle-walking meditation exercise. This practice made the young man much stronger and healthier, which the hermit hoped would keep him from ever again being in danger of dying of exposure while traveling. The young man was still a thief at heart, however, so he simply returned to the outskirts of his hometown of Beijing, where he developed his newfound skills into a unique personal martial art that helped him to become a better thief. This worked well for a while, especially in the burglary business, because his new lightness and techniques allowed him to scale walls and jump into windows. His new martial skills also helped him overpower security guards while plying the highwayman trade.

But eventually this behavior just brought more authorities after the thief, who then tried to escape capture by becoming a monk and hiding out in a monastery. Unfortunately, due to his nature and personality, the thief was quickly expelled from the monastery for practices of intemperance. Realizing that the imperial guards were now looking for him—and when they found him, his head would certainly roll—

the thief decided on one last desperate measure. He knew that he needed a good disguise and that hiding close to one's enemies was the best way not to be discovered. He therefore decided to become a eunuch, which would change his hair patterns and make his facial muscles go slack, giving him a perfect and permanent disguise. Being a eunuch would then allow him to work in the imperial palace and hide right under the noses of the guards. According to this one story, this is how Dong Hai Chuan came to be a eunuch in the palace of Prince Su Wang.

Another version of the story has Dong as a young revolutionary instead of a thief. In this version, he still learns his mysterious circling art from an old Daoist who has just saved the lad from exposure. And again, Dong is hiding from the authorities when he gets lost in the mountains; however, the reason for his trouble with the guards is different. The revolutionary Dong becomes a eunuch to gain entry to the palace in order to gather information for the revolution, the aim of which is to overthrow the Manchu dynasty and restore the previous Chinese dynasty. Once inside the palace, however, Dong finds himself cut off from his revolutionary friends and working as a lowly kitchen helper, a position that will never gain him access to military intelligence. This is where he finds himself on the day of Prince Su Wang's banquet.

Another version of Dong's story cites a romance with a lady of the court as young Dong's reason for hiding from the guards, being lost in the mountains, and subsequently meeting his Daoist teacher. In this version, after training with the Daoist in the mountains, Dong returned to the palace "disguised" as a eunuch so that he could reunite with his ladylove. Yet another telling of the story portrays Dong simply as a traveling martial artist who visits the masters of south China and learns something called Yin and Yang Palms from one of them. Upon his return to the Beijing area in the north, Dong adapts this art into his own circling and spiraling martial system. He then becomes a eunuch or disguises himself as one (which is rather unlikely due to the scrutiny of the Ching court of their eunuch servants), and gets whatever position he can within the court as a way to find out how to become a martial arts instructor there. He finally gets his chance on the day of the banquet.

The legends of Dong Hai Chuan's life after he became the martial arts instructor for Prince Su Wang's household are even more numerous than the stories of how he got there. There are many tales of Dong facing and defeating large groups of opponents while traveling beyond the Great Wall to collect taxes for the prince. One martial arts novel had Dong fighting three-day duels (both ending in draws), not only against Guo Yun Shen, "The Divine Crushing Fist" of xing yi quan, but also against Yang Lu Chan, the founder of Yang Style tai ji quan. There are also tales of Dong putting out the lamps and asking his students to find him in the dark—when they quickly relit the lamps, they found their teacher had attached himself to the ceiling using his lightness skills. Another story tells of how Dong only taught these lightness skills to one student and when the man used these skills to become a cat burglar, Dong had to personally run the him out of Beijing. Finding the incident distasteful, perhaps because it reminded him of his own past, Dong never taught his lightness skills to another student.

A particularly fantastic legend has an old Dong leaning his chair against a brick wall to have a smoke, only to have the wall suddenly collapse on him. His students frantically dug through the bricks, but when they got to the bottom, they didn't find Dong. When they turned around, they found the old master in his chair, leaning against the wall behind them and enjoying his smoke while watching them dig through the bricks. An even older Dong was said to have disappeared out from under a blanket that a student was spreading over the sleeping master, only to be discovered shivering and asleep on a cot on the other side of the room. At the end of his days, Dong is said to have been able to sit with his eyes closed and still correct his students' movement mistakes as they practiced in front of him. According to this legend, Dong didn't let up on his students even after his death. At his funeral, the pallbearers discovered that they couldn't lift the coffin. After they had tried three times, a voice from inside the coffin said, "See, I always told you that not one of you has a tenth of my skill." Then, there was silence, and they were able to lift the coffin on the fourth try.

Unfortunately, there are far fewer historical facts about the life of Dong Hai Chuan than there are stories and legends. Even the tale of the banquet is oral history, which was written down decades after the fact, at best. What consensus exists is that Dong was born in Zhu Jia Wu village, Wen An County, He Bei province, in Northern China in 1797 (although some writers say 1798). Most martial arts historians say that he died in 1882, but some set that date at 1879. There are no hard facts about Dong's early life and he appears in history at mid-life, as a servant of Prince Su Wang. It's true that Dong was a martial arts instructor and tax collector for the prince, and that he taught all of his early students the Luo Han Style of the Shaolin martial arts. It was only after his student Yin Fu had completely absorbed the Luo Han Style that Dong began to teach him and a few others his personal martial art, which was distinguished by its constant twisting and coiling of the body and its circle-walking patterns. Even then, Dong only accepted students into this new art if they were already highly accomplished in other martial arts; he then tailored their lessons in the new art to build on their previous skills, making each student's learning a little different from the others.

Dong called his new martial art ba gua zhang, or Eight Trigram Palm, in recognition of its Daoist roots and its correlations to the Chinese classic *Book of Changes,* the *Yi Jing* (also known as the *I Ching*). He would only reveal to his students that he had learned this art from an old Daoist, whose name he never seemed to remember, and that he had learned it on a mountain, whose name was also seemingly gone from his memory. Some of his students speculated that he learned his art on either Snow Flower Mountain or Nine Flower Mountain, but Dong never confirmed their suspicions. Many guesses were made as to who Dong's master was, but if Dong knew the old man's name, he took it with him to the grave. Professor Kang Ge Wu, who is currently the number-one martial arts scholar in China, has written that Dong must have studied one of the Daoist circle-walking meditation practices and then modified it into a martial art himself, as there is no historical evidence of a martial art resembling ba gua zhang before the time of Dong Hai Chuan.

Professor Kang Ge Wu with the authors at the Beijing Wu Shu Center.

In his old age, Dong retired from his work at the palace and lived with Yin Fu's student, Ma Gui the lumber merchant. His miraculous Eight Trigram Palm martial art did not become well known until after his death, when it was made famous by the exploits and teachings of Dong's two best students, Yin Fu and Cheng Ting Hua.

After the death of Dong Hai Chuan, Yin Fu and his other disciples buried him outside of the Eastern Wall (Dong Zhi Men) of Beijing, northeast of a hazelnut tree. Two years later, Yin Fu set up a memorial tablet for him there. In 1931 Ma Gui, a student of Yin Fu, set up a monument to show his respect for the teacher. Dong's tomb was vandalized and partially destroyed during the Cultural Revolution, but in 1980 Li Zi Ming and 442 ba gua zhang practitioners raised five thousand dollars to move the tomb from Beijing to Wan An Crematory, about sixty-five miles west of Beijing city. Since then, this location has become a famous cemetery and a sacred location for ba gua zhang practitioners, in large part because many third-generation masters of the art are buried near its founder.

The tomb of Li Zi Ming.

The ste-le of Wang Shu Jin.

From left to right: The tombs of Liu Xing Han, Liang Zhen Pu, and Guo Gu Min.

Frank and Tina in front of the tombs of the ba gua zhang masters.

The First Masters: Yin Fu and Cheng Ting Hua

Yin Fu was from a poor family that lived in a poor village. His humble beginnings probably had something to do with his being so underweight that he was known as "Thin Yin" throughout his life. He was born in Zhang Hua village of He Bei province in 1841. When he was in his late teens, droughts and then flooding drove him from his village to seek his fortune in the big city of Beijing.

Beijing was a different world from Zhang Hua village. It was fast, crowded, and cutthroat. If you couldn't make the grade, you would starve to death on the streets—the proof of that was all around you. Yin Fu was tenacious and industrious, so he survived. His first job was as an apprentice to a knife and scissor sharpener. Yin Fu learned quickly and did well at the trade, but his boss went bankrupt. Yin Fu then took his meager savings and invested in a business peddling hot cakes; he became known as the hardest-working hot cake hawker in Beijing. He was always the first person at the bakery in the morning, and he could often be found still selling cakes on the streets of the capital late into the evening.

Just as his finances were coming together, Yin was robbed one early morning on the misty streets of his new home. Needless to say, the young man was not happy about this turn of events. He decreased his work time slightly so that he could resume the practice of "Snake Tongue Boxing," which he had practiced as a boy in Zhang Hua village. Yin Fu knew that he needed more than this art to ensure his personal protection, though he wasn't sure just what he needed. He had become streetwise enough to realize that in Beijing it was often hard to tell the true martial arts masters from the charlatans.

Around this time, Yin Fu began to hear stories of the amazing eunuch that had become the martial arts master to the court of Prince Su Wang. No one was sure how the man did what he did, but they all said that Dong Hai Chuan had almost unbelievable martial skills. Dong taught his students a solid, basic, Luo Han Style Shaolin system, but this system didn't seem to explain the personal abilities of the master. Yin Fu was determined to discover the secrets of Dong Hai Chuan, so he moved his hot cake stand to a street near the palace that he knew Dong frequented. Each time the master passed by, Yin offered him a free cake and tried to exchange pleasantries with him. Dong was standoffish at first, but as time passed, and he saw how humble and hardworking Yin Fu was, he became intrigued and eventually even friendly. Upon finally listening to Yin's story, Dong invited him to become his first student from outside the palace.

On his first day of studying with Dong, Yin found
his suspicious nature rising to the surface. How could
he be sure that Dong wasn't just another martial arts
phony? Yin Fu approached the master, who was in
the act of opening a tobacco pouch. Rudely giving
Dong no time to finish what he was doing, Yin announced his doubts and asked for proof of Dong's
abilities. Dong stretched out his right arm and said,
"Attack me!" Yin launched a lightning-fast punch, but
the moment that his arm made contact with Dong's
arm, his punch was deflected, and Dong's right hand
shot in with a thrust to Yin's mouth, which knocked
out his front teeth. The tobacco pouch was still gently
nestled in Dong's left hand, where it had been at the
onset of the action—not a grain of the precious herb
had been spilled. Yin Fu dropped to the ground and
kowtowed, begging to become Dong's disciple, but
Dong refused.

Yin Fu

By chance, Prince Su Wang had been watching the encounter; the prince came
forward and said that this strange young man intrigued him. He asked Dong to accept
Yin as a student, as a personal favor to him. It was this act of kindness from Prince Su
Wang that allowed Yin Fu to get a second chance at being Dong's student. He would
eventually become the number-one student of Dong Hai Chuan. And for the rest of
his life, Yin Fu commemorated that first encounter by wearing a large, droopy mus-
tache, which covered his upper lip and missing front teeth.

Each afternoon Dong taught a class of guards, eunuchs, and scholars behind the
palace walls, and Yin Fu began his training with Dong by joining this class. It was
1865 and Yin was twenty-four years old. Yin spent the first year proving to Dong
that he was a worthy student—he studied harder and longer than anyone else. He
got to class first and left last. He stood in deeper stances and did more repetitions of
everything than anyone else. Yin Fu finally convinced Dong of his worthiness when
he sold his hot cake business so that he could study full-time with the master.

In early 1866 Prince Su Wang ordered Dong to lead an expedition to the prince's
land holdings in Inner Mongolia. He wanted Dong to stay for a few years and collect all of the back taxes owed to the prince by the locals. It was only logical for Dong
to bring his top student with him to be his assistant. He needed a fighter to watch

his back and a companion to keep him company (the locals would be a bit too rural for a man from the palace). There was nothing holding Yin to the capital now that he had sold his business.

Evidently, the prince was owed a lot of back taxes, because a "few" years turned into nine years. With only each other for company and nothing else to do, Dong and Yin trained incessantly. They had absolutely nothing in common with the local Mongolian folk, who probably hated them anyway (they were, after all, tax collectors from the far-away government in Beijing). Also, because Yin Fu was a married former-merchant and Dong was a eunuch servant from the palace, they found that they had very little in common with each other except for their love of martial arts. Therefore, when they weren't working or sleeping, they were working out. In the first couple of years, Yin Fu completed all of the Luo Han Style Shaolin system that Dong could teach him. Then, out of sheer boredom, Dong made Yin his first student in the Eight Trigram Palm style, ba gua zhang. Yin attacked the study of ba gua zhang furiously, as this was what he had been looking for all along. By the time they returned to Beijing in 1875, Yin Fu had mastered the entire ba gua zhang system, including the qi gong and Daoist meditation aspects of the art. At the time, Dong considered Yin Fu to be his one and only ba gua zhang student. Yin would be able to carry on the art and Dong could go back to teaching his regular Luo Han Style class at the palace.

Upon their return to the capital, Dong helped Yin Fu establish his own martial arts school and returned to his own duties at the palace of Prince Su Wang. Soon thereafter, he met a brash young coal merchant named Ma Wei Qi, and for some reason, Dong took a strong liking to the young man and made him his second student in the art of ba gua zhang.

With his school up and running Yin Fu developed a reputation as the thin, stern, new teacher with the calm and deliberate attitude; it was this reputation that brought martial arts master Yang Chun Feng to Yin Fu's door. Yang's reputation was fading and he hoped to revive it at Yin's expense. Yin confused Yang by politely inviting him in for tea and highly praising Yang's martial reputation. Yang decided that this man was decidedly too calm to actually fight with, so he proposed a martial arts contest instead, in which Yin would demonstrate his famous defensive footwork—by letting Yang attack him while Yin's hands were tied behind his back. Yin agreed to this seemingly ridiculous contest. Yang Chun Feng began with controlled attacks, but as it became apparent that he couldn't get near Yin, his frustration grew. Soon Yang was attacking with full force, yet he couldn't lay a hand on Yin Fu. Yang tried his best technique, the Poison Hand, but even that had no effect. Eventually Yang collapsed from sheer exhaustion. When he could speak again, Yang begged Yin Fu to accept him as a student and Yin agreed.

Yang Chun Feng learned ba gua zhang quickly; unfortunately, good manners and attitude don't always develop at the same rate. One day, Yin Fu's cousin, Shi Ji Dong, came to visit. He told Yin of a fight he had with Yang, in which Shi had been badly beaten; he wanted to know what Yin could do about this. This put Yin in a quandary: Shi was his cousin, but Yang was his disciple and had upheld the honor of Yin's style. Yin found the answer to his dilemma by asking Dong Hai Chuan to accept Shi as his disciple. Dong accepted, which gave Yin's cousin a superior lineage to Yang Chun Feng while assuring that Shi Ji Dong would receive a quality of training with which he could defend himself against almost anyone. In this manner, Shi Ji Dong became Dong Hai Chuan's third ba gua zhang student. Yang ultimately did not become a prominent member of Yin Fu's lineage.

While managing his school, Yin Fu also started a security agency. His students worked for him, guarding the homes and bodies of Beijing's wealthy and elite. The success of the agency hinged on the fact that each and every guard was backed by the reputation of Yin Fu. Each of the guards learned the Luo Han Shaolin system before learning ba gua zhang, which made each of them effective fighters in their own right. When he had become wealthy from his two businesses, Yin Fu began to send food and clothing to his village every month.

Yin Fu's reputation continued to grow. When a local wrestler named Hei Hu (Black Tiger) turned into a bully and a neighborhood nuisance, Yin Fu was called upon to discipline the young man. When they met, Black Tiger was dismayed to find that his opponent was such a thin man. Black Tiger quickly charged Yin and grabbed his arm, anticipating an easy throw, but Yin countered by seizing Black Tiger's wrist between his thumb and index finger, and used his internal strength to execute the Iron Bracelet move. Black Tiger fell to his knees screaming and begged to become Yin Fu's student. Always the gentleman, Yin Fu accepted the young wrestler as his student.

Not long after, a contingent of Yin's students came to him to complain about Black Tiger's behavior. It seemed that Black Tiger was still acting like a bully—just not to Yin Fu. In class the next day, Yin Fu called on Black Tiger to assist him in demonstrating a technique. Black Tiger attacked with lightning speed, but Yin sidestepped (using ba gua zhang footwork) and applied force in the direction of Black Tiger's movement; this move sent Black Tiger through a window with closed shutters, causing a shower of splinters. Black Tiger picked himself up off the ground and climbed back in the window, stating, "The skill of my teacher is very difficult to anticipate!" From that point on, Black Tiger became one of Yin Fu's most humble students.

Yin Fu's first wife had passed away while he was in Mongolia. Confucian etiquette demanded that a widower not remarry, though he could spend time with all the concubines and courtesans that he desired. Yin Fu committed the mortal sin of falling in love with one of his female companions and marrying her. As a eunuch, Dong Hai Chuan had little sympathy for Yin's situation and was appalled at his actions. Dong disowned Yin and stopped speaking to him. Fortunately for Yin, his personal reputation was strong enough that this falling out did not adversely affect his businesses, and he continued to quietly teach and run his security company.

With the loss of Yin Fu as his most honored pupil, Dong Hai Chuan decided to accept new ba gua zhang students. He no longer considered Yin Fu to be in his only lineage holder, and he wanted his teachings to survive, so he took on a number of students. He figured that each student could carry a piece of the knowledge so that together they would preserve the entire art of ba gua zhang. It was a good plan, but it was already 1876 and Dong would die in 1882. Therefore, no student would ever spend as much time with him as Yin Fu.

Dong's first new student was brought to him by Yin Fu's cousin Shi Ji Dong. Although fourth in lineage, Shi's friend was destined to become not only Dong's most popular student, but also the most ardent teacher in the history of ba gua zhang.

Cheng Ting Hua was born in 1848; like Dong and Yin, he was from He Bei province. As a youth, he was fond of martial arts and practiced broadsword and staff. Cheng developed into a short, stocky, powerful young man who was known for his aggressive yet gregarious and friendly nature.

Cheng moved to the capital in his late teens, where he started out as an apprentice to an eyeglass maker. As soon as he moved to Beijing, he began to study the art of Shuai Jiao (Chinese wrestling). Two styles of Shuai Jiao were popular in the capital at the time and Cheng studied both of them. He was good at the powerful and deliberate Mongolian wrestling, but his specialty was Bao Ding, a new, faster style of wrestling. In Bao Ding Style, the object was to explosively throw an opponent on first contact. Cheng felt that this fast style best suited his personality. Within five years, he was a known figure in the Beijing wrestling circles. He was known as "Cobra Cheng," because the cobra was known as the "eyeglass snake" and Cheng made and wore spectacles. Later in life, he would be known as "Invincible Cobra Cheng" because of his many victories. Throughout his life, due to his profession, Cheng was most often referred to simply as "Spectacles Cheng."

When he worked in the eyeglass shop, Cheng sat with one leg crossed over the other, as did his co-workers; however, Cheng, unlike his co-workers, never used a chair! He stood on one leg, and crossed the other leg over the thigh of his standing leg; the thigh of his support leg was always parallel to the floor. This was Cheng's major stance work throughout his life. He later augmented this practice by wearing a ten-pound weighted vest.

When he was twenty-eight years old and had ten years of Shuai Jiao under his belt, Cheng Ting Hua was brought to Dong Hai Chuan by Shi Ji Dong. When they were introduced, Dong asked to see a demonstration of Cheng's wrestling skills. He invited Cheng to attack him several times. Each of Cheng's explosive Bao Ding attacks found only air, as Master Dong was never quite where he seemed to be. Cheng Ting Hua immediately knelt at Dong Hai Chuan's feet and begged to become his disciple. Dong accepted and made Cheng Ting Hua his fourth ba gua zhang student.

Cheng Ting Hua

Cheng worked tirelessly on his ba gua zhang skills. He practiced his striking-palm techniques on a 300-pound basket filled with sand, which he hung from a beam in the back of his shop. Each day he would fill a wooden tub with water and tie a rope to the handle of the tub. He would practice his circling exercises while holding the tub by the rope. He kept the tub on the inside of his circle by switching hands when he performed his change of direction. He would practice this exercise for hours while never spilling a drop of water.

Dong was pleased with Cheng's hard work and the speed with which Cheng learned the foundations of ba gua zhang. Once Cheng had digested the basics of the art, Dong taught him a form of ba gua that best utilized Cheng's wrestling skills. It was quite different from the palm thrust--oriented ba gua of Yin, the kicking style of Shi, or the fist-oriented techniques of "Coal" Ma. Within a relatively short period of time, Cheng was Dong's new Thumb Student—the top student who assisted the master and who usually answered all challenges put forth to the school. Cheng never lost a match while defending the honor of his school. He defeated most of his opponents with his first technique, which was always Single Pounding Palm. This was when he became known as "Invincible Cobra Cheng."

Cheng befriended and became training partners with a number of the leading xing yi quan masters in Beijing. They probably found common ground in the emphasis all their arts placed on an explosive first move. Xing yi, Pao Ting wrestling, and Cheng Style ba gua are all known for employing this tactic, which is designed to end the encounter as soon as it begins. Cheng taught ba gua to Li Cun Yi, Liu De Kuan, and Zhang Zhao Dong. Because they were already recognized martial arts masters when they met Cheng, they were given the lineage of Dong Hai Chuan, even though they actually studied with Cheng. From these friendships began the tradition of students studying both xing yi quan and ba gua zhang.

Because of his connection to xing yi quan, Cheng received a visit from xing yi master Guo Yun Shen, also known as "The Divine Crushing Fist." Guo was the student of the famous xing yi quan master, Li Neng Jan, and a martial arts brother of the famous defender of Chinese martial honor, Che Yi Zhai. He was also a xing yi quan brother to Li Cun Yi and Zhang Zhao Dong. Guo was the master of the Half-Step Crushing Fist, with which he had sent men to heaven, hence the nickname "The Divine Crushing Fist." Guo spent time in prison for killing a highwayman, an incident that occurred when he worked as a bounty hunter. Laws at the time allowed for anything short of murder to capture an outlaw, but the penalties for crossing this line were quite severe. Guo might have been executed if it weren't for the testimony of the security guards whose lives he saved during the encounter with the roadside robber. During his confinement, Guo practiced his Half-Step Crushing Fist while dragging his ball and chain along. By the time he was released from prison, his primary technique was more powerful than ever. He was ready to test his skill against the famous ba gua zhang of Dong Hai Chuan, but first he wanted to speak with Cheng, who he considered to be an impartial ba gua boxer.

Over dinner, Guo expounded his theory that the Half-Step Crushing Fist could defeat anyone under heaven. Cheng begged to differ, saying that ba gua zhang might be of heaven not under it, and that Dong Hai Chuan was not an ordinary man. Guo tried to demonstrate his hand speed, only to find his hand pinned to the table by Cheng's chopsticks. Infuriated, Guo marched outside into Cheng's garden and challenged Cheng to come out and taste the power of his Crushing Fist. As Cheng crossed the threshold, Guo threw the Crushing Fist technique at him, but Cheng was suddenly behind him. Guo wheeled around and again launched an explosive Crushing Fist technique. Cheng effortlessly circled behind him and calmly went back into the house. He then called for Guo to come inside and finish dinner. His rage spent, Guo complied. As they finished dinner, Cheng explained that he didn't really want to fight the famous Guo Yun Shen, but that if he could avoid two of Guo's blows, perhaps Guo shouldn't risk his unbeaten record on Master Dong. Cheng explained that it was only because they were all from He Bei province that he didn't want to see anyone's reputation tarnished. Guo thanked him, rethought his position, and returned quietly to his job as the martial arts master in the household of one of the palace's dukes.

Cheng Ting Hua brought his younger brother, Cheng Dian Hua, to the capital to follow in his footsteps both as an eyeglass maker and a student of ba gua. Together, the Cheng brothers were successful in both endeavors, and every month, they returned to their home village for a few days to bring money to their family and to teach ba gua to the young men of the clan.

As Cheng Ting Hua's seventh year of Ba Gua training neared, Dong Hai Chuan's health became unstable, and he retired from his position at the palace. All of the ba gua students were sorrowful about Dong's health, but they were also apprehensive about who would now lead the school. The obvious choice was Cheng, but before he named a leader, Dong made the unexpected move of reconciling with Yin Fu. It was a tense situation—the old number-one student versus the current number-one student, both of whom expected to become the new leader of the style. In a moment of inspiration, Dong decreed that the capital would have four distinct ba gua zhang schools. His student Song Chang Jun, also known as "Flying Legs Song" and known for his lower-basin stances, would teach ba gua zhang in the northern section of Beijing. Liu De Kuan, also known as "Big Spear Liu," one of Dong's many students from his home province of He Bei, would teach ba gua zhang in the western section of the capital. Yin Fu would remain in the eastern sector of the city, while Cheng Ting Hua would teach in the southern section of Beijing. Dong Hai Chuan got to live out the rest of his days with Yin Fu's well-to-do top student, Ma Gui, the lumber merchant. In time, Cheng's Ba Gua became known as "Southern City Ba Gua," the grappling style, while Yin's Ba Gua was called "Eastern City Ba Gua," the striking style.

Not long after Dong Hai Chuan's death, Yin Fu became involved in a dispute between the city's Eastern Granaries and Western Granaries. The owner of the Eastern Granaries was an old friend of Yin's, so Yin offered to personally protect his friend and his friend's business. The head of security for the Western Granaries decided to visit his eastern counterparts and explain to them how business would now be done in the capital. When he arrived, he found Yin Fu waiting for him; each of Yin's hands had a Ba Gua Needle attached to it, spinning slightly in the palm. These needles were eight-inch spikes attached to rings by swivels. This allowed the needles to be firmly attached to the hands and still be able to spin 360 degrees under the palms and fingers. This type of weapon was a perfect complement to the trapping and counter-thrusting techniques of Yin Fu's Eastern City Ba Gua. Using his needles, Yin Fu was able to trap the man and effortlessly remove him from his friend's establishment.

Cheng Dian Hua

After this confrontation, the head of security for the Western Granaries decided that it was time to enlist some outside help. He hired a local swordsman named Mr. Yang, who had a reputation as a killer. Mr. Yang decided that the most prudent way to approach Yin Fu was with a roadside ambush. But Mr. Yang did not anticipate Yin's reflexes or his ba gua needles. In only two moves, Yin deflected the sword and delivered a counterthrust with a needle, killing Mr. Yang on the spot. When the owners of the Western Granaries heard of this encounter, they immediately negotiated with the Eastern Granaries for a peaceful resolution to the situation. It is safe to assume that the Western Granaries also hired a new security chief.

Dong Hai Chuan's former patron, the Prince Su Wang also heard the story of the granaries dispute. He was so impressed that he called Yin Fu to the palace and gave him Dong's old position of house martial arts instructor, as well as the job of inspecting the Revenue Collection Corps. These were both quite lucrative positions and represented a considerable step up in Yin Fu's career.

Meanwhile, Spectacles Cheng's reputation was growing in the south end of the city. One day, a local strongman nicknamed "Big Han" calmly walked into the courtyard of Cheng Ting Hua's school and announced that no one could match his strength. Cheng stretched out his right arm in the ba gua version of Unbendable Arm and flatly stated, "If you can lift my arm, I'll admit defeat!" Han put his shoulder under Cheng's arm, and with the combined power of his legs and back, he lifted with all his might. Minutes went by, but Cheng's arm didn't move a fraction of an inch. As soon as Cheng detected Han's loss of breath control, Cheng dropped his elbow half an inch, which promptly deposited Big Han onto the ground. Han lay on the ground gasping for breath for many minutes before he gathered enough strength to leave Cheng's school.

On another occasion, Cheng was walking just outside the walls of the Forbidden City when four burly wrestlers suddenly attacked him. They were old training partners of his from his Shuai Jiao days and were jealous of his success. As they approached Spectacles Cheng one by one, he retaliated by effortlessly tossing each wrestler into the Forbidden City's moat.

Cheng Ting Hua was also known for his abilities to make the best of a bad situation and to make a friend out of an enemy. One afternoon, while teaching basic circle walking to his students, Cheng was interrupted by the laughter and heckling of a rather large young man. "This is kung fu? It looks like a blind man feeling fish!" bellowed the young giant. He was known as "Tiger Zhou" and was from the south-end school of Wang Shen. Wang was a famous swordsman, who was called "Fast Broadsword Wang." He had faced ten martial masters of Beijing, and they had all tasted his blade. Reaching the position of Wang's number-one student had made Tiger Zhou quite confident.

"Strong Gentleman, please bestow a lesson upon us," called Cheng. Zhou looked with disdain at the short, middle-aged man with the glasses and arrogantly yelled back, "I'll show you something!" He then walked over to a huge stone plaque, which was half buried in the ground, and with a grunt, he wrapped his arms around it and pushed the thousand-pound stone over. Cheng looked over at Tiger Zhou and said, "You're certainly a strong young fellow, but I don't think that you could push over an old fellow like myself." Zhou couldn't believe his ears. Cheng continued, "If you can push me, I will bow to you as my teacher!" "Today, I accept an old disciple," countered Zhou. The Tiger pushed Cheng three times in rapid succession to no effect. Infuriated, Zhou screamed and attacked Cheng, but the stocky Ba Gua instructor seemed to simply raise his palm and Zhou flew backward and fell to the ground.

Cheng walked over and apologized, "If I, Spectacles Cheng, have hurt you, please forgive me." It was then that Zhou realized just whom he had faced. He felt that Cheng had set him up by not disclosing who he was at the onset of the encounter. He leapt to his feet and ran back to the south-end school of Fast Broadsword Wang to complain.

Upon arriving at his home base, Zhou went into a tirade about his loss of face and how it was his teacher's responsibility to get revenge for him. Wang knew who Spectacles Cheng was and wouldn't even grace his student with a response. A few days later, Tiger Zhou took a few of his martial arts brothers to Cheng's school and invited Cheng to visit their practice hall. Zhou then ran back to tell Wang that Cheng was on the way. Wang was apprehensive and not pleased with Zhou; however, when Cheng arrived, it was obvious he did not come for a fight. Cheng greeted Wang as he would any martial brother—with complete respect. The two of them spent the morning in friendly discussion. When Cheng was preparing to leave, Tiger saw that his plan falling apart and decided to take a last shot at revenge. As Cheng turned to leave, Zhou leapt forward and attempted to stab him in the back. Cheng turned his head quickly, which caused the coin embedded in the end of his braid to strike Zhou in the center of his right eye; Zhou dropped to the ground in a shower of blood. Cheng chuckled coldly and left.

Wang knew that Zhou was in the wrong, but he also felt that he had lost face by allowing his student to be blinded in their training hall. He felt a strong need for revenge, so one evening, he took his broadsword and set out to ambush Cheng. He hid in an alley near Cheng's home and waited for the ba gua master's return. "Cheng will pay for my student's eye with his two legs," Wang thought to himself. When Cheng appeared, Fast Broadsword Wang exploded from the shadows and chopped at his legs, but the sword cut only air. Cheng had disappeared. Suddenly, Wang felt a blow to the back of his right shoulder; his arm went numb and then it filled with pain, causing him to drop his sword. He turned to face a cold-eyed Cheng. "There was no problem between us," admonished Cheng. "The problem was your student, but now I understand why he didn't know how to act. Now, take your broadsword, and go home and behave!"

Wang didn't go home. He traveled China in search of a style that would allow him to defeat Cheng. He found and mastered Buddhist God Warrior's Iron Palm Technique, which strengthened his hands so much that he was able to chop wood with them. After five years of training, he returned to Beijing and found Cheng Ting Hua alone in his shop. Wang attacked immediately and his first chop split Cheng's bench, which exploded in a flurry of flying glass. But Cheng was gone again, and Wang knew he was in trouble again—he turned just in time to see Cheng's famous Single Pounding Palm heading toward his face. It was a potential deathblow, but Cheng recognized Wang at the last moment and pulled the blow by fractions of an inch. In a hurt voice, Cheng asked Wang why his mercy had been repaid with another vicious attack. He explained that he would show Wang mercy one more time, but if it happened again, no strikes would be pulled. Wang had fully expected to die and was amazed by Cheng's kindness. He begged for Cheng's forgiveness. Cheng was happy to oblige, stating that many a friendship began with a fight. From that day on Spectacles Cheng and Fast Broadsword Wang were best friends and all of their students referred to the other teacher as their martial arts uncle.

In 1900 a coalition of martial artists tried to drive the Western and Japanese armies off of Chinese soil during the ill-fated Boxer Rebellion. This revolution was mostly ignored by the top ba gua men, as many of them had connections to the palace that precluded their involvement. Cheng Ting Hua had no intentions of becoming involved in the conflict, but he was a passionate man. Upon returning home one afternoon, he found German troops raping and pillaging in his neighborhood and he lost his temper. He calmly walked into the middle of a group of Germans and drew his elbow knives—single-edged, forearm-length slashing weapons, which were Cheng's specialty. Cheng turned into a whirlwind of bladed death, and the Germans retreated, leaving a dozen of their comrades lifeless in the dirt. Oozing blood from a score of wounds, with his last stand successfully over, Spectacles Cheng sunk down among his defeated foes and joined them in the dust of destiny.

Cheng Ting Hua's eldest son, Cheng You Long, succeeded his father as the leader of their family's ba gua style. He was a stern teacher and an ardent martial arts student; he had studied tai ji quan for twenty years and combined it with his family's art to create Ba Gua Tai Ji.

Thin Yin did not intend to participate in the Boxer Rebellion either, but his lack of intention evaporated when he received a summons to the palace. Upon arriving, Yin Fu was asked if his security agency would protect the Empress Dowager as she made her escape from the capital. This was the most dangerous position of the campaign, but it was an offer that Yin Fu could not refuse. The Empress Dowager had been the patron of the Boxers, but had withdrawn her support under pressure from the foreign powers. Now she was despised by one group and hated by the other. Leaders of both

Cheng You Long

groups felt that their cause would be better off when the Empress Dowager was underground. Being her bodyguard was the last position in the capital that anyone wanted, but she was still the empress—a person that people did not say no to. With the help of his students, Yin Fu safely escorted the Empress Dowager to another palace. It was an act that would bring him undying fame.

The Empress Dowager returned to Beijing in 1901. She often called upon Yin Fu to appear at the palace and demonstrate the art of ba gua zhang for the amusement of her and her friends. For Yin Fu it was relatively easy work, the pay was exceptional, and of course, there was no way to turn it down. He simply made the best of the situation until one day, he got a little carried away and performed his very best set, the Swimming Body Continuous Returning Eight Trigram Palm. The empress was more impressed than ever. She asked Yin Fu if ba gua could be used for more than just fighting. When he answered that it was used to strengthen the body, she wanted to know if it could prolong life. When Yin Fu answered affirmatively, the Empress Dowager announced that she must learn this wonderful art and that she wanted Yin Fu to start instructing her soon. Yin Fu broke out into a cold sweat. The empress was over sixty, overweight, and out of shape. She didn't have the strength, flexibility, or willpower to learn ba gua zhang, but he knew that he couldn't say no to her and live. Yin Fu stalled for time by mumbling something about devising a special "royal study program" for her and left the palace to find a quiet place to think. Yin Fu knew that he couldn't avoid the empress for very long, and the thought of losing his head was beginning to depress him. Yin Fu's depressed state of mind was noticed by Dong Hai Chuan's old friend, Du Bao, the pharmacy eunuch. Upon hearing about and pondering Yin Fu's plight, the clever Du Bao came up with a solution.

The following evening Yin Fu presented himself to the empress at the Hall of the Everlasting Spring. She was not in a good mood and wanted to know why Yin Fu had been obviously avoiding her for some time. Yin Fu explained that when he left the hall the last time, he had realized he had a problem. He knew that the best way to instruct the empress was with a personal and secret ba gua manual of her own, which she could refer to in his absence, thereby allowing her to obtain perfect ba gua zhang. He had wallowed for days in the shame of his own illiteracy until he had remembered Du Bao, his ba gua brother. Du Bao had been a student of Dong Hai Chuan and he was literate; therefore, he was the perfect person to write the manual for the empress. Yin then presented the empress with a thin manuscript containing drawings of very simple martial arts stances with extremely elaborate written explanations. He explained that it was a secret ba gua zhang manuscript meant only for her eyes. The empress was thrilled, and she named her book *The Secret Art of the Palace.* When she could actually perform the stances after a couple of weeks of practice, she was beyond thrilled. She called Yin Fu to the palace and rewarded him with dozens of teals of silver. In this way, Yin Fu fooled the Empress Dowager while increasing his fortune and saving his head.

As Thin Yin spent more of his time guarding the capital's wealthy citizens, many of his regular teaching duties fell to his number-one student, the lumber merchant Ma Gui, who was often call "Wood Ma" because of his profession. (He was also occasionally referred to as "Crab Ma" because of his proficiency at the Revolving Crab Palms technique and "Ma the Dwarf" because of his diminutive size.) He had long been the champion of the Yin Fu's ba gua school and met all challenges for his master. One can imagine the ire of a challenger who has been informed that he will not face "The Thin Man," but the school champion instead. Expecting to fight a giant, young athlete, the challenger would instead find himself squaring off against the only man in the school who was smaller than Thin Yin. Ma the Dwarf never lost a match. Among the men he defeated were: Single Spear Liang Ching, a visiting Russian Strongman, a Japanese martial artist, and Yang Ban Hou's student Huang Chun.

Huang Chun's challenge to the Yin Fu Ba Gua Zhang School is the only time that top-rated internal martial arts masters crossed hands in recorded history. Huang was a guard at the imperial palace and one of the top six practitioners of Yang Style tai ji quan. He was known for his mastery of Peng energy (energy that expands upwards and outwards), which powered the *yang* aspects of his art. As their fight began, Ma Gui drew the tai ji boxer to attack him and then countered with a push that knocked Huang through an open door and into the courtyard. Huang Chun picked himself up, dusted himself off, walked back into the studio, and squared off with Ma the Dwarf for another try. Ma excused himself and circled around in order to shut and bolt the door behind Huang. When Ma had reset himself, Huang attacked him again; the results were pretty much the same, except that this time Huang went through the closed door, shattering the bolt and the hinges. It took Huang a bit longer to get up the second time, and when he finally did, he dusted himself off and went home.

When Dong Hai Chuan was very old, he went to live with Ma after retiring from the palace. Each day Ma would practice in front of Dong, while the old master sat with his eyes closed. Every tiny mistake that Ma made would be corrected verbally by Dong, even though the old master never opened his eyes. Ma Gui's lumber business always supported him well financially and therefore, he never had to accept very many students. Among the lucky few were the bodyguard Liu Zhen Lin, and Lin's student, Liu Hung Chieh.

Besides Ma Gui, the only other student to receive Yin Fu's complete ba gua system was the imperial guard Gong Bao Tian. Gong was originally from Shandong province; he inherited his position in the palace when his older brother retired. Even though he was Yin Fu's other top student, Gong's ba gua was very different from Ma's due to their different body types. Gong was long and lean and he specialized in lose, lightning-fast movements with extremely quick changes. Because of this, he was often referred to as "Monkey Gong." Like Ma, Gong was a master of vital points touching techniques, and like Ma, he was known for his volatile personality. During the Boxer Rebellion, Gong led an imperial army through Fu Jian and Guan Dong provinces. When Yin Fu retired from his work in the palace, Gong Bao Tian left his position as a palace guard and started a bodyguard and security guard service. When he was in his seventies, Gong retired and returned to Shandong, where he lived in a two-story house with no stairs—the old man jumped to reach the second floor.

After he had spent a number of years running his security agency and teaching a core of well-trained fighters, including his famous students Ma Gui and Gong Bao Tian, Thin Yin found that his fame had reached all the way to the Emperor Guang Xu. The emperor called upon Yin Fu to be received in audience and to perform the marvelous art of ba gua zhang for the royal retinue. Yin Fu was not sure why the emperor wanted to observe his martial art, but he was determined to put on an impressive show. When the time to perform arrived, Thin Yin stripped down to his light green pants and began to walk the circle. He moved slowly at first, but his speed soon increased, and he appeared to hover a millimeter above the ground. His hands moved like blowing clouds as he performed the techniques of White Snake Coils Upon Itself, Great Roc Spreads Its Wings, and Purple Swallow Opens the Scissors. He followed these with Unicorn Hands Over the Book, Black Bear Rolls Over on Its Back, and Lion Rolls the Ball. The emperor was duly impressed; he caught Yin Fu by surprise by asking to become his student. Yin Fu had been thinking about training troops or guarding palaces, not giving private lessons to the emperor. He didn't realize that the emperor had decided that the best way to build up China was to first build up himself. When Yin Fu understood the emperor's motives, he dedicated himself to training the Emperor of China in the most efficient way possible.

For the first six months of his training, Emperor Guang Xu was instructed to circle the arhat pine tree in the Imperial Garden three hundred times each morning. Yin would appear each morning to correct the emperor's form and movement. One morning, the emperor was not at the tree when Yin Fu arrived; a servant informed Yin that the emperor had taken the day off to go hunting. Yin Fu left the palace and refused to return until the emperor came to him to apologize and promise that it would never happen again. After all, being the emperor did not excuse Guang Xu from showing his teacher respect. From that day forward, the emperor was a model student and learned the skills of ba gua zhang quite quickly.

In his second year of training, the emperor was drawn into a situation that allowed him to practice his ba gua skills. A young maid, while relieving herself outside late one night was badly frightened by what she claimed to be two white ghosts. The young girl's constitution was so upset by her fright that she died within two days. The emperor had been rather fond of the girl, so he resolved to uncover the mystery of the two white ghosts.

A few nights later, at the stroke of midnight, two white forms appeared in opposite corners of the Imperial Garden. They both approached the Ten Thousand Springs Pavilion, where the two white forms met and combined into one. A black form leapt from a flowerbed toward the white form, which immediately split again into two forms. One white form screamed like a banshee and floated off; the other white form was snagged by the black form, and the two began to grapple. At one point, they separated and both threw off their cloaks (black and white, respectively) to reveal two men, one clad in green and the other in white. The white-clad man attacked with Fierce Tiger Scoops Out a Heart, but the green-clad man deftly circled away. The white fighter attacked with Jade Lady Works the Shuttles, and again, the green man was gone, only to counterattack with Close the Door and Push the Moon, which held the white fighter fast. "Arrest the thief!" called out the green fighter, and suddenly, the garden was filled with imperial guards. The guards' torches revealed the green fighter to be the Emperor Guang Xu. The white form was the eunuch Cui from the imperial kitchen. When questioned, Cui revealed that the other white form was a middle-aged maid, Yu Qiao. The pair had been meeting in the garden to play ghost and to perform whatever lewd and lascivious acts a eunuch and his girlfriend were capable of enjoying. They had frightened the little maid by mistake. Showing that he had no sense of humor—and perhaps why the Republic was soon to replace the monarchy—the Emperor Guang Xu promptly had Cui and Yu Qiao executed.

Late in life, Yin Fu became so wealthy from his involvement with the Royal Palace that he no longer needed to work. The peasant boy from He Bei province was able to spend his final days in leisure.

The *Yin* and *Yang* of Ba Gua Zhang

Thin Yin and Spectacles Cheng represent the origins of the opposite ends of today's ba gua spectrum. One was a thin, stern, deliberate, and poor man, who worked his way to riches through the patient development of his art and reputation. The other was a short and thick, gregarious and friendly, and passionate man, who didn't experience economic troubles once in his life. He simply liked to teach and to fight, and therefore, dedicated his whole life to ba gua zhang and to his honor. Yin developed the Ox Tongue Palm and the striking style of ba gua zhang, while Cheng developed the Dragon Claw Palm and the grappling style of ba gua. Together they fathered most of the styles of ba gua zhang that still exist today.

The philosophy of Daoism states that from nothing came the one thing, the Dao; from the one thing came the two things, *yin* and *yang*; and from the two things came the three things, the lines of the trigrams. From the three things came everything else. In ba gua zhang, from nothing came the one thing: Dong Hai Chuan. From Dong Hai Chuan, came the two things: Thin Yin and Spectacles Cheng. From those two men came the third thing: the mix of Thin Yin's and Spectacles Cheng's teachings. And from those teachings came most of the subsequent schools of ba gua, making Thin Yin and Spectacles Cheng the *yin* and *yang* of ba gua zhang.

The Other Masters

If the art of ba gua zhang was a tree, Dong Hai Chuan would be the trunk, and Yin Fu and Cheng Ting Hua would be the largest of the main branches. There would also be, of course, smaller main branches with smaller branches growing from each of them and even smaller branches sprouting of from each of them. Because Dong Hai Chuan taught each of his students a little differently depending upon their previous martial training, each of the branches of this ba gua tree would have leaves of a slightly different shape and color—and yet they would all grow from the same tree. The development of the smaller branches would often be as colorful as that of their larger siblings.

Ma Wei Qi

Dong Hai Chuan's second ba gua student was a brash, arrogant, and loud young bully, who was only in his early twenties when he began his studies. No one is sure why Dong decided to personally train the young coal merchant. Perhaps Dong was already becoming disenchanted with Yin Fu's seeming lack of social convention and chose Ma Wei Qi as the second student of ba gua zhang simply because his personality and temperament were the exact opposite of Yin Fu's quiet demeanor. Or perhaps the old master just sensed that the young coal peddler would be a diligent student. "Coal Seller Ma" certainly did not let Dong down—he practiced for many hours each day. Every morning, when he arrived at his coal shop by the Eastern Wall, he would shovel a man-sized pile of coal from the bins onto the center of the floor. Then he would circle walk around the pile all day long, practicing his ba gua zhang palm changes to change direction and striking the pile of coal with palm strikes, kicks, and fist techniques (his specialty).

Unfortunately, training with the old master did not improve Coal Seller Ma's personality, and he continued to be the bully of his neighborhood—only now he was more efficient at it! One story illustrating Ma's antisocial behavior tells of how the local acrobatic star, Hu San, was passing by Ma's shop one day when he spied the young merchant practicing his circle walking around the coal pile. The acrobat told Ma that he had noticed the coal seller doing this exercise each morning for a number of days, and he wanted to know why the young man was doing so. Ma replied that it was a martial arts practice, and Hu then made the near-fatal mistake of laughing and saying that Ma's practice certainly didn't seem like a method that could be used to beat people up.

Speaking to Hu as the spider speaks to the fly, Ma replied that he was certainly correct in assuming that circling around coal was no way to defeat anyone—why didn't the acrobat come into the shop and give this ignorant merchant a try? His chest filled with pride, the lithe acrobat entered the coal shop and attempted to throw the burly merchant to the floor, but each time he reached out to grab Ma, his hands found only air. Suddenly, a large fist landed in the middle of his chest and slammed him into the pile of coal. Gasping for air, Hu headed for the door, only to find his path blocked by Ma. Hu collided with the coal pile again, this time from the force of a technique that he never even saw. The next half hour seemed to last for years as that scene repeated itself over and over. Every time Hu tried to leave the shop, he found the burly coal seller blocking his way; somehow, each of his routes ended with him back in pile of coal. When Ma Wei Qi was absolutely sure that Hu San understood that he was a skilled martial artist, he allowed the acrobat to crawl out the door of the shop and limp home. The acrobat was not the only neighbor to suffer this type of fate at the hands of the brash young merchant, which made Ma rather unpopular, even in his own neighborhood.

Coal Seller Ma's antics almost earned him a royal beheading on the day that he was called upon to demonstrate his skills for Prince Su Wang. The prince had heard that Dong Hai Chuan's new student carried a family lineage of a wonderful spear style, so he asked Dong to have Ma show his miraculous Iron Spear techniques at the prince's next public function. When the day arrived, Ma performed at his highest level of ability. It is said that his techniques that day were like the flakes of a snowstorm, falling and rising with the course of the winds. Prince Su Wang was very pleased, and after the performance, he called Ma to him and asked what reward the martial artist would like in payment for entertaining the prince and his guests. As Ma pondered the question, he pulled out a bag of snuff and blew a handful of the tobacco mixture at the prince. Prince Su Wang immediately turned to leave in disgust, and Ma realized the dire consequences of his brash act. The coal merchant flung himself to the floor, banged his head loudly on the tiles, and cried out for the prince's forgiveness. He used the excuse that his martial brothers had dared him to do this outrageous act. Somehow, the prince accepted this apology, but he never called the coal seller to another audience.

As Ma Wei Qi's skills progressed, he began to fight regular challenge matches. The laws of the day stated that if a boxer killed an opponent in a challenge match, he would be charged with murder and executed. On the other hand, if a boxer's opponent made it home after the match and survived for a couple of days, the boxer would no longer be responsible for what happened to his opponent after that time. Therefore, Coal Ma became proficient at using his ba gua fist techniques to injure an opponent's internal organs to the point that they were sure to fail within a few days, but never before Ma's responsibility had lapsed. The young merchant was so good at this that he became known as "Ten Day Ma," because it was said that none of his opponents survived more than ten days after an encounter with him. Ma let it be known that his new motto was: "I hit you once and you are dead!"

This type of behavior does not earn one a lot of friends, though, and eventually Coal Seller Ma managed to make the wrong kind of enemies. Relatives of one of the young boxers who had succumbed to Ma's timed-release punches realized that sending anyone else to fight the burly young boxer would prove fruitless. They instead hired an unscrupulous herbalist to poison Ma. The coal merchant was twenty-nine when he was poisoned to death in 1880. He left behind a very small lineage, mostly because he was too quick to demonstrate the power of his techniques to his students—many of them were injured in the process and failed to complete their training. Few in the capital city of Beijing mourned the passing of the Ba Gua Bully, Ma Wei Qi.

Li Cun Yi

Li Cun Yi was born in Shen County of He Bei province, the same area that Dong Hai Chuan and Cheng Ting Hua came from. From a young age Li liked to practice martial arts, and his first style of choice was Northern Long Fist. He often gathered with friends to practice martial arts; this group included his cousin, Geng Ji Shan, and Li's friends Zhang Zhao Dong and Cheng Ting Hua. When the young men were all in their mid-twenties, Li, Geng, and Zhang began to study xing yi quan from the local master of that style, Liu Qi Lan. Around the same time, Cheng moved to Beijing, where he would meet and study with Dong Hai Chuan. Li

Li Cun Yi

Cun Yi and Cheng Ting Hua remained friends and eventually began to share their martial arts knowledge with each other. Through this exchange, Li became the first xing yi master to cross-train in ba gua zhang, and Cheng became the first ba gua master to absorb the art of xing yi quan. Because Li was a recognized martial arts master when he began to study with Cheng, Cheng Ting Hua brought Li Cun Yi to Dong Hai Chuan, who accepted Li as a formal disciple, even though Li continued to learn the art of ba gua zhang almost exclusively from Cheng. Eventually Li relocated to Tianjin, where he ran a very successful security service along with a martial arts school.

During the Boxer Rebellion, Li became famous for leading his students into battle against the Russian, German, and Japanese troops that besieged Tianjin. One story tells of how years after the revolution, Li went to visit a schoolteacher friend, and when his friend's students realized that the visitor was the famous "Single Saber Li" of the Boxer Rebellion, they begged the old man to demonstrate his skills. The old ba gua master held out his arms and let his long sleeves flow downward. He then announced that any student who could touch his sleeves could consider himself Li's master. The students chased the old master, who simply circled around them until each and every student lay exhausted on the ground. Not a single student had laid a finger on the old man's gown. Such was the ba gua skill of Li Cun Yi. The master died in 1921 at the age of seventy-five.

Li Cun Yi's most knowledgeable student was a peasant from Shandong province named Shang Yun Xiang. Shang moved to Beijing at age eleven, where he first studied Shaolin martial arts. At twenty-one, Shang met Li Cun Yi, who initially told Shang that he was too short to learn Li's style. Later, Li's cousin Geng Ji Shan convinced Li that Shang would be a worthy and loyal student. During his first years of training, Shang was taught the xing yi quan system by Li. Shang would practice the Hsing I Crushing Fist with Chicken Stepping technique during the entire journey to Li's home (a three-mile trip each way).

Li also taught Shang the ba gua zhang of Cheng Ting Hua. Shang Yun Xiang was known for the small limbs and large belly that graced his short frame. The strength of his round belly was legendary; many boxers broke their wrists by trying to punch this *qi*-filled orb. On some occasions, opponents tried to kick Shang's marvelous abdomen, only to get thrown across the room by a simple belly bounce.

Unfortunately, like Coal Seller Ma, Shang's manners left a lot to be desired—he is noted for thrashing a number of Cheng Ting Hua's students while "demonstrating" his skills for them. When Li Cun Yi demanded that Shang bow before Cheng to ask forgiveness for his disrespectful actions, Shang did as he was told; however, when Master Cheng went over to Shang to magnanimously raise him up from his bow, Shang rooted himself to the floor and refused to budge. When Cheng let go of him and stepped back, Shang rose and walked to the door, where he turned and challenged Cheng to "teach" him out in the courtyard. Despite all of his bravado, one a stern look from Li Cun Yi, was all it took for Shang to leave Cheng's school.

Shang was also known for his strict adherence to the principle that martial arts are for fighting. In 1928 he refused a teaching position in the Nanjing Central Martial Arts Academy because he did not like the popularization of martial arts as a health practice. In 1937 Shang died at the age of seventy-three. He did not have many students to carry on his legacy, because he killed a number of them during training by "answering" their questions by "demonstrating" his skills.

Zhang Zhao Dong

Zhang Zhao Dong was born in 1859 to a poor farming family in He Xin county of He Bei province. He left school at a very young age to help his father in the fields. In his spare time, he loved to practice martial arts. In his youth, Zhang studied the Lost Track Style that was very popular in North China at the time. Because his family was very poor, Zhang had many opportunities to observe how the strong and powerful took advantage of the poor and weak and this gave him a lifelong hatred of bullies of all stripes.

When he was in his mid-teens, Zhang began to travel to Shen County, also in He Bei province, in order to study the art of xing yi quan from famed master Liu Chi Lan. Liu had been the student of the most famous of all xing yi teachers, Li Neng Jan, who also taught the infamous xing yi master Guo Yun Shun and Guo's oldest brother, Che Yi Zhai, the master of the Chicken Step and xing yi sword. Shen County was famous for its martial arts--trained bandits and the martial artist bodyguards and cargo guards who kept them at bay. Cheng Ting Hua, Cheng's and Guo's student Sun Lu Tang, and Guo's student Wang Xiang Zhai (the founder of yi quan and da cheng quan) were all also from Shen County. Zhang became part of a xing yi study group at Liu's which included Li Cun Yi, who was yet another Shen County martial arts luminary in the making. Because he was the only member in his teens—the rest of the men were in their twenties—Zhang was known within the group as "Little Brother." Zhang Zhao Dong and Li Cun Yi would be friends for the rest of their lives.

When Zhang Zhao Dong was eighteen, his village experienced a year of bad crops just as the county government decided to raise taxes. When the tax collector came to the village, the local folk wined and dined him as a way to explain the crop failure and their subsequent lack of funds. The tax collector enjoyed the food, drink, and entertainment, and in the morning, he collected the full assessment from each villager and packed up to leave. Zhang Zhao Dong decided that such an injustice could not be perpetrated against his friends and neighbors, so as the tax collector was riding out of town, Zhang ran up to him and pulled the frightened official off of his horse. Zhang pummeled the man senseless and reclaimed the villagers' tax money. Zhang returned all of the money to the people, and this act began his reputation as a defender of the people and the scourge of all bullies, a reputation that would follow him for the remainder of his days.

Two years after the tax-collector incident, the famine in the village became so intense that Zhang could no longer manage to support himself there; he decided to move to the port city of Tianjin. When he arrived in the city, Zhang realized that his farming skills were useless—and his only other abilities were his martial arts. To make a living, he began to perform his martial techniques roadside, collecting coins from the onlookers. He worked alongside other roadside peddlers and came to despise the thugs and thieves who preyed on Zhang's new neighbors. These petty criminals reminded Zhang of the bullying officials that he had hated so much back in his home village, and Zhang began a regular practice of thrashing these thugs whenever they appeared and returning any stolen items to their rightful owners.

Needless to say, Zhang was quite popular with his fellow peddlers, and the local ruffians learned to avoid the large young man with the powerful martial techniques. When Zhang's reputation as the man that criminals feared reached the officials of Tianjin, they promptly hired Zhang Zhao Dong as the city's official "Thief Catcher." This position basically consisted of being a regularly paid bounty hunter. Whenever someone was wanted for committing a crime, Zhang was sent out to bring the culprit into custody. Zhang was very good at this job and it added to his reputation as a defender of the oppressed.

Shortly after Zhang became a thief-catcher, ba gua zhang master Cheng Ting Hua traveled from Beijing to Tianjin. Because they were from the same area and had many mutual friends, it was only natural for the two martial artists to become acquaintances. And while in Tianjin, Cheng Ting Hua encountered a problem that required Zhang's assistance. When Cheng asked Zhang what he would like in return for the favor, Zhang replied that he would like to learn the art of ba gua zhang from Cheng. Cheng not only agreed to teach Zhang, but also to introduce Zhang to Dong Hai Chuan. From that time on, whenever Zhang traveled to Beijing to bring an escaped bandit back to Tianjin, he visited Cheng and received instruction in ba gua zhang. When Zhang was introduced to Dong, the master decided that because of Zhang's existing martial skills and reputation, he would become an official disciple of Dong Hai Chuan. Despite having the honor of being one of Dong's disciples, Zhang probably learned most, if not all, of his ba gua from Cheng Ting Hua, as Dong was quite old at the time of the arrangement and passed away shortly thereafter.

Zhang Zhao Dong

While working as a thief catcher, Zhang liked to perform as many public martial arts demonstrations as possible, because these demonstrations enhanced his reputation and kept the local ruffians in fear of him. A fugitive who was in awe of Zhang's skills and feared his power was much less likely to fight when Zhang tracked him down. In one such demonstration, Zhang grabbed a horse by the throat and strangled it to death with one hand. Zhang's favorite public demonstrations were platform challenge matches against foreign fighters who had belittled their Chinese opponents in the local press. In the two most famous matches of this type, Zhang defeated a Japanese martial artist and bested a visiting German strongman. These matches were especially helpful to Zhang's reputation as a thief catcher, because whenever a Chinese boxer defeated a foreign martial artist, it was big news in the local newspapers and also on the streets—all of the local hooligans, literate or illiterate, would be aware of Zhang's latest exploits.

In 1918 a powerful Russian wrestler/boxer began touring China, and he defeated a variety of opponents in platform challenge matches. In September of that year, he reached Beijing, where he won a series of matches against local Chinese boxers. When news of these matches reached Tianjin, Zhang Zhao Dong was enraged at the loss of face the Chinese martial arts had incurred through these defeats. Zhang was nearly sixty at the time, however, and was no longer the man to meet such a challenge, so he contacted his old friend Li Cun Yi for advice.

The two masters quickly decided to select their top fighting students and head for Beijing to present a formidable challenge to the Russian. Shortly after their arrival in Beijing, Zhang and Li received a visit from a local police official who informed them that the Russian's matches were now "martial exhibitions" and no longer a "martial tournament," which meant that the events were no longer open to all challengers and the fighters from Tianjin were not invited to fight the Russian. After speaking with members of the Beijing martial arts community, Zhang and Li discovered that the Russian had been carefully matched with specific opponents; up until then, he had fought opponents with mid-level skills at best. The local officials were tolerating this arrangement as a method of Chinese and Russian détente. When Zhang realized that the Russian fighter and his people might not be in on the arrangement and might actually think that they were defeating the best China had to offer, he went to meet with them directly. The Russians had confidence in their man and were not pleased to hear of the officials' meddling, so they quickly agreed to an official meeting with Zhang

Han Mu Xia

and Li. At the meeting, both sides agreed that Zhang Zhao Dong's student Han Mu Xia would fight the Russian and that the match would take place in the Russians' hotel suite to avoid interference from the local officials.

A pact was signed at the meeting; it stated that if either fighter was killed, the other fighter and his attendants were not legally responsible for the death. When the match finally took place, the giant Russian immediately grabbed Han's elbow in a viselike grip in preparation for a throw. Han quickly pivoted and stepped in, hooking the Russian's leg with a toe-in step, which upset the Russian's balance. Han simultaneously slapped the Russian's hand off his elbow with an upward rising palm and quickly slammed his other hand into the Russian's ribs with a pounding palm. The leg lock, in conjunction with the pounding palm strike, was enough to send the large man sprawling to the floor. Han wanted to be sure that the Russian stayed where he was, so he glided over to the fallen giant and delivered a heel stomp to his stomach. The Russian promptly regurgitated the remnants of his luncheon banquet and rolled over onto his side with a loud groan. Han wanted to photograph the Russian lying in his vomit, but Li Cun Yi thought that would be in bad taste, so the Chinese boxers simply left the hotel. The Russian later went to the Beijing Martial Arts Association to find Han and congratulate him on his victory. Upon his arrival there, the Russian was advised to leave and avoid Han, who was likely to thrash the Russian again if he saw him. Upon his return home, the Russian fighter told his local newspaper that he never thought he would meet anyone as powerful as Han Mu Xia and that Han had "run over him like an iron ball on an iron track." He said that through this experience he had gained a deep respect for Chinese martial arts. Chinese officials later presented Han with a gold medal and a plaque for having defended the honor of Chinese martial arts.

Unfortunately, Han Mu Xia mostly gained respect for himself from this incident. One day, he went to the place where Zhang Zhao Dong was teaching and asked the old master for a sparring lesson. Apparently, Han had decided that his skills had reached a point that Zhang (at over sixty years old) could no longer handle. As they started to spar, Han pressed the older boxer with continuous attacks. Zhang circled, retreated, and played defense until he realized that his student was there only to show that his skills had progressed beyond Zhang's. With this realization, the old master changed his tactics, and entered right through his student's continuing attack—he sent the younger boxer crashing onto the floor. After the sparring match, Han was no longer associated with Zhang Zhao Dong, and he began to claim that he had learned much of his ba gua zhang from a traveling Daoist named Ying Wen Tian.

Zhang Zhao Dong continued to help organize martial arts events and to demonstrate his open and powerful style of ba gua zhang well into his seventies. In 1940, in his adopted home of Tianjin, Zhang Zhao Dong died of natural causes at the age of eighty-one. His martial arts were carried throughout China and spread to the entire world by his students Jiang Rong Qiao and Wang Shu Jin.

Jiang Rong Qiao

Jiang Rong Qiao was born in 1891 in He Bei province to a family that practiced the martial art Mi Zong Quan. Jiang practiced this style from a very young age and loved it. Mi Zong Quan became Jiang's obsession, and not only did he study it with his family and read all of the available material on the art, but while he was still in his teens, Jiang began to travel as much as possible in search of new Mi Zong Quan teachers. After Jiang became involved in the internal martial arts, he concluded that Mi Zong Quan had originally contained both hard and soft aspects, but the soft aspects had been lost, and so he endeavored to replace them. When he was thirty-eight, Jiang published a book containing all of the knowledge of Mi Zong Quan that he had gathered during his training and his travels. This book is credited with saving the art of Mi Zong Quan from extinction.

Jiang first began to hear of the power and depth of the internal martial arts at age twenty. He went to visit his local internal arts instructor, a man named Chen, who studied and taught tai ji, xing yi, and ba gua simply as a hobby. When Chen explained these arts, Jiang found the theory behind them to be fascinating; he wanted to find out if the theory worked in practice, so he asked Chen to spar with him. Jiang attacked ferociously, but Chen was able to neutralize each of Jiang's techniques, and after a while, Jiang noticed that Chen wasn't even trying to counterattack. Realizing that he was completely outclassed and that his Mi Zong Quan just wouldn't be able to find an answer to Chen's techniques, Jiang resolved to find an internal martial arts instructor to study with.

He began his study of the internal arts with a friend of his, Tang Shi Lin, who taught tai ji quan; soon, he also began to study ba gua and xing yi from Zhang Zhao Dong's student, Yao Fu Chun. Shortly thereafter, Yao introduced Jiang to Zhang Zhao Dong and Jiang became the formal disciple of Zhang. From that time on (around 1911), Jiang traveled often to Tianjin and studied with Zhang until Zhang's death in 1940.

Jiang's professional career was that of a railroad executive, and he used this position to travel extensively throughout China, meeting and exchanging knowledge with as many martial arts experts as possible. When he was thirty-five, Jiang met Wu Dang sword master Li Qing Lin and learned his art. This is how Jiang gained his reputation as a master of the three internal martial arts and the sword.

In 1928 Jiang founded the Committee for Respecting Martial Arts and Enhancing Morals. The committee was based in Shanghai and worked to present practicing Chinese martial arts as a method of strengthening the body and prolonging life to help the Chinese overcome their reputation as the "sick men of Asia." The committee published books on Chinese martial arts, and Jiang began his writing career to help get this information out to the people. Because of his work with the committee, the Central Martial Arts Academy in Nanjing hired Jiang to head their publishing department, as well as to help standardize forms. While at the academy, Jiang also edited their magazine and wrote a couple of articles for each issue.

Jiang Rong Qiao (seated) and Sha Guo Zheng

During the war with Japan, Jiang left Nanjing and taught in southwest China. After the war, he moved to Shanghai, where he spent the remainder of his life organizing his martial arts material and writing new books and articles. Jiang passed away in 1974 at the age of eighty-three. He is recognized as the most important internal martial arts scholar of the first half of the twentieth century. He is also noted for the fact that because he was a scholar, he would only fight an opponent until he had proved his point—he never pursued an encounter to the point of seriously injuring his adversary. Jiang Rong Qiao's top student was Sha Guo Zheng.

Sha Guo Zheng

Sha Guo Zheng was born in 1904 and began to study martial arts at a very young age. When he was sixteen, Sha met his first ba gua teacher, Wang Che Cheng, who had been a student of Dong Hai Chuan's student Wang Li Ti. Wang Che Cheng worked on merchant ships and traveled a lot, so whenever he was in Sha's hometown of Rong Cheng, Sha would study Wang's Lion Style ba gua. When Sha was twenty-two, he moved to Tianjin, where he met Jiang Rong Qiao and became his disciple. He worked hard and learned all the different arts that Jiang had to teach.

While living in Tianjin, Sha became famous for an incident in which he flattened three foreign sailors who were molesting a Chinese woman. At that time, Sha was known as "Small Stone" because although he was short, he was tough as a rock. A poem was written about him saving the woman, which read, "The foreign toads lusting after the swan's flesh; the small stone punishing the foreign devils."

In 1930 Sha moved to Inchon, Korea, to study further with his teacher Wang Che Cheng, who was living there. While living in Inchon, Sha defeated a Japanese soldier in a duel in which Sha had a sword while the Japanese martial artist wielded a long spear. Sha slid inside the spear's length and incapacitated his opponent with a blow to the shoulder. The Japanese soldier recognized that Sha could have easily killed him with that blow and admitted defeat. Sha later led a Chinese resistance against a Japanese incursion into Inchon's Chinatown, which further enhanced his reputation.

When Wang died in 1933, Sha returned to China. In 1946 Sha invited Jiang Rong Qiao to teach in Wuhu, where Sha was living. Jiang came and they lived, trained, and researched martial arts together for six months. Sha said that this was the period in which he greatly widened and deepened his knowledge of the martial arts. In 1949 the government made Sha an official martial arts instructor and he spent the remainder of his life promoting his arts and working to improve the health of the Chinese people. He passed away in 1992 at the age of eighty-eight. Sha Guo Zheng was the ba gua zhang master of Professor Kang Ge Wu, who has become the preeminent martial arts scholar.

Wang Shu Jin

Wang Shu Jin began studying ba gua zhang and xing yi quan from Zhang Zhao Dong in the early 1920s. Wang was in his late teens at the time, living in Tianjin and working as a carpenter. Wang continued to study with Zhang until Zhang's death almost two decades later. Wang Su Jin never managed to become an inner-door student of Zhang Zhao Dong and yet he was destined to spread Zhang's teaching farther than any of the inner-door students, with the exception of Jiang Rong Qiao.

In the early 1930s Wang had the opportunity to study for a year with Zhang's friend Wang Xiang Zhai, the xing yi quan disciple of the famed Guo Yun Shen and founder of da cheng quan, yi quan, and the Universal Post Standing Therapy. Until the end of his days Wang Shu Jin had all of his students arduously practice Wang

Wang Shu Jin

Xiang Zhai's Universal Post Standing Therapy as the foundation of whatever martial art they were learning. When Wang moved to Taiwan, he befriended the Internal Martial Arts master, Chen Pan Ling and became his student. Chen had studied ba gua with Cheng You Lung, xing yi with Li Cun Yi, Yang Style tai ji with Yang Shao Hou (the grandson of the art's founder), and Wu Style tai ji with its founder, Wu Jian Quan. Chen Pan Ling then linked the essences of these arts and created his own Combined Tai Ji Quan Form. Wang Shu Jin helped to spread the knowledge of this form by teaching it to students from many nations. Wang always believed and taught that Zhang Zhao Dong was the most knowledgeable and most powerful of his teachers, and Wang was proud to present Zhang's xing yi and ba gua to the world.

Shortly after starting his studies with Zhang Zhao Dong, Wang developed interests in philosophy and meditation. He became a vegetarian and joined a religious sect known as Yi Guan Dao. The outer teaching of the sect revolved around the belief that Daoism, Buddhism, Confucianism, Islam, and Christianity are all different expressions of the same universal and unwavering Dao, while the esoteric teaching of the sect involved various qi gong and other energy practices. This combination has been known to unsettle the local authorities, so the sect is often partially underground, and their energy practices are kept in the strictest confidence. Wang became a leader of the sect, and it was in this capacity that he was invited to move to and teach in Taiwan in 1948.

Wang Shu Jin moved to Tai Zhong, on the island of Taiwan, which is about eighty miles south of the capital of Taipei, and opened his first martial arts school there during his first year on the island. He also ran a Yi Guan Dao group there and taught at other Yi Guan Dao temples around the island. From the late 1950s to the late 1970s Wang made many extended trips to Japan where he taught both the internal martial arts and the philosophy of Yi Guan Dao.

Wang gained fame worldwide for his ability to absorb blows with his five-foot-eight, nearly three-hundred-pound body. Martial artists from around the world tried their techniques on Wang's rotund frame. American martial arts experts Robert Smith and B. K. Frantzis have both written about having Wang simply stand in front of them and let them rain blows on him until they were sore and tired; all the while, Wang never showed any ill effects from the exercise.

Wang was also known for being able to use Shang Yun Xiang's favorite trick to shatter the wrist of his attacker with a roll of his talented paunch. He especially liked to employ this technique when allowing karate experts in Japan to strike him. This led to a number of challenge matches with karataka, none of which turned out well for the Japanese men. While teaching and demonstrating in Japan, Wang also managed to attract and ultimately impress members of the Western martial arts community who he met there. Perhaps the most skilled of all the Western masters of Japanese martial arts to go up against Wang was Donn Draeger, who once tried to engage in a semi-friendly sparring match with the stocky ba gua zhang master. As Draeger gripped Wang and set himself up to deliver an explosive throw, he was suddenly hit with a powerful palm strike from a hand that had been less than an inch away from his body. The blow caused Draeger to buckle over in pain—and to become the tai ji quan student of Wang Shu Chin. When Wang went to Donn's house to instruct him, the entire house shook from the power of Wang's punching practice; the corpulent Chinese master would end each session by bouncing Draeger off the walls of his own home in what passed for Push Hands practice.

Wang once injured the wrist of Dutch judo champion (and Mas Oyama's best foreign karate disciple) John Bluming when the giant Dutchman tried to blast the ba gua master's bulbous belly. When Robert Smith questioned Bluming about the incident some time later, the Dutch martial arts master remained skeptical of Wang's overall martial skills, noting that even a great defense doesn't make a complete fighter. Smith arranged for another meeting of Wang and Bluming and asked the ba gua master to please demonstrate his corkscrew punch for the Dutchman. Wang gently placed his finger tips on Bluming's solar plexus and then coiled his hand into an upward corkscrew motion. Bluming doubled over in agony and developed a sudden belief in the defensive and offensive balance of Wang Shu Chin's martial arts. Wang was also known to use his belly as an offensive weapon, rendering opponents unconscious by pulling them into him and bouncing them off this awesome orb.

Wang Shu Chin continued to teach in Japan, as well as in Taiwan, until three years before his death in 1981 at the age of seventy-seven. Many of the Western students who studied with Wang in Taiwan first heard of him and perhaps studied with him in Japan, where he had more students than he did in Taiwan. Wang's students

Wang Fu Lai and Huang Jin Sheng carried on his arts after Wang's death. In 1994 Wang Shu Jin's Japanese students raised the funds to have a tablet erected in honor of Wang by Dong Hai Chuan's tomb. Wang wrote two books on his style of ba gua zhang. His book on his Linked Palms set was published privately in 1978, and his book on his Swimming Body Palms set was published in 1980 by the Taiwan Physical Education Division of the Ministry of Education.

Liang Zhen Pu and His Disciples

Liang Zhen Pu was one of the last and youngest students of Dong Hai Chuan. Because Dong was quite old at the time of his learning, Liang also studied ba gua zhang with both Yin Fu and Cheng Ting Hua. Liang's own style of ba gua zhang is clearly a perfect mix of both teachers' styles. Liang was originally from He Bei province. In Beijing, he ran a successful textile appraisal business; because of his success in business, local gangsters picked Liang as a victim for their kidnapping

schemes. When Liang received a ransom note, which informed him that his family had been taken and told him where he should bring money to retrieve them, he was infuriated. He immediately started out for the destination mentioned in the note, but instead of money, he brought with him a three-foot-long bamboo rod. When Liang arrived brandishing a stick—instead of kowtowing with money held over his head—the entire gang armed themselves with knives and swords and attacked the ba gua master. With his circling movements flowing faster than a run-away whirlwind and his bamboo stick cracking like the bolts of the thunder god, Liang promptly thrashed the entire lot of them and brought his family home. Liang's teachings were carried on by his disciples Guo Gu Min and Li Zi Ming.

Liang Zhen Pu

Guo Gu Min came to Beijing from Ji Zhou in He Bei province, where he was born in 1887. At the age of fourteen he became an apprentice in Liang Zhen Pu's clothing shop and began to learn ba gua zhang from Liang. At age twenty, Guo was accepted by Liang as an inner-door disciple, and he began his career as a martial arts instructor. When China was invaded by Japan in 1937, Guo was invited to teach martial arts at the Japanese Embassy. Considering this position to be traitorous, Guo fled to Shandong province where he taught martial arts to the troops of the local warlord, Han Fu Ju. Guo Gu Min was a short and thin man who devoted his whole life to martial arts. He mastered the ba gua teachings of Liang Zhen Pu and exchanged knowledge with other luminaries of the ba gua community, such as Dong Hai Chuan's disciple Liu De Kuan; Yin Fu's fourth son, Yin Yu, the Snake Palm expert; and Yin Fu's best student and school champion, Ma Gui. Guo was also an educated man who spoke English and wrote *The Complete Book of Ba Gua Boxing*, as well

Li Zi Ming

as a text on Ba Gua Rotating Palms. After the Liberation of 1949, Guo spent the remainder of his days teaching ba gua in the parks of Beijing. He passed away in 1968 at the age of eighty-one. In 1984 two of Guo's students had his ashes relocated to the side of Dong Hai Chuan's tomb.

Li Zi Ming began his study of ba gua zhang with Liang Zhen Pu in 1921 when Li was seventeen. He went on to become one of Liang's inner-door disciples and the student who would spread Liang's teachings the widest.

Li also studied ba gua with Li Cun Yi's disciple, the much-feared Shang Yun Xiang and often exchanged ba gua knowledge with his senior brother in the Liang Zhen Pu Style of ba gua, Guo Gu Min. In 1979 Li Zi Ming began to work

to save Dong Hai Chuan's tomb from being completely destroyed by the Cultural Revolution and an upcoming construction project. His fundraising efforts were a success, and on August 2 and 3, 1980 hundreds of ba gua practitioners, under the direction of Li Zi Ming, moved Dong's remains and accompanying stone tablets to their current location in Beijing's Wan'an Public Cemetery.

The authors practice ba gua zhang at the tomb of Dong Hai Chuan.

A year later in 1981, China's first single-style martial arts research association, The Beijing Ba Gua Zhang Research Association, was established, and Li Zi Ming was elected its first president. He held this position until his death in 1993 at the age of ninety-one. Li Zi Ming left many followers behind to carry on his art, along with a textbook detailing his style of ba gua entitled, *Liang Zhen Pu Eight Diagram Palm.* Prominent among Li Zi Ming's successors are Ma Chuan Xu, a later president of research association, and Sui Yuan Jiang, who carries on the traditional ways of teaching in the park and is the instructor of Li Zi Ming's granddaughter. Li Zi Ming was buried near his teacher Liang Zhen Pu's grave at the site of Dong Hai Chuan's tomb, which Li was responsible for preserving.

Gao Yi Sheng

Gao Yi Sheng, also known as Kao I Sheng, was born in Shandong province in 1866 and grew up practicing his family's style of martial arts, Da Hong Quan. When Gao was still a youngster, his family moved to He Bei province, near the city of Tianjin, and Gao began to study Hsing I Chuan from famed master Li Cun Yi. At twenty-six, Gao began to study ba gua zhang from Dong Hai Chuan's disciple, Sung Chang Jung, known as "Flying Legs Sung," master of low-basin circle walking. Sung was the master who, upon Dong's retirement, inherited the northern section of Beijing in which to teach ba gua. He insisted on teaching the techniques to students very slowly, and after three years of study, Gao was still working on the single palm change. When Gao questioned this style of learning Sung told him that there were infinite aspects of ba gua to be gleaned from the single palm change and that Gao needed patience.

Gao Yi Sheng decided that what he really needed was a new ba gua teacher, and shortly after his enlightening conversation with Sung, Gao met Cheng Ting Hua's student, Zhou Yu Xiang. They were both xing yi quan students of Li Cun Yi and were both known for their fighting abilities, so it was only natural that when they met they immediately wanted to test each other's skills. Gao attacked Zhou three times in rapid succession, and Zhou evaded each attack while coming into counterstrike range. Gao immediately recognized Zhou's superior skills and asked to become his student. Zhou was uncomfortable with this arrangement as he and Gao were close in age and in training time, so he brought Gao to Beijing and asked Cheng Ting Hua to accept Gao as a student. Because of this recommendation and Gao's previous martial arts accomplishments, Cheng accepted Gao as an official disciple. Whenever Gao happened to be in Beijing he studied with Cheng, but he actually learned most of his ba gua zhang from Zhou Yu Xiang in Tianjin. After six years of study with Zhou,

Gao had absorbed the eight basic palm changes, with all of their prerequisite training exercises, and five or six weapons sets. This seemed preferable to spending the same amount of time learning the infinitesimal nuances of the single palm change. In fact, Gao now felt ready to begin developing his own version of ba gua zhang.

Gao Yi Sheng

Gao returned to his original home in Shandong province to begin teaching his form of ba gua zhang. At that time, almost every village in the area had its own martial arts training hall and village style, most of which were based on Shaolin styles. The accepted method of opening a school in the area was to defeat one of the prominent teachers. Gao quickly set up a contest with a local named Wu Hui Shan and just as quickly settled the matter, thoroughly convincing Wu which of them was the superior boxer. Gao followed this victory with quick wins of local notables "The Tiger of Da Shan Street" and "Iron Palm Li." These three victories established Gao in the Shandong province martial arts scene and brought him students from all of the villages in that area.

In 1917, when he was about fifty years old, Gao left his home village in Shandong and moved to Yang Village in He Bei province, about ten miles outside of Tianjin. He began to teach his ba gua in Yang Village, returning often to his home village to teach his students there, and started to travel to Tianjin city to also teach there. At the time, Tianjin had a problem with street crime, along with an array of the finest martial arts bodyguards and security guards ever assembled to deal with the rise in crime. In a town where Li Cun Yi and Zhang Zhao Dong were setting the example of what a martial arts guard should be no newcomer went untested. Gao hadn't been there long when Wu Meng Xia, a noted fighter and xing yi and ba gua student of Han Mu Xia (who had stomped the Russian Giant), came calling. Wu was there to test Gao's skills and determine if the Shandong man deserved to become a member of the Tianjin martial arts community. Gao defeated Wu so soundly and thoroughly that Wu Meng Xia not only accepted him, but also bowed to Gao and became his first disciple in Tianjin. Because Wu was a fighter with a big reputation in Tianjin at that time, many students came to study with Gao because he was Wu's teacher.

In 1927 Gao began recording his ba gua system in a handwritten book, which would be finished in 1936 (by which time it would consist of six volumes). Gao allowed many of his students to copy his book by hand, and subsequently, much of his material has appeared in a number of ba gua books over the years. When the Sino-Japanese war began and was then followed by World War II, life in Tianjin became difficult and the foreign concessions were sealed off. In 1942 Gao retired to Yang Village where he only taught a few select students in the back of a medicine shop owned by one of these students. In 1951 Gao Yi Sheng passed away in Yang Village at the age of eighty-five. Gao Yi Sheng left Wu Meng Xia and Liu Feng Cai to carry on his art in Tianjin. His student He Ke Cai brought the art to Hong Kong, and Zhang Jun Feng brought Gao's style of ba gua zhang to the island of Taiwan. Thanks to the efforts of these teachers, the ba gua zhang of Gao Yi Sheng is one of the best-known styles of the art still in existence.

Zhang Jun Feng

Zhang Jun Feng was born in Shandong province and moved to Tianjin in 1911 when he was about ten years old. By age twenty-one, Zhang was a successful manager of an alcohol, groceries, and tobacco wholesale business and had enough spare time to begin seriously studying martial arts. It was about this time in his life that he met the ba gua student of Han Mu Hsia and Gao Yi Sheng, Wu Meng Hsia. Wu introduced Zhang to Gao Yi Sheng and the two men from Shandong province immediately got along well, so Gao accepted Zhang as a student. Because he worked during the day when Gao held public classes, Zhang studied with the master privately both in the morning before work and in the evening after work. Gao also often held classes at Zhang's home, and Zhang became a major supporter of Gao and his teachings. Zhang Jun Feng also spent a lot of practice time sparring with his senior brother in the art, Wu Meng Hsia, and thanks to this and his many hours of private instruction, his progress in ba gua zhang was quite rapid. Over the years, Zhang gained a reputation as a talented martial artist and a fearless fighter. In his mid-thirties, although he was still quite busy with his business, Zhang began to teach ba gua zhang. At one time, he was the chairman of the Tianjin City Martial Arts Association.

In 1948, when the political climate in Tianjin became too unstable, Zhang relocated to Taipei, on the island of Taiwan. The island's economy was in bad shape and this kept Zhang from restarting his wholesale business. Instead, he started a business selling flour and rice, but when he hit a slow sales period, his flour turned moldy and he lost all of his capital and was forced out of business. Luckily for Zhang, he had already gathered

a small core of martial arts students and was able to
make a smooth transition from merchant to martial
arts instructor. While trying to make a go of his rice
and flour business, Zhang had spent his spare time
practicing his martial arts in the Round Mountain
area of northern Taipei. Zhang was a large man and
his power was obvious, so he often drew a crowd
during his practice sessions.

Zhang Jun Feng

This, of course, led to a number of local wor-
thies trying their hand at humiliating the big
mainlander. When Zhang easily defeated each
challenger one by one, it quickly generated interest
in his art. Zhang soon gained a core group of ten
students, three of whom were the Hung brothers.
When Zhang's rice and flour business completely
collapsed in 1950, he began to live part of the time
with his student Huang Er Hou and spend the rest of his time with the Huang family. This was also when he became a full-time martial arts instructor.

Zhang held open classes at various locations around Taipei and would teach his
arts to anyone who was serious and had the tuition. This was an unpopular attitude,
as it was customary in Taipei that Northern Chinese only teach their arts to other
Northern Chinese. Also, most of the mainlanders believed that their stay on the island was temporary. Zhang agreed that they might not be there forever, so he taught
his early students dense sections of information that they could continue to work on
for quite some time in his absence, if he happened to suddenly return to the mainland. Regardless, he continued to teach to everyone whether they were Northern
Chinese, Southern Chinese, or native Taiwanese. Martial arts were his livelihood,
not his hobby, and Zhang had no time for stuffy attitudes. That Zhang taught students who were native to the island, including the Hung brothers, brought a wave
of displeasure from the local Taiwanese martial arts masters, which was even more
intense than the chagrin of the local Northern Chinese. These Taiwanese masters
taught the Southern Shaolin, Monkey, and White Crane styles in secret classes while
carefully guarding their personal techniques. It irked them that someone would
teach martial arts so openly, and it infuriated them that a teacher from Northern
China was teaching his arts to native Taiwanese boxers. A number of these local
masters felt compelled to appear at Zhang's classes and try to provoke or spar with

the outsider. When Zhang not only easily defeated all of them, but also managed to do so without seriously injuring any of them, both his reputation and his student enrollment grew.

After Zhang Jun Feng had been teaching full-time for about a year, he realized that his stay on Taiwan was probably a permanent one, so he began to teach his students at a more measured pace in which they were required to complete each stage fully before moving on to the next level. He also began to teach each of his senior students a bit differently, matching each student's style to their physical and mental capabilities and personality types. It was about this time that his students decided the master was lonely; a number of them chipped in and bought him a bride. The girl was a sixteen-year-old relative of Huang, who Zhang had seen at Huang's house and apparently liked the looks of. Eighteen of Zhang's students, including the three Hung brothers, went to the girl's village to bring her to Zhang, but upon their arrival, they discovered that the men of the village did not agree with the girl's parents and were willing to fight to keep the young girl in the village. They were especially upset that she had been sold to a Northern Chinese man twenty-five years her senior and viewed this as a disgrace to their village.

Unfortunately for the villagers, the money had already exchanged hands and the young martial artists were not going to be denied their rightful due, so they pounded the village men into dust and took the girl to Zhang. The girl, Xu Bao Mei, was extremely angry at having been sold by her parents to an old Chinese man from far away. When she discovered that her new husband required that she practice martial arts every day, she found the situation intolerable. Her only solution was to focus on her martial arts practice in the hopes that she would develop a high level of skill by the time her husband began to age and his skills were diminished. Initially, she dreamed of the time when she could kill Zhang and return to her village, but as the years passed, the dream faded and she became accustomed to her older husband. After they had children, she decided that he was actually a good man and she instead used her martial skills to teach tai ji quan classes and the female students of Zhang's school.

Zhang began teaching in Taipei around the same time that Wang Shu Jin began teaching internal martial arts in Tai Zhong in central Taiwan. The two internal arts teachers were martial arts cousins and were also very closely connected through their involvement in the Yi Guan Dao sect. Wang lived in a particularly volatile area of the island, where challenges from local martial artists were common, so he often invited Zhang to come down and help him handle the local instructors and assorted ruffians. Stories of these encounters were wild and numerous, though unfortunately, none of them seem to have been written down. Besides assisting Wang in the actual confrontations, Zhang was always useful after the scuffle for his bone-setting, massage, and herbal-medicine skills. Wang never pulled his punches in the way that Zhang did and simply went full blast until the affair ended. He was then happy to have Zhang there to repair the damage left in his wake.

When not dealing with local troublemakers, Zhang and Wang would spend their hours together practicing and researching the arts of ba gua zhang and xing yi quan. In the late 1950s the president of Taiwan, Jiang Jie Shi, also known as Chang Kai-shek, invited a number of well-known martial arts masters to put on a demonstration in the presidential building. After the demonstrations, one of Jiang Jie Shi's assistant's came up to Zhang Jun Feng and presented him with a letter of employment and two bolts of fine cloth. Zhang began to give the president private lessons in tai ji quan and qi gong; he had the cloth made into two suits that he only wore when teaching the president. These lessons led to Zhang becoming the martial arts instructor for a number of different government institutions including the Taiwanese Air Force headquarters, Central Investigation Bureau, the Intelligence Bureau, and the Department of Defense.

In the mid-1960s an old friend of Zhang's from the mainland came to visit. When Zhang mentioned that he thought he had become slightly diabetic, the friend produced an herbal formula for diabetes. Zhang took the medicine right away, and that evening he became so ill that he had to be hospitalized. It took a blood transfusion and a number of days of intravenous feeding to save Zhang's life—he never fully recovered his strength. From that time on, his wife taught most of his classes, although he would instruct her each morning in exactly what he wanted her to teach and would often watch classes and yell instructions from his chair. In the early summer of 1974 Zhang told his wife that he had only three days to live. He called each of his children to him and told them his hopes for their future. As he had predicted, he died on the third day.

The best known of Zhang Jun Feng's students was the Taipei martial arts instructor Hong Yi Xiang, also known as Hung I Hsiang. Hong was one of the few students who became a professional martial arts instructor. His school, which he oversaw during the 1970s, had over two hundred students including many foreigners. Hong was a member of a wealthy Taiwanese family who had made their fortune in candles, incense, oils, and fireworks. To protect their wealth, Hong's father, and all of Hong's brothers, studied martial arts. They all learned Shaolin Boxing, but only Hong Yi

Xiang and his brothers Hong Yi Mian and Hong Yi Wen went on to study internal martial arts from Zhang Jun Feng. The three Hong brothers were members of Zhang's first ten-student class, and when Zhang became a full-time teacher, he often lived at the Hong household and instructed the brothers privately. Because he was large and powerful, Hong Yi Xiang's specialty was xing yi quan; his small brother Hong I Mian specialized in ba gua zhang, and the middle-sized Hong Yi Wen studied Zhang's tai ji quan.

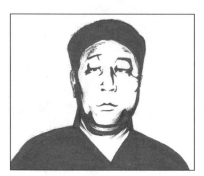

Hong Yi Xiang

And because he was large and strong, Hong Yi Xiang was often chosen to demonstrate techniques with Zhang Jun Feng. He credited this hands-on training for him having absorbed more of Zhang's teaching than most of the students. Hong thought that to actually feel a teacher's power in training was the only way to truly understand the subtle aspects of that teacher's art. At one point in Hong's training, he questioned Zhang as to the martial viability of the internal arts. Zhang suggested that Hong go and challenge the senior students of other teachers and see what happened. Twenty-five fights and twenty-five wins later, Hong was back at Zhang's school and his question had been answered.

Hong went on to be an undefeated fighter both in and out of the studio. He was often involved in street battles in which the use of weapons was common, but the big ba gua xing yi boxer never came home any worse for wear. In the mid-1960s Hong Yi Xiang opened his Tang Shou Tao School in Taipei. Students there began their studies with Shaolin Boxing, followed by xing yi quan, ba gua zhang, and tai ji quan. Hong did not teach the tai ji of Zhang Jun Feng but the same combined-form tai ji of Chen Pan Ling that Wang Shu Chin taught. Senior students often received their hands-on training in late-night private sessions when Hong was feeling his oats and his cups. This rough-and-tumble training produced a number of champions in the All Taiwan Full Contact Tournaments. Hong Yi Xiang passed away in the mid-1990s a little shy of seventy years old, but his martial arts continue to be taught around the world.

Fu Zhen Song

Fu Zhen Song was born in the village of Ma Po in He Nan province in 1872. At that time, many villages hired martial arts instructors to teach the men of the village how to defend their homes and families—police protection was non-existent. When

Fu was a boy, a master from Chen village came to Ma Po and taught Chen Style tai ji, which the young Fu loved and absorbed quickly. When Chen Yan Xi returned to Chen village, the village of Ma Po then hired one of Dong Hai Chuan's ba gua disciples to teach them. Jia Feng Ming traveled from Beijing to Ma Po village and taught the villagers there. His most ardent student in Ma Po was the young Fu Zhen Song, who later became Jia's formal disciple. When he was seventeen and had studied ba gua zhang with Jia for a number of years, Fu moved to Beijing to further his studies in the art. He was in the capital for three years, during which time he studied with both Cheng Ting Hua and Ma Gui. When he had added Ba Gua Push Hands (Rou Shou), free fighting, and ba gua spear to his list of ba gua skills, he returned to his home village of Ma Po.

Fu's reputation continued to expand in his native village. For a while, Ma Po village was continually terrorized by a family of bullies known as Old Tiger Yen and His Boys. This situation went on until the Old Tiger decided one day to show his superiority to the young martial arts instructor in town. He simply walked up to Fu Zhen Song and launched a lightning-fast attack at the young instructor. Fu instinctively deflected the blow with a White Crane Spreads Its Wings technique from his tai ji training and followed that move with a ba gua double palm counterstrike, which left the Old Tiger rolling in the dust of the village square. Tiger Yen was not going to stand for such treatment in his village, so he rushed home to retrieve his staff—and his four sons. The five bullies surrounded Fu and began to menace him with their staffs, but as soon as one of Tiger's boys actually lunged in for an attack, Fu dropped into a low stance and deftly removed the staff from the young tiger's pudgy paws. Fu then exploded into motion—circling, twisting, turning, rising, and dropping down—and with each movement his staff would crash into yet another extended extremity belonging to the Tiger Clan. With their arms and legs swollen masses of blue and purple flesh, Old Tiger Yen and his sons retreated to their home and were never again seen bullying the natives of Ma Po village.

Fu's fame grew even greater when a band of armed marauders invaded his home village and defeated the Ma Po village defense force. Just as the local men were losing their ground, Fu Zhen Song appeared on the scene. As to what happened next, there are a number of different versions. The bandits numbered somewhere between twenty and two hundred. One version has the fight start out with two hundred ruffians, but Fu meets the challenge of a select twenty of them. In that story, Fu faces the twenty men empty-handed, and using his Hurricane Palm, repeatedly knocks down multiple opponents with single blows until the bandit leader is so impressed that he and his men withdraw. In another version, Fu kills the bandit leader and injures twenty of his men using a steel rod; the remaining invaders leave in confusion. In yet a third rendition of the tale, Fu arrives on the scene with a long spear that has an iron shaft. He cuts through the sea of bandits like a whirlwind in a wheat field. Bandits and body parts fly in all directions as Fu dispatches scores of ruffians on his way to the center of the group, where he decapitates the gang leader, thereby scaring the remaining group members into a full retreat. Whatever the details were, it is certain that Fu Zhen Song single-handedly routed a group of bandits who had invaded his home village, and in doing so, he will always be remembered as one who stood against many in an act that echoes throughout eternity.

Fu Zhen Song

In the early 1900s, Fu became a bodyguard and caravan guard for a short while, but he gave it up with the coming of the Boxer Rebellion. He began to spend his time traveling in search of students, training partners, and martial arts teachers and met Sung Wei Yi, a Wu Dang tai ji quan master, who was well known for his Lightning Palm and Rocket Fist techniques. Sung taught these skills to Fu, who later used both techniques in some of the forms that he created.

In 1913 Fu Zhen Song became a martial arts instructor for the Revolutionary Army and held the position for three years. Upon leaving the Revolutionary Army, Fu resumed his life as a traveling martial arts instructor. This is when he met and exchanged knowledge with General Li Jing Lin, known as "Magic Sword Li," and the spearmaster Li Shu Wen, who was nicknamed "God Spear Li." This spearmaster was so skillful that he could kill a fly on a windowpane with the point of his spear without breaking the glass. Using his Four Faced Ba Gua Spear Style, Fu dueled the "God Spear" to a draw, which increased the fame of both masters.

In May of 1928 Fu took part in a national martial arts demonstration in Beijing. The government held a number of martial arts events in a number of different locations that year for the purpose of selecting instructors for the Central and Provincial Martial Arts Academies. Fu Zhen Song's demonstration was so well received that he was awarded the position of Head Ba Gua Zhang Instructor at the Central Martial Arts Academy in Nanjing. Sun Lu Tang was the xing yi master of the academy, and Yang Cheng Fu presided over the tai ji program. Fu became good friends with both of these great masters and spent many hours trading techniques and sharing knowledge with them. He helped Sun with the development of his Sun Style tai ji quan, and when Fu later created his own tai ji style, the influences of both Sun Lu Tang and Yang Cheng Fu could be detected in the form.

Later, the Central Academy sent Fu, along with four other instructors, to teach in Southern China. Fu Zhen Song became the Director of the Provincial Academy in Guangdong. These five instructors of the northern styles of the Chinese martial arts were on a mission to introduce their styles to the south. Needless to say, the local masters of the southern styles were not pleased with this turn of events and challenged the northerners whenever they had the opportunity. After a few years had passed and the southerners had yet to win a single match, they grudgingly gave their due respect to the northern masters and began to refer to them as "The Five Northern Tigers." In this way, the martial arts instructors of the south could give respect to these particular five northern masters without saying that the southern styles were inferior to the northern arts.

Fu Zhen Song spent the remainder of his life living and teaching in Southern China. In the summer of 1953 Fu was asked to demonstrate his Dragon Ba Gua Zhang at a festival in the Cultural Park of Guangzhou. Thousands of spectators turned out to see the old master perform his thrilling art. Fu's demonstration was even better than the crowd had expected, and they were amazed at the speed and power of the eighty-one-year-old master. At the end of his performance, the crowd exploded into a thunderous applause, which moved the old master to return to the stage for an encore. Fu's second set was even faster and stronger than the first one, and at its completion, the crowd erupted into another ovation and screamed for a second encore. Fu returned to the stage, and his third set was a flawless exhibition of power, grace, and speed. As the crowd stood for their third standing ovation, however, the old master realized that he had pushed his octogenarian body too far. Fu Zhen Song collapsed and was taken to a hospital; he passed away that evening. The master who could defeat an entire gang by himself had succumbed to an encore. Fu Zhen Song left his lineage to his eldest son, Fu Yong Hui.

Sun Lu Tang

Fu Zhen Song's friend from the Nan Jing Central Martial Arts Academy, Sun Lu Tang, was born into dire poverty in He Bei province, near the city of Bao Ding. Records from that time were spotty, so this event either happened in 1859 or 1861. Either way, it was the late years of the Qing dynasty, and the farmers of China were laboring under extraordinarily heavy taxes. Sun's father worked from dawn until dusk every day in able to care for his family and pay his exorbitant taxes. When the young Sun Fu Quan, as he was known then, turned seven, his father was having a good year, so he traded a scholar friend farm crops for reading and writing lessons for the young Sun. Sun Fu Quan exhibited a great talent for scholarly learning and this arrangement with the scholar lasted until Sun was nine. That year, disaster struck in the form of a bad crop season, and Sun's father had to sell everything he owned in order to pay his taxes and avoid prison. The strain was too much for the elder Sun, and soon after his farm was sold, he passed away. Sun and his mother were penniless, so she talked a local merchant into taking Sun on as a lower-level servant who would work for only room and board.

The merchant was bad-tempered and abused the boy continually. His son was even worse and made Sun's life miserable. The following year, when Sun was ten years old, he was tending sheep on a hill when he heard the sound of men yelling. Upon closer inspection, he discovered a martial arts class in progress. The boy fell in love with martial arts virtually at first sight and begged the teacher to instruct him. When the old teacher, who was a former Tai Ping rebel, heard Sun's sad story, he accepted him as a student; however, he immediately began to lecture the boy on the evils of revenge and the glory of martial virtue.

Over the next couple of years, Sun spent every free moment studying and practicing the arts of Shao Lin Quan and Ba Ji Quan. When Sun was twelve, the merchant gave all his servants a half-day off on New Year's Day to visit their families. As Sun was about to leave to visit his mother, the merchant's son suddenly confronted him and taunted, "I hear you've been studying martial arts! Well my cousin's Shuai Jiao can still tear you apart!" Then, out came the merchant's twenty-year-old nephew, a brawny wrestler. The older and larger boy immediately grabbed Sun by his best shirt and flung the boy into the air, but Sun rotated as he sailed upwards and was able to land on his feet. Looking down at his torn shirt, the young Sun exploded forward and blasted a Ba Ji fist into the wrestler's solar plexus. The merchant's nephew dropped into the dirt and promptly vomited his New Year's dinner all over himself.

At that moment, the merchant himself appeared with a long pole and attacked Sun while screaming that the ungrateful boy had insulted his family and that he was going to kill him. Sun quickly turned and ran from the area.

The loss of his job, as bad as it had been, was a tragedy for Sun—it left him with no way to support himself or to help his mother.

At first, Sun tried to survive by simply practicing martial arts all day and eating roots and things he could find. But the lifestyle was depressing and the villagers frequently taunted him about how his martial arts were worthless, as he couldn't even earn food with them. One day, in complete despair, the boy hung himself. As luck would have it, a couple of friendly travelers happened upon the scene in time to cut the boy free and save his life. They took him to his mother, and when they heard the plight of the boy and his mother, the kindly strangers brought them to the boy's uncle, who owned a scholar's supply store in Bao Ding. Young Sun went right to work for his uncle making brushes, tending to customers, and keeping the shop as neat as a pin. In his spare time, Sun was free to practice his martial arts, as well as practice reading and writing.

The boy was a great help to his uncle, and after he had been there a few years, his uncle arranged for him to study both with a scholar friend and with another of the uncle's friends, Li Kui Yuen, who was an expert in xing yi quan. For the first year, Li had Sun simply stand in the San Ti stance. Over the course of the second year, Li taught Sun most of the xing yi quan that he knew. Aware that the lad had potential for greatness in the martial arts, Li took Sun to his own xing yi quan teacher, the infamous Divine Crushing Fist, Guo Yun Shen. In 1882 Sun became the formal disciple of Guo and studied xing yi quan with him for the next eight years.

In 1890, when Sun was about thirty, Guo decided that the young man had mastered the art of xing yi quan. Therefore, to further Sun's martial arts education, Guo introduced Sun to his longtime friend, ba gua zhang master Cheng Ting Hua. In his first lesson, Cheng had Sun attack him with his best xing yi offensive techniques. Each of these attacks left Sun facing an empty space, with Cheng behind him. When Sun tried a quick hundred-and-eighty-degree turn to find his target, he ran directly into Cheng's double pounding palms and found himself on the floor. Sun was highly impressed with this technique, but Cheng instructed him to simply start by practicing the circle walking, which is what Sun did for the next year.

Sun couldn't get Cheng's explosive double palm technique out of his mind. So, shortly after he began his circle walking practice, he began to supplement this exercise by practicing palm strikes on some extremely heavy old cannons that he found by the edge of a city wall. He was very happy when he could move the cannons a few inches. When Sun had been at these practices for about a year, a martial artist from Southern China arrived in Beijing (where Sun was studying with Cheng) and challenged the entire Cheng Ting Hua Ba Gua school. Many of Cheng's students went to meet the challenge; the southern boxer soundly defeated them all. As Cheng was preparing to go and fight the southerner himself, Sun suggested that he be allowed to try first. When Cheng protested that Sun only knew the walk, Sun pointed out that it wouldn't make any difference if another member of the school lost before Cheng met the challenge personally. When Sun faced the southern fighter, the man launched himself at Sun with a ferocious attack, but Sun simply circled behind the attack and hit the man with the same double palm strike that he used on the cannons. The southern boxer flew right out the window of the room they were in, and when Cheng saw this, he was so overjoyed that he slapped the bench he was sitting on and broke it in two. The southerner honorably returned to the room and bowed down to Cheng in defeat.

Sun spent the next two years learning Cheng's ba gua, and during that time, he was allowed to copy all of Cheng's ba gua notes (upon which Sun based his later ba gua writings). At the end of three years of training, Cheng announced to Sun that he had learned all of Cheng's ba gua zhang. If Sun wanted to learn the deepest secrets of the art, he would have to travel to the sacred mountains of southwest China to study the teachings of the Daoist masters on the Chinese *Book of Changes,* the *Yi Jing.* Cheng Ting Hua then gave Sun the new name of Lu Tang and sent him on his way.

In 1894 Sun Lu Tang traveled to southwest China, where he studied the *Yi Jing* and Daoist Immortality Skills with the monks of the Wu Dang and E Mei mountains. In 1896 he returned to Bao Ding and began his full-time teaching career. In 1899 Sun moved to Xing Tang, eighty miles from Beijing, where he taught for the next eight years. In 1907 the governor of the northern provinces invited Sun to teach in the northeastern region. Sun took his martial arts younger brother from the Cheng Ting Hua School, Li Wen Biao, with him and moved to Feng Tian, where the two teachers set up shop. While teaching in Feng Tian, Sun was challenged by a local bandit leader known as "Invincible in the Eastern Provinces." When Sun easily defeated the bandit chief, his fame grew greatly in the northeast of China. After three years in Feng Tian, Sun and Li Wen Biao returned to Beijing, where they opened a martial arts school, followed by another school in Tianjin. Traveling between the two schools kept Sun and his young friend very busy.

In 1914 Sun discovered that tai ji quan master Hao Wei Zhen was ill and staying in a cheap hotel in one of the poorer districts of Beijing. Hao had come to town from the countryside to visit his fellow tai ji master Yang Jian Hou but had somehow been unable to locate his friend. The country master was lost, had become ill, and was running out of money. Sun promptly brought the tai ji master to his home and got a doctor to come and help Hao. Hao didn't even know who his benefactor was, but when he regained his health and discovered that his savior was none other than the famous Sun Lu Tang, he was overjoyed. Before leaving for his country home, Hao Wei Zhen taught Sun Lu Tang the art of Hao Style tai ji quan. Sun would later combine Hao style with techniques from his ba gua zhang and xing yi quan training to create Sun Style tai ji quan.

In 1915 Sun published his first book, *A Study of Xing Yi Quan.* This was the first time that someone put in print the idea that ba gua zhang, xing yi quan, and tai ji quan are one family of martial arts. Sun had picked up this concept from Cheng Ting Hua, who had promoted this outlook in the 1880s when he ran a school with Li Cun Yi and Liu De Kuan that offered all three arts. Sun took Cheng's idea a step further and related all three arts to Daoist skills and philosophy. Sun's writing began the popularization of the idea that ba gua, xing yi, and tai ji are the three members of a martial arts grouping known as Nei Jia Quan or Internal Family Martial Arts. Much later, in 1928, the idea took on new dimensions when the Nan Jing Central Martial Arts Academy had divisions of Shaolin and "Wu Dang" arts. The Wu Dang arts were the three arts of Nei Jia Quan, although they had erroneously been linked with an old Ming dynasty art also called Nei Jia Quan and claiming its origins on Wu Dang Mountain, which actually had nothing to do with ba gua, xing yi, or tai ji.

In 1916 Sun completed his second book, *The Study of Ba Gua Boxing,* and three years later, he finished *The Study of Tai Ji Boxing,* which was published in 1921. From 1919 to 1924 Sun Lu Tang taught for the Chinese government, even teaching in the president's palace. In 1921, when Sun was about sixty, a Japanese martial artist arrived in China, sent there by the emperor of Japan to prove the superiority of Japanese martial arts over those of China. The Chinese government asked Sun to defend the honor of their country, and a meeting of the two martial arts masters was held in a government office. The Japanese fighter was surprisingly tall and towered above the five-foot-seven-inch Sun; he also greatly outweighed the Chinese master. Sun offered to lie down with one arm behind his back and allow the Japanese master to apply a lock in that position. As soon as the Japanese warrior began to apply a lock to Sun's arm, Sun lifted his whole body, freeing the arm that was beneath him. With the free hand, he quickly applied a finger strike to the delicate nerves of his opponent's solar plexus. When the Japanese master flinched in pain, Sun pulled his other arm free from the lock and jumped to his feet. Undaunted, the Japanese fighter tried to throw Sun back down, but Sun quickly struck a few more nerve points on his opponent; as the Japanese fighter retreated, Sun threw him into a bookcase, which promptly fell on top of the foreigner. The Japanese fighter's manager cried out that his man was injured, but Sun replied that such a great warrior could obviously take more that and that he was ready for the repost. The Japanese warrior declined to continue and the fame of Sun Lu Tang spread even wider.

In 1923 Sun finished his fourth book, *The Real Meaning of Boxing,* which was published in July of the following year. In 1924 Sun retired from his government post and went to teach in Shan Xi province. The following year, he completed his fifth book, *The Study of Ba Gua Sword,* which was published in 1927. In 1928 Sun Lu Tang became a senior advisor at the Nan Jing Central Martial Arts Academy and also began to teach in Shanghai and Su Zhou; he spent his time traveling between these three teaching assignments. When the Japanese invaded China in 1931, Sun returned to Beijing to live quietly.

Sun Lu Tang

In 1933 Sun announced to his wife and daughter that through his study of the *Yi Jing,* he had discovered that he would die that year. Sun had recently been examined by a German doctor, who proclaimed that Sun had the body of a forty-year-old, so his wife and daughter didn't take his prediction seriously. Sun set about completing the studies of his students and moved back to his home village near Bao Ding. He returned to the home he was born in, and on December 16, he told his wife and daughter that this was his day to die. He refused to dress or eat and spent the day meditating while sitting in a chair. Because Sun had recently lost an old friend, his wife and daughter assumed that he was simply depressed and went about their daily business. Three times that day Sun asked the time, and after the third response, he replied that his time was near, and he said, "Goodbye." The next time his wife and daughter checked on him, they discovered that Sun Lu Tang had quietly passed away sitting in his chair, exactly when he said he would.

It took thirty-five years after Sun Lu Tang's death before his beloved art of ba gua zhang began to be widely known among the martial arts circles of the Western world. For many early ba gua enthusiasts in the West, their interest began with Robert W. Smith's 1967 book, *Pa Kua: Chinese Boxing for Fitness and Self-Defense.* Smith had worked in Taiwan for three years in the early 1960s and studied ba gua with Wang Shu Jin, Paul Kuo, and Hong Yi Xiang while he was there. Around the same time, Lee Ying Arn's English translation of Yen De Hua's 1937 book *Ba Gua Zhang's Martial Applications* was released with its myriad of seemingly cryptic drawings.

In the 1970s John Painter began to publish articles on ba gua in major American martial arts publications. As a boy, Painter had studied a family style of ba gua zhang from his neighbor Frank Li in Texas in the 1950s. Frank Li was from a traditional, security-guard family from southwestern China. Painter's articles were very informative and contained some of the first stories of the early ba gua masters to ever be read by many Western martial artists. In 1975 B. P. Chan arrived in New York City and became the first ba gua teacher there to teach non-Chinese students. He taught a variation of Cheng Style ba gua from the Jiang Rong Qiao School at the William C. C. Chen School of Tai Chi Chuan in New York for the next twenty-seven years. In the early 1980s the ba gua books of Sifu Jerry Alan Johnson, who had studied the art with Chinese masters at home and abroad, began to circulate. These teachers presented the art of ba gua zhang to the West and created the "early days" of the art in America.

2

The Basic Training of Ba Gua Zhang

Perfecting the basic stances of ba gua zhang is one of the most important components of training in the art. The stances are the foundations of the postures, which in turn provide the framework for the individual movements of the art. Training these stances is also a common way to improve body conditioning, to learn proper positioning and footwork, and to start to feel internal energy flow.

Learning ba gua zhang without first going through this important stance training would be like trying to learn English without first learning the alphabet. If you don't learn the correct stances, you will never excel at the art, because you will never obtain a deep understanding of correct internal body mechanics, which is tantamount to reaching a high level of skill in ba gua zhang. The concepts of ba gua zhang movement, internal breathing, and rooting while walking are all contingent on developing skill in the basic stances and basic stepping patterns. This training is also important for the development of flexibility, stability, coordination, speed, and internal strength and breathing—essential elements for good health in general.

There are clear requirements for each stance and each stepping pattern. Correct stance and stepping training can greatly enhance form practice as well as aid the development of fighting skills, which also depend on correct postures, proper alignment, and rooting. Lastly, the discharge of internal power is initiated from a base of solid stance work.

Part One: Basic Stances

Horse Stance: The horse stance is the most basic stance, not only in ba gua zhang, but also in all the Chinese martial arts. In the horse stance, the feet are shoulder-width apart, parallel, and flat on the ground. Body weight is distributed evenly, with fifty percent on each foot. Tuck the tailbone slightly inward, and keep the spine, neck, and head straight. Keep the chest and face relaxed and the mind calm. Your focus is soft and relaxed, too—let the images come into the eyes instead of projecting your vision out onto the images in front of you. Lower your center of gravity by breathing in the abdominal area instead of the upper chest. This breathing is continuous—never hold your breath. The breathing, focus, and state of mind described here are used throughout all ba gua zhang training. To complete the horse stance, gradually settle into a sitting position.

Figure 2-1: Horse Stance

Half Horse Stance: As the name suggests, this is similar to the horse stance. In the half horse stance, however, the body weight is distributed sixty-forty, with sixty percent of the weight on the foot that points forward and forty percent of the weight on the foot that points to the side. Twist your body slightly toward the side that supports less weight.

Figure 2-2: Half Horse Stance

Front Stance: This is often referred to as the bow stance. The front foot bears seventy to eighty percent of the body weight. The bent knee of the front leg should line up with the foot; the knee should never extend over the toes in this stance. The back foot bears only twenty to thirty percent of the body weight. Keep the knee of the back leg relaxed and slightly bent. Square your hips so that they are at right angles to your thighs. (Note that there are variations on the hip positions and on how deeply you bend the front knee, according to the style used and the application of the stance.) Sinking the waist and hips downward and opening up the inner side of the thighs serves to root the feet in order to transfer power from the feet to the legs and then to the whole body. This is a powerful stance for training in releasing energy and a very useful position for fighting.

Figure 2-3: Front Stance

Crouching Stance: Bend one knee and put eighty to ninety percent of your body's weight on it. The other leg steps out to the side with the knee slightly bent and the toes pointing forward. Lower your center of the gravity as much as possible within your own range of strength and flexibility. This stance is for the maximum opening of the hip joints and the Kua (the pelvic area in general, and the inguinal crease in particular), which plays an important role in all Chinese martial arts training. Opening the Kua begins to open the tissues and joints of the body, which is essential to flowing movements and energy discharge as well as to your overall strength and general health. Activating this area is essential for maintaining a good connection between the lower body and upper body. The benefits of long-term flexibility and internal strength will be greatly increased though continuous training in the crouching stance. The ability to fight in lower positions and an increase in leg power and range of motion are also benefits that come from training in this stance.

Figure 2-4: Crouching Stance

Empty Stance: Sink down slightly and sit on the back leg, which bears the entire weight of the body. The front leg does not bear any weight; the toes or the heel of the front foot lightly touch the ground. This stance has its substantial and insubstantial parts clearly defined, and it is used for balance training and as an easy method of shifting weight from one leg to the other.

Figure 2-5: Empty Stance

Crane Stance: This stance trains balance and rooting with a single leg. Bend the knee of the support leg slightly, and sink down into a slight sitting position. The raised leg can be in different positions, depending on which form and application is being used. This stance is a great training method for improving centering and balance.

Figure 2-6: Crane Stance

Cross Leg Stance: Bend both legs and cross one over the other so that your knees touch. The front leg bears most of the body's weight and the heel of the back foot is lifted. Usually, the front leg takes a step to cross over the back leg to form this stance. The cross leg stance is used for training a quick 180-degree turn in a tight space or as a method to use the back foot to step on an opponent's foot.

Figure 2-7: Cross Leg Stance

Back Step Stance: This stance is similar to the cross leg stance in that you cross your legs when you settle into the stance; however, in this one, you always start by taking a step backward, stepping behind the front leg. Note that the knees don't touch as they do in the cross leg stance. The ball of the back foot touches the ground first to form the stance. Most of the body weight is on the front leg, and the body is twisted toward the front leg. Training this stance provides practitioners with a quick way to step backwards and the ability to pivot the feet and turn the body 180 degrees to make continuous strikes.

Figure 2-8: Back Step Stance

Toe-in Step (*Kou Bu*): This is a special way to step, turn, and change direction when walking in ba gua zhang practice. The foot that steps forward has the toes pointing inward (the ankle is turned inward as well) and travels forward on an inward curving path. Touch the ground with the ball of the foot first; the knees are bent and close together. The foot that makes the toe-in step should be close to the other foot, no farther apart than the width of your own foot, and can be closer than that if necessary.

The toe-in step in ba gua zhang is normally performed as a gradual transfer of weight onto that foot, with the knee, hip, and upper body turning in the direction the toes are pointed. The toe-in step allows for a very fast yet stable change of direction. The toe-in step is used in different ways: it can be a hooked step to the back of the opponent's foot to upset his balance or it can be used as a quick change of direction to step in back of the opponent and strike. The toe-in stance internally helps the qi to sink down to lower *dan tian* (the area two inches below the navel and in the center of the body), which is a gathering center for qi as well as the body's optimal center of gravity. Centering your energy at this point helps to stabilize the body and increase your rooting abilities. The toe-in step also helps to open the lower back, which increases your ability to generate power from there.

Figure 2-9: The stance created
by doing a toe-in step

Toe-out Step (*Bai Bu*): The toe-out step is another way to change direction while walking in ba gua zhang, and it's as important as the toe-in step. The foot that steps forward has the toes pointing outward (the ankle is turned outward as well) and travels forward on a curved outward path. Usually, you touch the ground with the ball of the foot first, then slide the foot a little farther, but in some cases, you touch down with the heel first and pivot the foot as it makes contact with the ground (this allows for a wider stance or for the step to be used as a way to hook an opponent's foot). Transfer your weight onto the toe-out foot, with the knee, hip, and upper body following the direction of the toes.

The toe-out step can be big or small and use various angles and distances, depending on the fighter's needs. In fighting, the toe-out step is used to go around an opponent to avoid a direct attack. It can also be used as a curved step with which to change angles, enabling you to get closer to an opponent's centerline to attack. Like the toe-in step, the toe-out step can also simply be used as a very fast way to change direction. Internally, the toe-out step opens the inner side of the hip joint to make energy flow in this specific area.

Figure 2-10: The stance created
by doing a toe-out step

V Stance: This is a special stance often used in ba gua zhang, which is formed by a toe-in step. Both feet pointed inward to form a V; the knees are bent and close together. The body weight is evenly distributed on both legs. In this stance training, you compress and relax all the joints, open the lower back, and sink downward. This stance is for cultivating the spiraling energy that runs from the rooted feet, up the back of the legs, and up through the hips into the spinal cord. The energy continues traveling vertebra by vertebra up to the neck and head, while flowing sideways to the shoulders, through the opened shoulder blades, and out to the arms, palms, and fingertips. The arms are crossed, compressing and gathering energy, as you sink into a sitting position. The *dan tian* should be totally relaxed.

In ba gua zhang form practice, this position is almost always practiced with the weight transferring from one leg to the other because in a martial application, the toe-in step turns into a hooked step used to lock the opponent's foot while simultaneously applying a shoulder strike. This complete posture (upper and lower body) is often called Conceal the Flowers under the Leaves to refer to an important concept in ba gua zhang, which is hiding the compressed and coiled parts of the body before launching a sudden change or release of a hidden palm strike.

Figure 2-11: V Stance

Ba Gua Zhang Scissors Stance: This is the trademark stance of the art of ba gua zhang. In the scissors stance most of the body weight is on the back foot. The center of the crown (also known as the acupuncture point "Bai Hui") should always be in alignment with the bottom of the torso (the acupuncture point "Hui Yin"). You should maintain this straight vertical line, which travels all the way down through your central core, regardless of how many degrees or angles you twist sideways with your waist and hips. The basic requirements of this special ba gua zhang stance are as follows:

Head: Hold your head upright, keeping your chin parallel to the floor.

Chest and back: Relax the chest inward naturally, and keep the back rounded yet straight and natural.

Spine: Keep the spine straight.

Shoulders: Relax and drop the shoulders.

Arms: Extend both arms out from the shoulder blades.

Elbows: Drop the elbows; strength reaches the heels of hands.

Hands and fingers: Spread the thumb outward, and extend the forefinger. Keep the forefinger relaxed. This forms the Tiger's Mouth, the slightly rounded space between the thumb and forefinger.

Waist: The waist is relaxed and coils to the side.

Hips: The hips are in a sitting position, while the buttocks are tilted slightly forward. The sacrum is flat and there is a crease where the legs join the torso.

Legs, knees, and feet: The legs are close together, and the knees are bent and over the feet. The feet are flat on the ground—you should have the sensation of being rooted to the earth.

Breathing: Breathe into the *dan tian*. Never hold your breath.

Mind: You should be calm, clear-headed, and aware of your entire environment.

This posture is also called Green Dragon Stretches Its Claws. It is an opposite posture to Conceal the Flowers under the Leaves (the V stance). It opens up the body and spirals energy from the bottom of the back foot up to the palms. For instance, as the left foot steps back, the energy goes up through (and slightly inward) to the bent knee, travels to the hip, and with a coiling and twisting movement, then travels through the entire body to the extended right arm and palm. The front foot (in this case, the right foot) also channels energy up through the leg and slightly inward to the bent knee, then to the hip and through the twisted body to the extended left arm and palm. Make sure the hips remain in a sitting position, connecting the lower body and the upper body, and that they do not collapse (i.e., drop too low, arching the sacrum backward) during the twisting motion. The scissors stance posture contains all the elements of ba gua zhang. The spiraling energy developed from this primary posture is associated with all the powers in nature and gives practitioners a foundation that can be extended, changed, or transferred to any ba gua technique.

Figure 2-12: Ba Gua Zhang
Scissors Stance

Basic stance training cultivates qi. It gets rid off stiffness and hardness in the body, building the softness that helps you to easily gather qi and channel it throughout the body. When qi can flow through an entire body that has flexible joints and can hold all of the positions that transmit power throughout the body and into the mind and the willpower, then internal power can begin to develop properly. But the stances are just the first step and only one aspect of training. No one can have internal power just by standing still—you have to move!

Ba Gua Zhang Palm Positions

A wide variety of palm positions are used in stance training as well as in the movement practices of ba gua zhang. Below is a sampling of these palm positions along with some of their corresponding stances. In all of these palm positions, the hands are stretched, open, and never tensed.

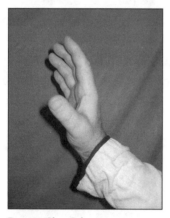

Dragon Claw Palm

Thrusting Palm

Pushing Out Palm

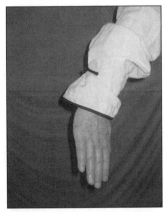

Yin Palm

Yang Palm

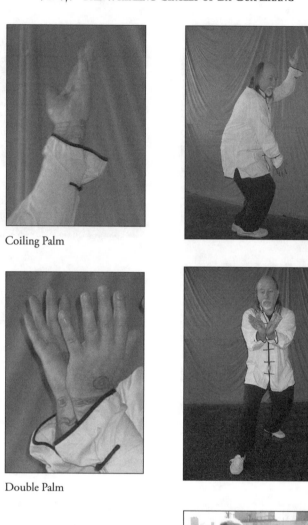

Coiling Palm

Double Palm

Fist Palm

Part Two: Circle Walking

Circle walking requires the practitioner to bring into play all of the various aspects of his or her art. The walking and changing of direction itself develops the quick evasive footwork that made ba gua zhang famous as the martial system of the Beijing bodyguards in the late 1800s and early 1900s. This footwork, combined with the art's alert and aware mindset, allowed the early ba gua zhang boxers to contend with several opponents at once while staying aware of their clients' well-being. The twisting, spiraling, and coiling movements of the arms, torso, and legs can become an astonishing array of hand, elbow, shoulder, hip, knee, and foot strikes, as well as the mechanics of powerful throws and standing joint locks. These same movements create a wide variety of defensive blocks, deflections, and evasive techniques that work in conjunction with the stepping patterns to create an impenetrable defense. Walking the Straight Mud Tread Step discussed below develops a front kick that steps forward instead of snapping back. Toe-in steps can become roundhouse kicks and sweeps. Toe-out steps can be raised to become outward crescent kicks. All of the effective fighting techniques of ba gua zhang are contained within the circle-walking and change-of-direction practices.

Ba gua zhang training also enables the practitioner to execute this footwork with stability, firmness, and nimbleness while maintaining flexibility and liveliness in the waist, arms, and palms. Ba gua zhang trains the body to follow the steps—the palms follow the body through the changes and the whole body twists together like a rope—enabling practitioners to put all the strength of their bodies into every technique, an important aspect in the development of internal power.

Circle walking is also a very useful tool for the development of one's health. The constant shifting of the body weight regulates blood flow and helps regulate blood pressure. The squeezing and stretching of the lymph nodes in the inguinal crease (where the legs join the body), along with the constant twisting of the muscles, increases the flow of lymphatic fluid, thereby strengthening the immune system. Maintaining proper alignments, and compressing and expanding the joints, helps keep the skeletal system healthy. The constant relaxation of the mind and body increases stamina and awareness.

The act of continuous walking or continuous changing, and the practice of making smooth transitions through those changes without interrupting the qi flow, actually increase one's energy in a unique way. The continuous walking and non-stop movement make it so easy to feel an energy boost in the very first stages of walking training that newcomers are often very encouraged by it and continue their practice. Circle walking easily opens a door for internal martial arts practitioners to have an awareness of their body's energy systems. The practice of circle walking will open up all the energy passages and channels in the body while increasing the amount of qi. This practice also heightens one's sensitivity, which allows him or her to feel, and thereby control, this life-force energy.

Mud Tread Walking Step

Tang Ni Bu or Mud Tread Step is one of the common ba gua zhang stepping techniques. This excellent training step is practiced in many schools, and it is the foundation step in most of the ba gua zhang styles, including Cheng Style. Step forward with the lead foot, touching the ground with the ball of the foot first and then sliding (extending) the foot slightly forward, like you're walking on thin ice. The foot is never lifted very high from the ground, hence its name—it's like walking through mud. Each step should slide as far forward as you can comfortably cover while still being able to move quickly; this is different than taking as series of small steps, which simply resembles running fast.

The Mud Tread Step trains balance and stability while in motion and increases energy flow from the bottom of the foot up through the entire body. When you start to take a step with the left foot, keep your body weight on your right foot (Figure 2-13). Then, shift your weight to your left foot and pick up your right foot, keeping it parallel with the ground (Figure 2-14). The right foot then takes a step out, with ball of the foot touching the ground first, while the weight is on the left foot (Figure 2-15).

Figure 2-13   Figure 2-14   Figure 2-15

To walk in a circle, the inner foot (the foot closest to the center of the circle) always travels straight forward. The outer foot (the one farther from the center of the circle) always travels on a slightly curved, inward path toward the center of circle to direct the circular pattern (Figures 2-16, 2-17, and 2-18).

| Figure 2-16 | Figure 2-17 | Figure 2-18 |

Changing Directions while Walking

The change of direction is the most important component of basic circle walking; it manifests the concept of the endless changes of the *Yi Jing* (*I Ching*). During the changes of direction, the techniques of ba gua zhang are usually shifted from one side to the other. The walking and change of direction practices will increase coordination, internal and external integration, and functional flexibility of the ankles and legs, which eventually develops into beautiful footwork, the power source of ba gua zhang.

Beyond simply paying attention to the footwork itself, you must train the torso to be relaxed, coiled, and coordinated with the footwork and palm positions, and you must train the mind to be focused and to direct the changes. In a basic stance, your body weight is on the right foot (Figure 2-19). Step forward with right foot toe-in, and as the weight is transferring from the left foot to the right foot, start turning your body in the opposite direction (Figure 2-20). When the weight is completely transferred to your right foot, take a step out with your left foot (Figure 2-21). Shift your weight onto your left foot and step your right foot forward until it is close to the left foot and parallel to the ground (Figure 2-22). Then, step forward once again with the right foot (Figure 2-23).

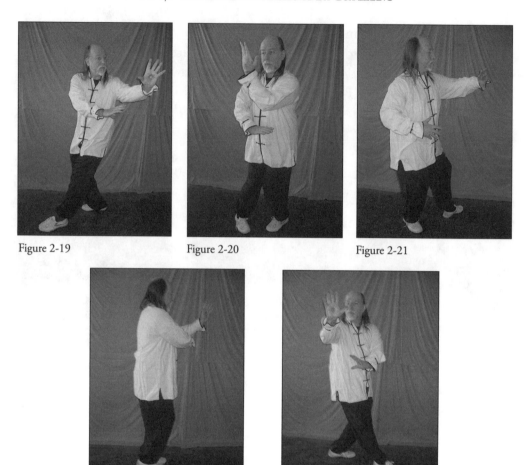

Figure 2-19   Figure 2-20   Figure 2-21

Figure 2-22   Figure 2-23

Eight Palm Postures Circle Walking: A Unique Practice of Ba Gua Zhang

Circle walking is the most important step of training in ba gua zhang. Traditionally, students would dedicate three years to mastering the essentials of holding these eight different postures while walking in a circle. In today's high-speed world, however, very few instructors still have the option of teaching in this manner. Instead, the eight postures circle walking practice actually becomes a lifelong practice that benefits all levels of ba gua zhang practitioners.

Each of the eight basic palm postures has its own unique and simple palm technique—the foundations upon which complicated ba gua zhang fighting skills are built. Some schools of ba gua zhang believe that each posture has a different energy related to one of the eight trigrams of the *Yi Jing*. Within the different schools of ba gua zhang, you'll find many similarities between the eight basic postures taught by each, as well as many variations on the basic postures. Here we would like to introduce the eight postures of the Cheng Style, a widely recognized and respected branch of the art. The trademark of Cheng Style circle walking is the coiling and spiraling movement of the body as you walk in a circle using Mud Tread steps. This set has been passed down by Cheng Style Grandmaster Liu Jing Ru.

Posture 1: Fierce Tiger Comes Out of the Mountain. Both palms press down in front of the *dan tian.* Twist your waist toward the center of the circle (Figure 2-24).

Figure 2-24

Figure 2-25

Posture 2: Big Roc Spreads Out Its Wings. Open both arms and lift them up to about ear level (palms facing upward). Twist the waist toward to the center of the circle (Figure 2-25).

Posture 3: Lion Opens Its Mouth. In this posture, one palm is curved and held up in front of the head, and the other palm is thrust toward the center of the circle. Twist the waist toward to the center of the circle (Figure 2-26).

Figure 2-26

Posture 4: White Ape Presents the Peach. Bring both palm heels together and keep your palms open; both elbows coil inward in front of the body. Twist the waist toward to the center of the circle (Figure 2-27).

Figure 2-27

Posture 5: Embrace the Moon. Let both elbows drop, and push the palms outward in front of the chest. Twist the waist toward the center of the circle (Figure 2-28).

Figure 2-28

Posture 6: Black Bear Stretches Out Its Paw. Thrust the front palm forward, keeping the wrist bent backward. Press the rear palm downward next to the front arm's elbow—it should point in the same direction as the front palm. Twist the waist toward to the center of the circle (Figure 2-29).

Figure 2-29

Posture 7: Pointing to Heaven and Plunging to Earth. One arm coils upward and outward, pointing to the sky; the other arm coils downward and inward, pointing to the ground. Twist the waist toward the center of the circle (Figure 2-30).

Figure 2-30

Posture 8: Green Dragon Stretches Its Claws. This is the signature posture of ba gua zhang. The front arm extends forward from the shoulder and the palm opens. The rear arm is bent at the elbow and the palm is held close to and below the leading arm's elbow. Both palms point toward the center of the circle, and the waist also twists toward to the center of the circle (Figure 2-31).

The way to train these basic palm postures is to simply walk in a circle while holding each posture one at the time, changing directions to walk in both directions of the circle. This practice can be done in different sequences and for different lengths of time.

Figure 2-31

Circle Walking

Circle Walking Tips

Below are a few tips to help you walk correctly and gain the maximum benefits of this training.

Twisting, Coiling, and Turning

It is extremely important that the twisting and coiling of the whole body is maintained while walking in a circle, specifically in the torso area, which provides the connection between the upper body and lower body. The hips do not twist with the waist; they turn only slightly, mostly staying in line with the feet and knees for rooting and positioning. The spiral energy of the whole body is maintained by physically coiling from the bottom of the feet, through the energy channels up to the ankles, legs, hips, waist, chest, shoulders, and arms, and on to the hands, neck, and head. This always keeps you centered, in line with your central core.

Proper twisting of the waist increases the flexibility and looseness needed to create ba gua zhang's spiraling energy power; it also builds coordination, which allows you to move your whole body in one piece and with full force. Lastly, it helps you understand the principle of internal power, which comes from the legs, is directed by the waist, and is expressed in the hands.

External and Internal Aspects

The practice of walking in a circle gives you both external and internal exercise at the same time. Externally, circle walking exercises all of the body's muscles and connective tissues. It increases coordination, helps develop speed, and has an aerobic effect, which helps develop stamina. Internally, the postures help relax the mind, release the tension in the internal organs, open the energy channels, and sharpen your focus (by drawing your focus to the center of the circle while walking). The result can be even better than a full therapeutic massage, because the flow of energy and movement comes from your own qi and helps to increase your energy naturally. Physicians can only help heal specific issues, but you can increase your own natural energy, which will make a positive change inside you—a greater harmony between body and mind can create long-term good health.

Mind and Body Integrations

The mind plays a very important part in circle walking. The mind should remain calm, relaxed, and focused on the center of the circle. The physical movements of circle walking and changing direction will naturally move your energies to where they need to go as the mind becomes more aware of how energy naturally moves the body and reminds the body of many important points of practice. An increased energy flow throughout the entire body (including the brain) integrates power and grace, which will make the circle walking smooth, continuous, and high quality. The longer you train in circle walking, the quicker brain response will develop. Eventually, a strong relationship will be established, bringing together the coordination of the mind, the contractions and relaxations of the muscles, the movements of the body, and the functions of the internal organs. Even when encountering a sudden attack (emotional or physical), the highly coordinated body and mind will not collapse—one should be flexible to change and take control of every situation.

Rooting

Rooting is also built up through circle walking. Rooting allows the energy to sink down to the lower *dan tian,* makes the mind calm, and makes the body feel centered and perfectly balanced. Without a rooted step to support every move, ba gua zhang training is an empty and bad dance form, and its practitioners will never be free from stiff, off-balance steps that cause movements or fighting techniques to fail. Real ba gua zhang skill is based on stepping training and body training, not just the shape of the palms or the strength of the strikes. Well-rooted steps reduce or completely negate the need to think about footwork when concentrating on other aspects of the art such as fighting. If practiced diligently, the footwork of circle walking will eventually become second nature, at which time you are absolutely free to place your foot anywhere. If your steps are not well rooted, you will not be able to hold simple postures long enough and strong enough for them to be of any real benefit. Also, if your steps are not rooted, you won't be able to move and strike at the same time with decent power, because you won't be connected to the ground and will, therefore, be easily thrown off-balance.

Rooting in ba gua zhang is different than rooting in other internal martial arts. Whereas tai ji quan and xing yi quan require you to root deeply like a tree, due to its constant motion, the rooting of ba gua zhang is more akin to that of strawberries, which have shallow roots that travel along with the vine. The rooting of ba gua circle walking draws energy up the rear weighted leg, across the hips, and down the light forward leg. As your weight shifts forward, this energy travels underground and back up your rear leg to complete a circle. When the rear foot rises from the ground and begins to step forward, energy then begins to shoot up the other leg—which has just become the rear weighted leg—and the process starts all over again. Walking very slowly and focusing on feeling the energy in your legs helps to develop this rooting process. When this circle of energy is firmly inserted into your circle walking technique, you'll begin to project energy forward from the tips of your toes. This energy travels in front of the walker and under the earth, creating the sensation of being pulled from underground, to stabilize the structure of the walker.

Rooting also requires proper alignment that harmonizes the shoulders and hips, elbows and knees, hands and feet. These six harmonies compose a functional position that helps the body remain centered.

Speed and the Three Basins

Within the same walking techniques, the center of gravity can be lowered to different levels. "San Pan," in Chinese, describes three different levels of bending the knees to make three different height positions in walking. The most commonly practiced is the middle level, in which the center of the gravity drops to a comfortable level and the knees are slightly bent. The upper level is used simply as an introduction for new practitioners or for practice among the aged and students who have physical limitations. Walking at the lowest level is a great exercise used by advanced practitioners to strengthen their legs, but it is somewhat impractical in actual combat situations. These three levels in ba gua zhang are often referred to as the three basins.

The length of the steps in circle walking can be long or short, depending on your physical condition and training experience. However, the walking step should be long enough to get your speed up and yet short enough to not loose your rooting and stability. The speed of walking can vary depending on what the practice is focusing on at that moment. It is important to remember that speed is increased by lowering the hips and lengthening the steps and not by running.

A slower speed of walking is used by beginners or for meditation purposes; a normal speed of walking is used for energy building; and the fast, strong, and extra light steps of high-speed circle walking are used for fighting, power training, or getting a high-energy boost. The most balanced training regimen incorporates them all—intermediate and advanced practitioners should practice each version in both directions. In the beginning, circle walking should be done slowly and precisely to learn how to relax and concentrate, keeping in mind, of course, that relaxation and concentration are training methods, not the goal of ba gua zhang. Slow-motion training is a way to build a smooth, balanced walking style, but understand that rooting, speed, and lightness of step are important parts of developing the hidden power behind the postures.

The other hidden powers of ba gua zhang derive from the momentum of continuously flowing, full-body movement and from the proper discharge of energy directed by an intense focus of the mind and a pumping of the body's fluids. For the discharge of power, the primary fluid pump is that of the synovial fluid of the joints. This flow is achieved by the expansion and compression of the joints. In the expansion phase, every place in the body where two or more bones come together is slightly spread apart. This involves slightly stretching the ligaments, which connect bone to bone, as well as the tendons, which connect muscle to bone and other muscles. When the ligaments are stretched, the synovial membrane that encapsulates the joint is also stretched. When stretched, this membrane secretes synovial fluid into the joints, which allows the skeleton to work like a well-oiled machine and vastly improves skeletal health. When the joints are compressed by drawing the bones together, the synovial fluid is forced against the walls of the joints; when suddenly released with an expansion, these fluids create an internal hydraulic compression power, which is extremely useful in short-range techniques. The standard method of using this short-range power is to compress a line of joints through a hand and arm, across a shoulder, down the spine, across a hip, and down a leg into a foot. When this line of joints is simultaneously expanded, tremendous short-range power can explode from the hand at the end of the line. Advanced practitioners can use this technique with any line of joints, granting any part of their body short-range power.

In ba gua zhang, a specific walking practice is used to develop the compression and expansion of the joints. This is a four-part walk in which all of the joints of the body are expanded as the lead foot steps forward. These joints are then compressed as the body weight shifts forward eighty-percent and expanded once again as the weight shifts forward even more from eighty-percent to one-hundred-percent. The joints are compressed again as the rear foot steps up to the lead foot. When the rear foot steps forward, the process begins again. One hundred practice hours of this four-part walk are required to program this compression and expansion into the automatic nervous system. After this has been accomplished, the four-part compression and expansion cycle will take place in your circle walking without you having to think about it. Periodic returns to the four-part walking practice are necessary to maintain this compression and expansion of the joints.

The martial aspects of the four-part compress-and-expand walk are trained and tested in a simple two-person exercise. One practitioner stands firmly rooted while the other practitioner pushes them with a single hand by simply stepping out and expanding into their space. The second push is set up by the compression (the eighty-percent-forward weight shift) and then released with the expansion (the shift from eighty percent to one-hundred percent). The third push is accomplished by compressing as the feet come together. As the joints in the back of the hand compress, the heel of the hand is driven a little forward, delivering a shocking short-range push, which has a different quality to it than the preceding expansion pushes. It is important that only the expansion and compression of the joints is used to push the partner and not an extension of the arms and legs. This may seem somewhat powerless at first, but by sticking to the principles of the technique, short-range internal power will be developed over time.

Ba gua zhang practitioners must stay focused on the fact that a good foundation in the basic training practices of the art is the only route to attaining proficiency in it.

3

The Forms of Ba Gua Zhang

Forms are prearranged patterns of movements comprised of various techniques in the style being practiced. They are arranged in patterns that both make martial sense and create the posture structure and energy-flow patterns that improve the practitioner's health, physical conditioning, and development of the art. These prearranged movement patterns are indigenous to most styles of Asian martial arts and are also known as "sets," as well as by a number of colloquial names. Forms are the textbooks of Chinese martial arts practices. In this analogy, learning the basic postures and breathing techniques is like learning the alphabet, and learning the circle walking exercises is akin to learning how to read. Having mastered those basic skills, the student is ready to move on to studying the textbooks of the art, the forms. In the early days of martial arts, the forms were often the only textbooks available to students, as most of the earliest martial arts practitioners were illiterate.

When fully studying any subject, a student usually reads more than one textbook. During a long-term study, a student will usually read a number of books on the subject, put a select few on the front shelf for constant rereading and simply commit the useful information from the other texts to memory for use when they are needed. Often the student will discard any texts that don't answer his or her questions or continue to meet his or her needs in the long-term, while carefully guarding, cherishing, and constantly rereading his or her favorite texts. This study pattern is very prevalent in a lifelong practice of martial arts.

After reading a text thoroughly, a student must always take the knowledge gleaned from the text and bring this knowledge into his or her daily practices in order for the text to have any real use. In martial arts, this means taking the physical, energetic, martial, and emotional techniques from the forms and moving them into one's daily life, as well as into one's fighting and meditation practices. The downfall of martial artists who spend their entire martial arts practice simply repeating their forms is that they have simply become readers who never actually use the knowledge that they have learned from their books.

In ba gua zhang, most forms are expressed as eight methods of changing direction while circle walking. Each of the eight sets of movements vary in length and the number of techniques included, but they all end the same way—the practitioner has turned around and is walking in the opposite direction around the circle. Each of these change patterns can be done from either direction to turn the practitioner in either direction. Because the object of each is to change direction, and because the patterns are the basis of the Eight Trigrams Palm system, these prearranged movement patterns are usually referred to as The Eight Palm Changes. Often the title also comes with a descriptive phrase, such as "The Old Eight Palm Changes," "The Basic Eight Palm Changes," "The Original Eight Palm Changes," "The Dragon Claw Eight Palm Changes," and so on. Some styles of ba gua zhang have linking or cascading forms where there are no circle walking breaks between changes, and a few styles have straight line sets, but most styles of the art emphasize The Eight Palm Changes pattern. (The correlations between the art of ba gua zhang and the Chinese *Book of Changes,* the *Yi Jing,* will be explored more fully in Chapter Eight.)

Within the Chinese martial arts, most styles have a number of forms and variations on these forms. Over time, each instructor's personal nuances slip into his forms and are passed on to his students. This happens even when instructors try their best to pass on the forms exactly as they've learned them from their teachers. In addition, each generation of each style usually has a few instructors who set out to create new forms for their styles (and occasionally whole new styles). Because their martial art is based on the Chinese *Book of Changes,* many ba gua instructors feel that they have carte blanche to create changes within their forms. This has led to a wide variance in ba gua zhang forms, sometimes even among the followers of a single teacher. When studying ba gua zhang, a student should realize that if a teacher's art exhibits constant movement; the coiling, twisting, and changing patterns of ba gua zhang; internal power principles; some circle walking; and a basic knowledge of the history of the art and credible origins, then that art is ba gua zhang, no matter how unfamiliar the forms may be.

The Story Behind the Cheng Style Eight Basic Palms

Later in this chapter, we will illustrate the Cheng Style of the Eight Basic Palms form. First, we'd like to explain our introduction to ba gua zhang forms and then how the Cheng Style Eight Basic Palms was passed down to us and why we chose it to be included in this book.

As we mentioned in Chapter One, B. P. Chan arrived in New York City in early 1975 and quickly began teaching ba gua zhang in the studio of famed tai ji quan master William C. C. Chen. This was an eventful class, because until that time no one in the area had ever offered ba gua zhang to non-Chinese students. Chan was a quiet and humble gentleman of small stature, who still managed to exude power and confidence in his arts. Chan had spent his early life in Fujien province in China, where he had done his primary martial arts training. He then moved to Manila, in the Philippines, when Japan attacked China in the 1930s. In Manila, young Chan Bun Piac was known commonly as Guillermo, which means "William" in Spanish. Having a William Chan teaching in William Chen's studio seemed to be a bit too confusing for the American students, so Chan Bun Piac became simply known as B. P. Chan.

Chan Bun Piac

Word of Chan's class spread like wildfire through New York's tai ji community. "It's ba gua, man! That new guy at William Chen's is actually teaching ba gua!" was the word that passed among the local tai ji enthusiasts. Many in the tai ji clan had read Robert Smith's and Lee Ying Arn's books on the art of ba gua zhang and had long been intrigued by the mysterious style.

Co-author Frank Allen was privileged to attend classes during the early years of B. P. Chan's ba gua classes in New York City. After teaching students the basics of posture, breathing, and Mud Tread stepping, Chan introduced a form, which was known in the old Wade-Giles system of the day as Pa Kua Chang. His students knew him simply as "Mr. Chan," as his inherent humility had him deny that he even was a teacher. He always stated, "I'm not the teacher. We just practice together." Meanwhile, he had the widest knowledge of martial arts that any of his students had ever encountered, and soon, he was teaching—in addition to his ba gua class—Yang and Chen forms of tai ji quan, xing yi quan, Qin Na, a couple of Shaolin forms, and Chi Kung.

Mr. Chan's ba gua zhang was based on an Eight Palm Changes form, which he taught along with a matching two-person form for martial applications, an eight-section meditation set, and a ten-exercise qi gong set to develop the basic body alignments, openings, and strength. At first, the entire system was simply referred to as Pa Kua Chang, but later Chan told his early students that the form was the Combined Form of the Jiang Rong Qiao School. He told us that he knew the famous Original Form of the Jiang Rong Qiao School, but he wouldn't teach it because an older teacher somewhere in Chinatown was teaching that form to his Chinese students.

Twenty years later, Chan told his later students that the form he taught was a Cheng Style Dragon Claw form that had been the specialty of Cheng Ting Hua's son Cheng Yu Long. It is easy to see how the same form had two names, as the Jiang Rong Qiao School taught Cheng Style ba gua zhang. In the 1990s Chan also began to teach students Jiang's Original Form.

Although usually quiet and a bit vague as to the origins of his arts, Mr. Chan did divulge that his primary ba gua teacher was Liu Hing Chow and that he had begun his martial arts career under the Shaolin tutelage of Chan Jing Ming and progressed in these arts under Lian Dak Fung. As a youngster, Chan studied xing yi quan with Chow Chang Hoen and then learned the combat aspects of xing yi in the Chinese army during the Sino-Japanese War. He never spoke directly about his war experiences but seemed to have intimate knowledge of the Chinese Broad Sword Brigade, which was made up of martial artists of small stature who rolled in under the Japanese machine gun fire and then jumped into the machine-gunner's trenches and went to work with their broadswords.

B. P. Chan's ba gua consisted of quick, small, circle movements that clearly illustrated the martial aspects of the art, especially when the form was practiced in conjunction with the two-person set. Chan was very careful that students understood the martial application of each movement within the form. He taught how the power within these movements was contingent on posture, breathing, and full-body motion.

Mr. Chan continued to teach his arts at William Chen's studio and at other venues in the New York area right up until a couple of weeks before his death. After twenty-seven years of passing on his arts to his students in New York, B. P. Chan quietly passed away at the age of eighty on March 17, 2002.

In 1989 Master Bruce Kumar Frantzis finally agreed to begin teaching ba gua zhang to his students in New York City and San Francisco. Frantzis had been teaching on and off in New York City since the early 70s, and following his return from an extended trip to China in 1987, had been teaching regularly in New York, as well as in Boston and San Francisco. Over the years, Frantzis had offered his students a varied menu of qi gong, Wu and Yang styles of tai ji quan, internal Shaolin, and xing yi quan, but had always deemed his students unready for the intricacies of ba gua training. His students—co-author Frank Allen among them—were ecstatic to finally receive instruction in what Frantzis had always referred to as the highest level of martial arts.

Frantzis had spent almost three quarters of his forty years immersed in a study of the martial arts. While attending college in Japan, he trained and re-tested for the karate, judo, and aikido black belts that he had first acquired during his high-school years in New York. He was also a member of an All Japan National University Championship Karate team. In 1968, at the age of nineteen, Frantzis began to travel to the island of Taiwan, where he studied ba gua zhang and other internal martial arts, first from Wang Shu Chin and later from Hong Yi Xiang. On subsequent visits to Hong Kong, Frantzis met and studied with a young internal martial arts master named Bai Hua.

B. K. Frantzis and Frank Allen in 1992

In his youth, while living in Beijing, Bai Hua had been honored to be one of the few students of Internal Martial Arts and Daoist Grandmaster Liu Hung Chieh. When Frantzis traveled to Beijing in 1981 to study Yang Style tai ji quan at the Beijing Sports Institute, Bai Hua gave him a letter of introduction to present to Liu Hung Chieh.

While still in his teens, Liu Hung Chieh became the disciple of ba gua master, Liu Zhen Lin. Liu Hung Chieh first studied with Liu Zhen Lin when Liu was teaching in the school of Cheng Ting Hua's son Cheng You Lung and Dong Hai Chuan's student Liu De Kuan. Liu Zhen Lin was a famous fighter and bodyguard who first studied ba gua under Yin Fu's student Liu Yong Qing (who was a close friend and training partner of Yin Fu's top student, Ma Gui). The young Liu Zhen Lin learned all of his basic ba gua from these two masters, but his teachers brought him to bow before and become the disciple of court minister Liang Zhai Wen; in this way, Liu Zhen Lin received entry into the third generation of ba gua masters, which was the same generation as his foundation teachers. Liang Zhai Wen was a military man who had been the chief guard at the most important fire gate on the Great Wall before becoming a court minister. Due to Liang's position in the court, his associa-tion with the palace eunuch servant Dong Hai Chuan was not widely known until after Liang's death. Because he was the top student of Liu Zhen Lin, it is safe to as-sume that young Liu Hung Chieh also received training under his teacher's kung fu "uncles," Liu Yong Qing and Ma Gui.

Liu Zhen Lin School, Nov. 11, 1962. Second from the left in the front row is Liu Zhen Lin and to his right side is Liu Hung Chieh. The first student in the third row is Zhu Bao Zhen, who currently teaches in Beijing.

After teaching at the Nan Jing Central Martial Arts Academy and studying tai ji quan with Grandmaster Wu Jian Quan, Liu Hung Chieh devoted most of the remainder of his life to his spiritual pursuits. He followed an intense study of Tian Tai Buddhism with ten years of training with the Daoist masters in the mountains of southwest China. While there, Liu felt that he had discovered the Daoist circle walking meditation system that Dong Hai Chuan had studied and used as the basis of the art of ba gua zhang.

Upon his return from the mountains of southwest China, Liu Hung Chieh became an urban hermit in Beijing and accepted only three private students. His three students were his own son, the son of his classmate in the Liu Zhen Lin School, Zhu Bao Zhen, and Bai Hua. B. K. Frantzis had the extreme good fortune to be chosen as the old grandmaster's last private student. Frantzis studied with Liu for a few months in 1981 and again when he returned to China in early 1983. During this return trip, Frantzis studied with Liu every day until Liu passed away in December 1986.

Although the influences of his early ba gua training on Taiwan occasionally trickled in, B. K. Frantzis primarily taught his students the ba gua zhang of Liu Hung Chieh. This was not the Yin or Cheng styles of the Liu Zhen Lin School, but a form developed by Grandmaster Liu Hung Chieh, the foundation of which was his training with the Daoist masters of southwest China. It is a free-flowing, large-circle form, which when used in martial applications, spirals down to small circles at the moment of impact. Frantzis made sure that his students were trained in an array of conditioning exercises, posture and breathing exercises, and circle walking before they began to learn this form. Because of its foundation in Liu's studies of Daoist circle walking meditation, this form has some of the strongest *Yi Jing* correlations and meditation applications of all the variations of ba gua zhang. Frantzis continued to teach his style of ba gua zhang in New York until his senior students there had learned all of the Eight Palm Changes, including their auxiliary exercises and martial and meditative applications. It took a decade. Co-author Frank Allen was privileged to be the first ba gua zhang instructor certified by Master B. K. Frantzis.

Lao Ba Zhang, or Old Eight Palms set, is reputed to be the basic training set of the original Dong Hai Chuan school; several variations of the set were developed and Jiang Rong Qiao taught one of these which he passed down to his top student Sha Guo Zheng. Sha taught the set to Professor Kang Ge Wu, who in turn taught it to thousands of students, one of whom was Master Jiang Jian-ye of Albany, New York, who in turn taught it to the authors of this book in 2002 in a series of private lessons at his school. Later, on a subsequent trip to Beijing, we had the honor of discussing the Old Eight Palms set—and ba gua zhang in general—with Professor Kang Ge Wu.

The Old Eight Palms set is a perfect beginning form, which trains the body in the postures and movements needed in more advanced ba gua sets. It is a simple set that is easy for a student to learn while he or she learns all of the basic skills of the art. This set is an extremely efficient method of training the student's waist to twist and stretch in the manner necessary for the correct application of advanced ba gua techniques. The Old Eight Palms set also presents the student with the basic techniques and strategies of ba gua fighting and acts as a basic qi gong regimen for improving his or her health. We were very pleased to learn this beneficial set from Master Jiang and add it to our ba gua regimen.

In 2003 co-author Tina Zhang began to offer martial arts study trips to the public and organize and lead annual internal martial arts training trips to Beijing. After a lot of research and a couple of false starts, Tina brought her group to study ba gua zhang with Cheng Style Ba Gua Zhang Grandmaster Liu Jing Ru.

Tina Zhang and Frank Allen study with Grandmaster Liu Jing Ru in Beijing.

Liu Jing Ru holds an eighth-degree ranking in China's national martial arts rankings. There are no current ba gua masters in China with higher rankings; there's only one ba gua master in all of China with the same ranking. Liu Jing Ru is from an esteemed lineage with only two masters between himself and the founder of Cheng Style ba gua zhang, Cheng Ting Hua.

Liu Jing Ru's lineage starts with Li Wen Biao, who was an inner-door student of Cheng Ting Hua. Li Wen Biao was known for his size and for the power of his rolling palm-heel strike, known as Ta Zhang. In this palm strike, the hand rolls into the opponent, touching first with the fingertips, then with the surface of the palm, and ending with a power release from the palm heel. It was said of Li that if he hit an opponent with thirty percent of his Ta Zhang power the opponent was sure to be injured; if Li used fifty percent or more of his power, it always brought blood from the opponent's mouth. As a young inner-door student in the Cheng School, Li sometimes accompanied and assisted his senior martial arts brother Sun Lu Tang on his teaching journeys. Later, Li became an imperial guard of the late Qing dynasty and served as a martial arts instructor to the troops. Due to their traditional hairstyle, Li's top military students were known as Li's Twenty Best Braids.

Li Wen Biao's death was a result of an offer he made to guard his post alone over a holiday in order to allow the other guards to go home and celebrate with their families. This left Li completely out-numbered when a bandit gang decided to pick that day to raid the post and steal the arms there. Li didn't lie down quietly, though, and legend has it that he exterminated a dozen of the brigands before they shot him to death. Both its circumstances of the empty hands of a master versus the firearms of a group and the number of deceased attackers make Li's demise strangely reminiscent of that of his master Cheng Ting Hua.

Luo Xing Wu was one of Li Wen Biao's Twenty Best Braids. Luo managed to make the transition from the Imperial Qing army into the army of the new Republic of China. During the Sino-Japanese War of the 1930s, Luo was in Manchuria, and it was there where his most famous encounter took place. At some point Luo was attacked by a Japanese man wielding a Japanese katana sword. This warrior was considered the best swordsman in the entire area. Having no weapon on his person, Luo picked up a slender tree branch. Although his weapon was vastly inferior to the katana, Luo's clever ba gua footwork completely confused his attacker, allowing him to disarm the Japanese warrior and beat him into submission.

After the liberation of the People's Republic of China in 1949, the first martial arts school to open in Beijing had two sections. The tai ji quan section was headed by Wu Tu Nan, the famous student of Yang Shao Hou and Wu Jian Quan, and the third-generation Northern Wu Style tai ji master Yang Yu Ting. The xing yi and ba gua section of the school was led by Liang Zhen Pu's top student, Guo Gu Men, and Luo Xing Wu. Luo was one of the few martial arts masters to bridge not only the Late Qing and Republican eras, but also from the Republic to the People's Republic.

Liu Jing Ru began to study with Luo Xing Wu in 1957 at the age of twenty-one. In 1963 the last national martial arts tournament before the Cultural Revolution took place and twenty-seven-year-old Liu Jing Ru won the gold medal in ba gua zhang. When there was finally another national martial arts tournament in 1979, a forty-three-year-old Liu Jing Ru again took the ba gua gold medal. Liu says that he felt like a youngster in that tournament, as the average age of the competitors was forty-seven. The following year, Liu again won the national Ba Gua Championship after which he became a martial arts teacher. Even as he enters his seventies, Liu Jing Ru is fast, loose, powerful, and full of energy. He has trained many champions in China, and he now teaches regularly in Europe as well as at home in Beijing.

Liu Jing Ru teaches the entire system of classical Cheng Style ba gua zhang, which contains the following forms: Eight Palm Postures Circle Walking, a foundation of ba gua zhang; Eight Basic Palms, the basic techniques of ba gua zhang in eight foundation palm changes; Swimming Body, a cascading set of palm changes; Sixty-Four Palms, eight variations of each of the eight basic palm changes; Sixty-Four Hands, sixty-four palm techniques taught in line drills and in a two-person drill; and the weapons techniques of Ba Gua Sword and Ba Gua Deer Horn Knives.

Liu always starts his students off with the Cheng Style Eight Basic Palms set right after they have learned the Eight Palm Postures Circle Walking (introduced in

Chapter Two). The first three palm changes in this Eight Basic Palm set are somewhat similar to the Jiang Rong Qiao Old Eight Palms, but while they teach the same basic principles and training postures of ba gua, they also add greatly to the martial repertoire and advanced flavor of the art. Although the Eight Basic Palms is an older and more original basic training set than the Old Eight Palms, it can be used as an advanced set to be learned only after a beginner has absorbed the lessons of the Old Eight Palms.

Because it so well illustrates the essence of the art of ba gua zhang while presenting some of the original methods of the Cheng School, we have picked the Cheng Style Eight Basic Palms of Liu Jing Ru as an example of the forms of ba gua zhang. This is a large-frame open set—large frame forms work like machines that have small, fast gears on the inside that move big, powerful gears on the outside. The set clearly shows ba gua's basic requirements: some high, some low; some fast, some slow; and some release of Fa Li (shaking) energy. This form teaches the student the agile footwork, quick turns, and subtle coiling that provide the foundation of ba gua's martial excellence. The set also showcases a number of ba gua's more unique fighting techniques, while providing all of the health benefits that are derived from the practice of the internal martial arts.

Liu Jing Ru and Frank Allen discussing the palm changes
in Beijing, December 2004

The Cheng Style Eight Basic Palms Form

Beginning

Stand in a basic internal posture with your feet one-fist distance apart (Figure 3-1). Raise your arms to shoulder height with your palms facing upward (Figure 3-2). Raise your hands above your head, with your palms facing downward (Figure 3-3), then bring your hands down your centerline (Figures 3-4 and 3-5). Step forward with the inner foot, coil your hands toward the center of the circle, and assume the basic ba gua zhang posture (Figure 3-6).

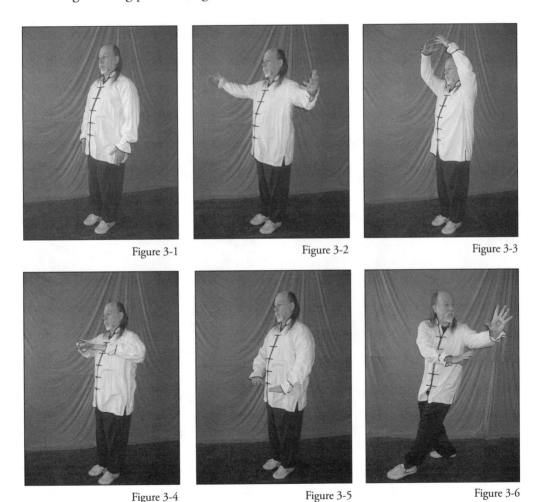

Figure 3-1   Figure 3-2   Figure 3-3

Figure 3-4   Figure 3-5   Figure 3-6

The First Palm Change: Single Palm Change

1. Green Dragon Stretches Its Claws
2. Close the Door and Hide the Elbow
3. Open the Window and Look at the Moon
4. Conceal the Flowers under the Leaves
5. Green Dragon Stretches Its Claws

Start in a basic ba gua posture (Figure 3-7). Take a toe-in step with the outer foot while sweeping the inner hand across the face with a blocking motion (Figure 3-8). Take a toe-out step with the other foot, and bring the corresponding hand to the line of the circle, keeping your palm out and your little finger up; the other hand turns, palm up, at the waist (Figure 3-9). Step around in a V stance, and bring the lead arm under and past the opposite elbow (Figures 3-10 and 3-11). Sweep the bottom arm toward the center of the circle while stepping forward on the inner foot and returning to the basic ba gua posture (Figure 3-12).

Figure 3-7

Figure 3-8

Figure 3-9

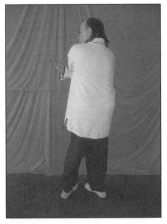

Figure 3-10

Figure 3-11 (Front view
of Figure 3-10)

Figure 3-12

The Second Palm Change: Double Palm Change

1. **Green Dragon Stretches Its Claws**
2. **Close the Door and Hide the Elbow**
3. **Open the Window and Look at the Moon**
4. **Conceal the Flowers under the Leaves**
5. **Pointing to Heaven and Plunging to Earth**
6. **Swallow Skims the Water**
7. **Sweep the Rider from His Saddle**
8. **Conceal the Flowers under the Leaves**
9. **Green Dragon Stretches Its Claws**

Start in a basic ba gua posture (Figure 3-13). Take a toe-in step with the outer foot, sweeping the inner hand across the face with a blocking motion (Figure 3-14). Take a toe-out step with the other foot, and bring the corresponding hand to the line of the circle, keeping your palm out and your little finger up; the other hand turns, palm up, at the waist (Figure 3-15). Step around in a V stance, and bring the lead arm under and past the opposite elbow (Figure 3-16). Coil the lower hand past the upper elbow and up above the head (Figure 3-17). Pull the lead foot to the rear foot while lowering the body, thrusting the lower hand downward, and pivoting toward to the center of the circle (Figure 3-18). Step out to the line of the circle while dropping into a crouching stance; the lead hand goes, palm up, over the lead leg, and the palm of the rear hand faces the chest (Figure 3-19). Expand the joints of the weighted leg, raising the body slightly, and drop the rear hand into a palm-down block below the groin, while raising the lead hand into a knife-edge-up cutting palm (Figure 3-20). The rear hand then sweeps, palm down, over the rear knee and coils around to the front of the torso palm up (Figure 3-21). Step around into a V stance and bring the lower hand under the upper elbow (Figure 3-22). Coil back into a basic ba gua stance (Figure 3-23).

Figure 3-13

Figure 3-14

Figure 3-15

Figure 3-16

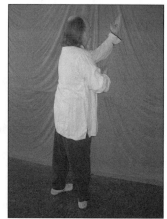

Figure 3-17

Figure 3-18

Figure 3-19

Figure 3-20

Figure 3-21

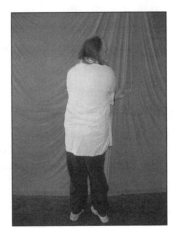

Figure 3-22

Figure 3-23

The Third Palm Change: Flowing Along the Direction Change

1. Green Dragon Stretches Its Claws
2. Pick Up the Helmet from behind the Head
3. White Snake Lies in the Grass
4. Sweep the Rider from His Saddle
5. Conceal the Flowers under the Leaves
6. Green Dragon Stretches Its Claws

Start in a basic ba gua posture (Figure 3-24). Step forward with the outer foot (Figure 3-25). Take a toe-in step with the inner foot to face outside the circle (Figure 3-26). Take a toe-out step to the line of the circle, shift your weight onto that leg, and bring your rear hand behind your head (Figure 3-27). Take a toe-in step with the other foot and execute a palm strike, bringing your hand over your head (Figure 3-28). Shift your weight again, cross your hands, and look in the opposite direction (Figure 3-29). Drop into a crouching stance, extending both arms outward, with palms out and fingertips down (Figure 3-30). Circle the rear hand past the rear knee (Figure 3-31). Coil the rear hand past the waist, and step up into a V stance, bringing that hand under the opposite elbow (Figure 3-32). Coil to the center of the circle and return to a basic ba gua stance (Figure 3-33).

To transition into the change of direction, take a toe-in step with the outer foot (Figure 3-34), and then step out of the line of the circle with the same foot (Figure 3-35). Lastly, bring the feet together and bring the inside hand under the outside elbow (Figure 3-36). Coil back to a basic stance (Figure 3-37).

Figure 3-24   Figure 3-25   Figure 3-26

Figure 3-27   Figure 3-28   Figure 3-29

Figure 3-30   Figure 3-31

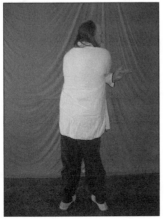

Figure 3-32   Figure 3-33

Figure 3-34

Figure 3-35

Figure 3-36

Figure 3-37

The Fourth Palm Change: Turning the Body Back Palm

1. Green Dragon Stretches Its Claws
2. Cutting Clouds
3. White Snake Spits Out Its Tongue
4. Green Dragon Leaves the Water
5. Swallow Skims the Water
6. Snake Leans Back and Spits Out Its Tongue
7. White Ape Presents the Peach
8. Two Snakes Spit Out Their Tongues
9. Push the Mountain into the Sea
10. Sweep the Rider from His Saddle

11. Conceal the Flowers under the Leaves
12. Green Dragon Stretches Its Claws

Start in a basic ba gua posture (Figure 3-38). Step forward with the outer foot, coiling the inner hand inward (Figure 3-39). Step forward with the inner foot, bringing the inner hand forward in a cutting palm strike (Figure 3-40). Take a toe-in step with the outer foot, and twist your body to face the opposite direction while bringing your inner hand, palm up, close to the chin (Figure 3-41). The next sequence completes a circle-and-a-half and is as follows: toe out, toe in, toe out, toe in, toe out, and thrust (Figures 3-42 to 3-44). Step the rear leg forward and thrust (Figure 3-45). Step the forward foot directly back and drop into a crouching stance (Figure 3-46). Rise and step forward, thrusting the lead hand, palm up, to throat level. The rear hand is, palm forward, at the lead wrist, and the torso leans back slightly (Figure 3-47). Take a toe-in step with the lead foot (the one facing the outside of the circle) while bringing the forearms and wrists together; the palms are extended upward and outward (Figures 3-48 and 3-49). Complete another circle-and-a-half using the following sequence: toe out, toe in, toe out, toe in, and toe out into a long front stance with the arms fully extended in a palms-up thrust (Figures 3-50 to 3-54). Step through with the rear leg and execute a palm-up thrust (Figure 3-55). Coil the lead hand into the body and the lead leg into the standing leg (Figure 3-56). Step out with the front leg into a half horse stance; bring the lead hand out with the palm out and the little finger pushing up. The rear hand is palm down at the centerline (Figure 3-57). Sweep the rear hand over the rear knee (Figure 3-58). Step up into a V stance, bringing the lead hand under and past the opposite elbow (Figure 3-59). Coil back to a ba gua basic stance and walk the circle (Figure 3-60).

Figure 3-38   Figure 3-39   Figure 3-40

Figure 3-41

Figure 3-42

Figure 3-43

Figure 3-44

Figure 3-45

Figure 3-46

Figure 3-47

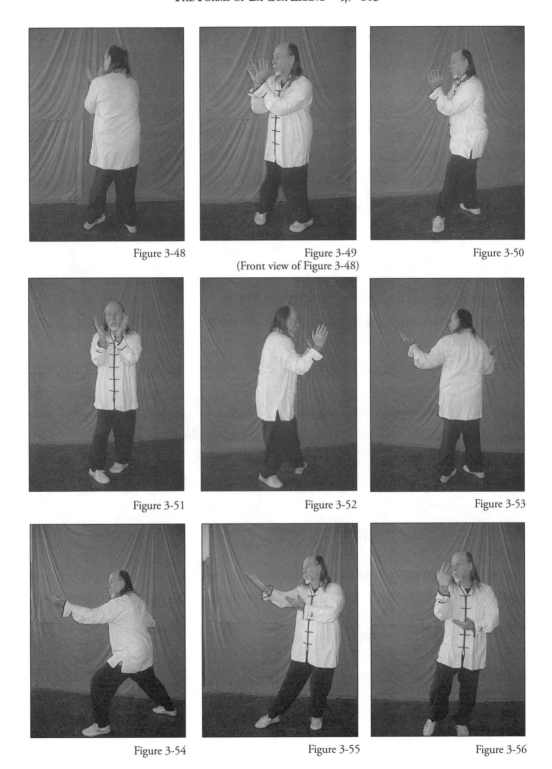

Figure 3-48

Figure 3-49
(Front view of Figure 3-48)

Figure 3-50

Figure 3-51

Figure 3-52

Figure 3-53

Figure 3-54

Figure 3-55

Figure 3-56

Figure 3-57

Figure 3-58

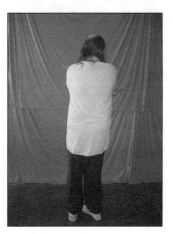

Figure 3-59

Figure 3-60

The Fifth Palm Change: Turning the Body around Palm

1. Green Dragon Stretches Its Claws
2. Pulling in Palm
3. Warlord Ties Your Elbows
4. Elbow Crashes into the Chest
5. Yin and Yang Fish
6. Push the Mountain into the Sea
7. Sweep the Rider from His Saddle
8. Conceal the Flowers under the Leaves
9. Green Dragon Stretches His Claws

Start in a basic ba gua posture (Figure 3-61). Take a toe-in step with the outer foot, change direction, and drop into a back-weighted stance. The heel of the front foot is raised. The lead arm is extended forward with the elbow bent and the hand in a palm-up grasping position. The rear hand is at chest level with the hand in a palm-down grasping position (Figure 3-62). Take a half-step forward, thrusting the rear elbow past the lead wrist in a vertical elbow strike (Figure 3-63). Step forward with the rear leg and toe in, striking horizontally with the same elbow (Figures 3-64 and 3-65). Step backward, bring the lead foot behind the rear foot, sink your weight onto that leg, and bring the corresponding hand, palm up, to the thigh (Figure 3-66). Draw the lead foot in toward the rear foot and into an empty stance, dropping the hand, palm up, at the thigh (Figure 3-67). Take a toe-out step with the lead foot toward the outside of the circle, coiling the body, and bring the lead hand, palm out, behind and below the lower back. The rear hand is palm out in front of the chest. This is known as the Yin and Yang Fish posture (Figure 3-68). Toe in and toe out to complete three full yet tight circles, which should maintain their position along the line of the master circle (Figures 3-69 and 3-70). Drop into a half horse stance—your body should face the center of the circle, while your head and eyes focus along the line of the master circle. The lead hand is in a knife-edge up, palm-out push, while the rear hand is palm down, blocking below the groin (Figure 3-71). Sweep the rear hand over the rear knee and back around in front of the chest so that it is palm up (Figure 3-72). Step around into a V stance, bringing the lead hand, palm up, under the opposite elbow (Figure 3-73). Coil back into a basic ba gua stance and walk along the master circle (Figure 3-74).

Figure 3-61   Figure 3-62   Figure 3-63

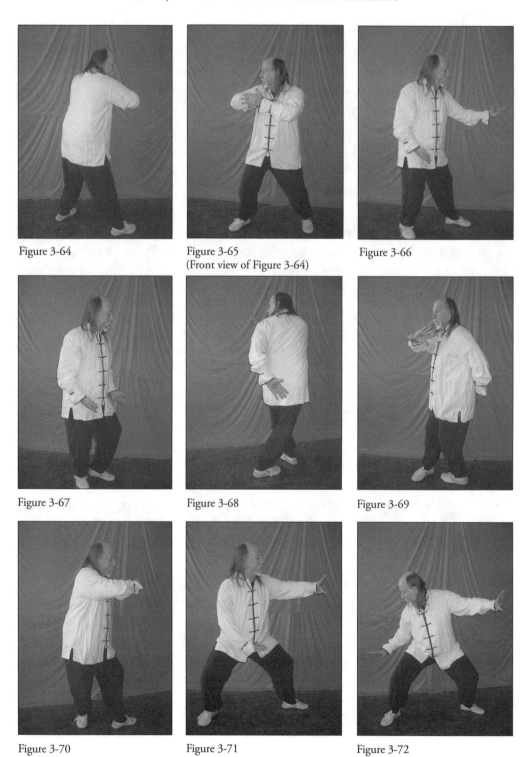

Figure 3-64

Figure 3-65
(Front view of Figure 3-64)

Figure 3-66

Figure 3-67

Figure 3-68

Figure 3-69

Figure 3-70

Figure 3-71

Figure 3-72

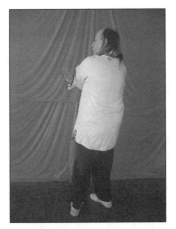

Figure 3-73   Figure 3-74

The Sixth Palm Change: Grinding the Body Palm

1. **Green Dragon Stretches Its Claws**
2. **Cutting the Grass**
3. **Green Dragon Swings Its Tail**
4. **Golden Snake Coils around the Tree**
5. **Conceal the Flowers under the Leaves**
6. **Green Dragon Stretches Its Claws**

Start in a basic ba gua posture (Figure 3-75). Step forward with the outer foot, cutting the outer hand, palm up, to the center of the circle (Figure 3-76). Bring the inner foot up to the outer foot while cutting the inner hand, palm down, along the line of the outer arm and past it (Figure 3-77). Take a toe-out step with the inner foot toward the center of the circle while bending forward and coiling the lead hand (palm up) behind the back and the rear hand (palm up) in front of the chest (Figure 3-78). Take a toe-in step with the opposite foot, and bring the hand by the chest to the opposite armpit (Figure 3-79). Take a toe-out step with the other foot while bringing the hand past the armpit and coiling it upward above the head. The opposite hand moves from behind the back to a palm-down position at the chest (Figure 3-80). Take a toe-in step with the rear foot, dropping the upper hand, palm down, over the lower elbow of the arm that is resting at chest level (Figure 3-81). Take a toe-out step with the other foot, coiling the upper hand, palm up, below the other elbow; the upper hand is palm down above the lower elbow (Figure 3-82). Step around into a V stance, bringing the lower hand, palm up, past the upper elbow (Figure 3-83). These eight steps complete a small circle, which sits on the edge of the master circle. Now, coil back to the basic ba gua posture and walk the master circle (Figure 3-84).

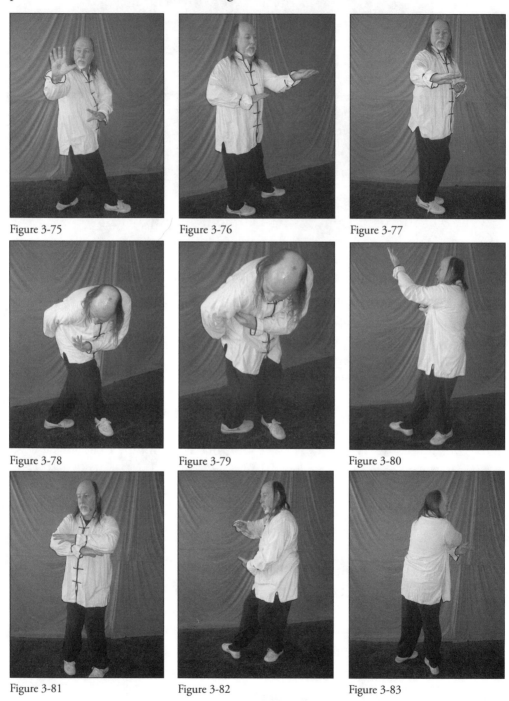

Figure 3-75

Figure 3-76

Figure 3-77

Figure 3-78

Figure 3-79

Figure 3-80

Figure 3-81

Figure 3-82

Figure 3-83

Figure 3-84

The Seventh Palm Change: Overturning the Body Palm

1. **Green Dragon Stretches Its Claws**
2. **Point the Toe Kicking**
3. **Swallow Skims the Water**
4. **Python Overturns Its Body**
5. **White Snake Lies in the Grass**
6. **Eagle Spreads Its Wings**
7. **Push the Mountain into the Sea**
8. **Sweep the Rider from His Saddle**
9. **Conceal the Flowers under the Leaves**
10. **Green Dragon Stretches Its Claws**

Start in a basic ba gua posture (Figure 3-85). Step forward with the outer foot, coiling both hands in toward the body (Figure 3-86). Kick the inner foot straight out (point the toes), while thrusting both hands forward, palms up, along the line of the leg (Figure 3-87). Sweep the kicking leg directly back and drop into a crouching stance, with the lead hand (palm up) above the lead leg and the rear hand (palm up) at the chest (Figure 3-88). Take a toe-in step forward into a bent-forward stance, with the lead hand hanging down, the lead arm extended, and the rear hand at the opposite armpit (Figure 3-89). Step around and toe out, extending the inner leg. The inner arm coils around the front of the body and up over the head, while the outer hand thrusts forward palm up (Figure 3-90). Swing the inner hand around, past the body, to the opposite shoulder (Figure 3-91). Swing the outer hand, palm up, back along the line of the circle (Figure 3-92). Coil the body, circling the outer hand above the head and the inner hand to the side of the chest (Figure 3-93). Sweep the inner foot backward into a horse stance (facing in the opposite direction), and thrust both hands outward with palms out and fingertips down (Figure 3-94). Take a half-step forward into an upright stance, coiling the arms in, up, and down into back-of-hand downward strikes (Figure 3-95). Coil the lead foot into the standing leg to create an empty stance while coiling the lead hand into the body (Figure 3-96). Take a half-step out into a half horse stance, with your lead hand pushing out, knife-edge up, in front of your chest and your rear hand blocking, palm down, below the groin (Figure 3-97). Coil the rear hand past the rear knee (Figure 3-98). Coil the body in other direction, and bring the rear hand, palm up, to the chest (Figure 3-99). Step around into a V stance, bringing the lead hand, palm up, under the opposite elbow (Figure 3-100). Coil into a basic ba gua stance and walk the circle (Figure 3-101).

Figure 3-85

Figure 3-86

Figure 3-87

Figure 3-88

Figure 3-89

Figure 3-90

Figure 3-91

Figure 3-92

Figure 3-93

Figure 3-94

Figure 3-95

Figure 3-96

Figure 3-97

Figure 3-98

Figure 3-99

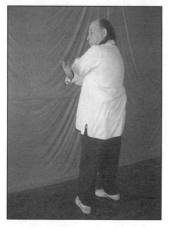

Figure 3-100

Figure 3-101

The Eighth Palm Change: Returning the Body Palm

1. Green Dragon Stretches Its Claws
2. Step Forward and Palm Strike
3. Swallow Skims the Water
4. Green Dragon Leaves the Water
5. Running Horse Suddenly Turns Back
6. Thrust the Little Flower Forward
7. Push the Mountain into the Sea
8. Sweep the Rider from His Saddle
9. Conceal the Flowers under the Leaves
10. Green Dragon Stretches Its Claws

Start in a basic ba gua posture (Figure 3-102). Step forward with the outer foot, palm striking with the outer hand to the center of the circle; keep your palm forward and your fingertips up (Figure 3-103). Bring the inner foot to the outer foot while striking to the center of the circle with the inner palm; again, keep your palm forward and your fingertips up (Figure 3-104). Turn to the outside of the circle and drop into a crouching stance, with your lead hand palm up above the lead leg and your rear hand palm up at chest level (Figure 3-105). Step forward with the rear leg into an empty stance while thrusting the rear hand, palm up, under and past the lead hand (Figure 3-106). Take a toe-in step with the lead foot, turning to face the center of the circle, while dropping the lead arm over the other arm and keeping both hands palms up (Figure 3-107). Turn and step towards to the center of the circle, rolling the hands to bring the wrists together at the centerline, with palms forward and fingers extended to the sides (Figure 3-108). Step through toward the center of the circle, thrusting the hands and arms forward (Figure 3-109). Step the rear leg forward to the line of the circle, draw the lead foot into it in an empty stance, and coil the lead hand into the body (Figure 3-110). Take a half step out into a half horse stance, and push your lead palm out in front of your chest, knife-edge up. The rear hand blocks, palm down, below the groin (Figure 3-111). Coil the body to sweep the rear hand past the rear knee (Figure 3-112). Coil the rear hand around to the chest, and then step around into a V stance, bringing the coiling hand palm-up under and past the opposite elbow (Figure 3-113). Coil back into the basic ba gua stance and walk the circle (Figure 3-114).

Figure 3-102

Figure 3-103

Figure 3-104

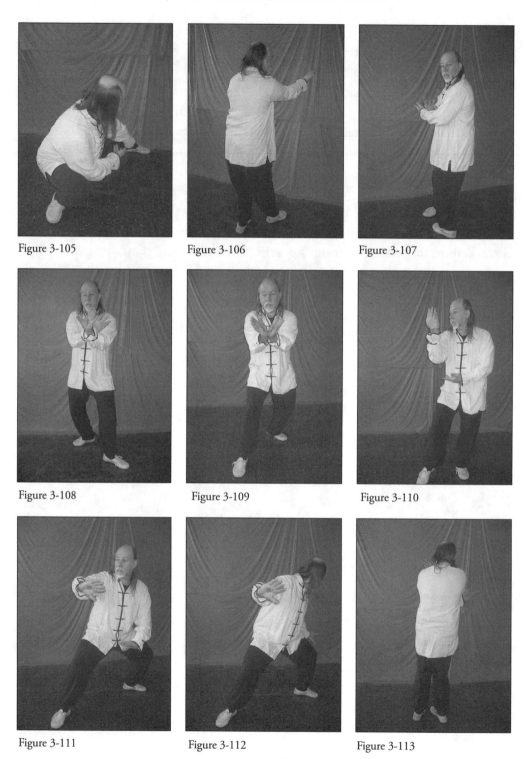

Figure 3-105

Figure 3-106

Figure 3-107

Figure 3-108

Figure 3-109

Figure 3-110

Figure 3-111

Figure 3-112

Figure 3-113

Figure 3-114

Closing

Step the inner foot up to the outer foot and raise the hands to the sides (Figure 3-115). Continue raising your hands until they are above your head, and turn your palms down (Figure 3-116). Lower your hands down the centerline (Figure 3-117). Bring your hands to hip level and spread them apart until the thumbs align with the hip joints (Figure 3-118). Finally, lower the hands to the sides of the thighs, palms facing inward (Figure 3-119).

Figure 3-115 Figure 3-116 Figure 3-117

Figure 3-118

Figure 3-119

4

Twisting, Coiling, Circling, and Spiraling: The Fighting Techniques of Ba Gua Zhang

The emergence of ba gua zhang in the mid-1800s was noticed solely because of the martial abilities of Dong Hai Chuan and his disciples. Their techniques were characterized by the continuous twisting, coiling, circling, and spiraling nature of their movements and the way in which these movements cascaded over one another to form a continuous flow of motion. This continuous flow of techniques and circling movement, with its constant changes in position and posture, allowed ba gua boxers to defend themselves and their clients from multiple opponents while always being aware of the location and safety of the clients. This ability made the early ba gua boxers the preferred bodyguards of Beijing's royal, rich, and famous citizens. The fame of the various ba gua zhang–oriented guard services was greatly enhanced by the many challenge-match wins of the companies' star guards. When famous ba gua boxers such as Chang Chao Tung and Ma Gui defeated foreign fighters from Russia, Japan, and Germany in challenge matches, they made the art of ba gua zhang respected throughout China. The exploits of various ba gua boxers during the Boxer Rebellion of 1900 also enhanced the martial reputation of the art.

Unlike some other Chinese martial arts, ba gua zhang has been lucky that most of the masters who brought the art to the West carried the martial traditions of ba gua zhang with them. B. P. Chan taught at least one martial application for every movement in his ba gua sets. He also taught a two-person martial application set, two-person circling and technique-exchange exercises, and a stylized ba gua sparring practice.

During his early years of teaching in the 1970s, B. K. Frantzis often demonstrated his ba gua martial skills while sparring with his Internal Shaolin, tai ji quan, and Hsing I chuan students. Students would try their best techniques, often ones that they had recently learned from Frantzis himself, but always to no avail. Students could never understand how Frantzis always seemed to be behind them or how he always seemed to be able to upset their balance and send them flying through the air and crashing into the floor.

When Frantzis began to teach ba gua in 1989, he explained to his remaining students from the old days that it was the art of ba gua zhang that had left them bruised and confused in the 70s. The focus of Frantzis' ba gua zhang teaching became health and meditation, but his classes retained the martial flavor of his ba gua teaching in New York City. In an interview in the September/October 1991 *Pa Kua Chang Newsletter*, Frantzis said, "New York is right now the designated Pa Kua area on the East Coast. I live in Marin County, in the San Francisco Bay Area, but some of my original students are in New York, such as Frank Allen who teaches there. I went back to teach Pa Kua there because I'm from the town and know the people. The physical realities of self-defense are more appreciated in New York City than in laid-back California!" In New York, Frantzis not only taught the martial applications of his form movements, but also the foundations of ba gua fighting, including such subjects as circling around an attack, twisting the muscles and connective tissue to spiral into and through an attack, diverting the attention of an opponent, and hiding one's own weak angles while finding the weak angles of an opponent. The foundation of Frantzis' ba gua martial teachings was the Rou Shou, or Soft Hands, exercise, which was augmented with two-person martial application exercises and a liberal amount of graphic demonstrations by Frantzis himself.

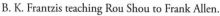

B. K. Frantzis teaching Rou Shou to Frank Allen.

Although modern China has a reputation for teaching its martial arts as health exercises, cultural arts, and movement systems, Grandmaster Liu Jing Ru (of Beijing) teaches his Cheng Style ba gua zhang in the traditional manner—presenting an effective and proven efficient martial art. He makes sure that every student understands the martial applications of each movement that he teaches.

Liu Jing Ru explains ba gua martial applications to Frank Allen in Beijing.

Liu's specialties are the close-range coiling motions of the Cheng Style, which bombard the opponent with an array of elbow, shoulder, and wrist strikes; short thrusts; and quick joint locks (which often set the hapless opponent up for a devastating throw). He shows minimal interest in the meditation aspects of ba gua, and although Liu has trained many forms champions, he makes it a point to tell students that his interest is in carrying on the tradition of the martial art of ba gua zhang. The martial skills demonstrated by Liu Jing Ru are amazing for a man in his seventies and bring to mind stories of the ba gua masters of a hundred years ago.

The foundation technique of ba gua zhang is circling around an attack. Although this skill is developed through hours of circle walking practice, the technique is not used to simply run around the opponent in full 360-degree circles. A ba gua fighter doesn't begin to circle until the opponent attacks, at which time the ba gua boxer circles the attack with a 90-degree, 180-degree, or 270-degree turn. As soon as he has reached the position where he has found the opponent's weak angle or blind spot, he executes his counterattack, which could be a push, a strike, or a throw. When practicing these techniques, students begin to understand the ba gua terminology, which refers to all body parts facing the inside of the circle as the inside hand, inside foot, and so on, and all of the body parts facing the outside of the circle as the outside hand, outside foot, and so on.

Common and simple methods of practicing these basic techniques begin with a student making a simple, controlled attack on a classmate. The student being attacked circles the attack and practices either a 90-degree turn followed by a push to the opponent's side or an 180-degree turn followed by a push to the opponent's spine. Other ways to practice circling an attack include making 90-degree circles to either palm strike or punch the opponent's side, throwing hip checks from 90-degree turns, or using throws from that same angle. One common throw from the 90-degree turn is accomplished by catching the opponent's chin with the inside hand while sweeping the opponent's weighted leg with a backward inside leg movement. This moves the opponent's head backward and down as his or her legs go forward and up. Another common throw from the 90-degree turn is accomplished by stepping the inside leg over and behind the opponent's lead leg while the inside hand pushes his or her near shoulder back and down and the outside hand reaches over and pulls the top of his or her leg forward and up. Another common ba gua throw begins with a 270-degree turn: when the opponent's blind spot is reached, the ba gua boxer grabs the opponent's chin with his or her outside hand, while he or she uses the inside hand to grab the opponent's forehead. The opponent is brought to the ground by the twisting of the head that occurs as the ba gua boxer continues to circle walk.

Most martial arts that use circular techniques apply the ideology of being the center of the circle and moving the opponent's force around you. The circling-around-an-attack techniques demonstrate the ba gua boxer's ability to become the edge of the circle and to contain the opponent within the center of the circle. Ba gua zhang also teaches how to spiral right across the diameter of the circle—and through an opponent who is in the center of the circle.

Circling around an attack.

In ba gua zhang, as in other internal martial arts, techniques simply become methods to apply the basic fighting skills of awareness, angles, speed, and power. Internal boxers are always conscious of every moment and aware of an opponent's every movement. They never rely on unconscious, reflexive action. In the beginning of this training, conscious movement is usually slower than unconscious, reflexive action, but as the internal boxer disciplines himself to only use conscious movement—even if it means losing encounters at first—slowly, the trend is reversed and conscious movement becomes faster than unconscious action. This happens because the spaces between see, think, and do narrow as the internal boxer continues to practice only conscious movement. When these spaces are short enough, the internal boxer can then consciously change his or her movement while their opponent is still attempting to complete their unconscious, reflexive action.

As well as maintaining his or her own continuous flow of conscious awareness, the ba gua boxer works to discover and create gaps in his or her opponent's awareness. Once these gaps in awareness are detected, the ba gua fighter will attempt to overcome the opponent's defense, enter the opponent's space, and deliver his or her technique by way of the opponent's gap in consciousness. Often gaps in an opponent's awareness can be created with feints and other subtle distractions. Some ba gua masters claim to be able to create gaps in an opponent's awareness through subtle manipulations of the opponent's energy field.

Ba gua fighters also use their conscious awareness to constantly be on the lookout for their opponents' weak angles—and to be aware of and hide their own weak angles. Each and every stance and posture has eight angles, of which there will always be strong and weak angles. No posture has less than two weak angles, and most postures have many more weak angles than that. Ba gua boxers begin to understand the nature of the angles by testing their stances. A boxer will stand in any of the postures or stances that he or she commonly uses and have a partner push on each of the eight angles to see which ones hold and which angles, when pushed, make the boxer immediately fall over. The eight angles are: middle of the front, middle of the back, straight through the right side, straight through the left side, a 45-degree angle through the right front, a 45-degree angle through the left front, a 45-degree angle through the right back, and a 45-degree angle through the left back. Through the process of testing the angles of their stances, ba gua boxers begin to recognize weak and strong angles within the stances, their movements, and those of their opponents. Ba gua boxers also begin to realize that because of their constant movement, they have the advantage over opponents who use stationary stances. Any single stance the ba gua boxer uses can only be analyzed and have its weak angles attacked for a mere moment, after which the ba gua boxer will be in another posture.

Once one of an opponent's weak angles is found, power is applied to that angle. The internal power used in ba gua zhang is developed in a number of different ways. Primary among these methods are weight momentum, twisting and lengthening the muscles and connective tissue, and activating the pumping of the synovial fluid through the joints—all of which are directed by conscious intent. Grandmasters of the art can also use a discharge of pure energy as a power source, but few ba gua fighters ever reach this level. The development of these power sources is contingent on the ba gua boxer having spent many, many hours practicing their basic training exercises.

Speed in ba gua zhang is a by-product of relaxation and not nearly as important as timing and positioning, which are created by the boxer's constant motion and continuous changing. The stamina of a ba gua boxer comes from diaphragmatic breathing and the ability to relax the body and mind. There is also an aerobic element to long periods of circle walking and other continuous movement training exercises, which helps build up a fighter's stamina.

The primary training exercise used to develop the skills of awareness, angles, and power in ba gua zhang is called Rou Shou, which simply means Soft Hands. This exercise is somewhat similar to the Push Hands exercise of tai ji quan, but it allows for a much wider variety of techniques and is somewhat rougher and more aggressive than its tai ji counterpart. Practitioners face each other in opposing front and back stances, join their wrists together, and spiral their arms in a figure-eight pattern while shifting their weight forward and backward. When they are familiar with working this pattern in a solid stance, they begin to walk back and forth in a straight line while maintaining the spiraling pattern of the arms, which is driven by a coiling of the legs and body. When the Rou Shou practitioners can maintain their arm spirals while moving in a straight line, they begin to work the pattern while walking in a ba gua circle, changing directions periodically. When the steady, straight line, and circling patterns have been mastered, practitioners begin to see if they can find each other's weak angles and try to push and uproot each other during the exercise. When the practitioners have become accustomed to the uprooting aspect of the practice, they begin the soft hand striking that gave the exercise its name. The idea is to keep the hands relaxed and light—and definitely not loaded with qi—and strike the opponent whenever the Rou Shou practitioner can do so without breaking the general flow of the exercise. This allows a practitioner to practice most of the palm strikes of his or her art without injuring his or her training partners. When the palm-striking aspect of Rou Shou has been mastered, practitioners go on to add sweeps, kicks, and throws to the exercise. Only the most advanced practitioners of Rou Shou use these final techniques within the practice. Advanced ba gua practitioners will use all of the techniques of the Rou Shou practice in the stationary, straight-line, and circling versions of the exercise. Some Hsing I chuan systems also practice the Rou Shou exercise, but only with the stationary and straight-line variations.

Rou Shou

The basic stepping patterns of ba gua zhang contain intrinsic training for ba gua kicking techniques. This is referred to in the old ba gua adage, "A step is a kick and a kick is a step." Because the basic Mud Tread Step puts the foot forward while keeping it weightless, the practitioner only has to pick the leg up to turn this step into a forward toe kick. This is the most basic example of "a step is a kick." Often, after a kick is delivered, the ba gua practitioner will not retract the foot but simply use the momentum from the kick to step forward with the foot that has just kicked, hence the idea of "a kick is a step." Because most ba gua steps land weightlessly, the "step is a kick" principle can also be applied to ba gua steps other than the Mud Tread Step. Classic examples are how the toe-in step can be used as a roundhouse kick, a sweep, a leg lock, or an inward crescent kick, and how the toe-out step can become an outward crescent kick, a sweep, or a leg lock. Walking the circle and changing directions with these steps will train the body in the movements necessary for these kicks, but only practicing the steps as kicks on an opponent or training partner will teach the ba gua practitioner how to actually perform the martial functions of these low or high kicks.

Kicking techniques of ba gua zhang.

Every movement in every ba gua form has at least one martial application. In some movements, the martial applications are very obvious, while in others, the martial techniques could never be gleaned from their corresponding form movements without the help of a qualified instructor. Practitioners must first carefully learn the martial possibilities of the forms they practice and then specialize in the techniques and variations that best suit their own physical, mental, and emotional states and capabilities. B. P. Chan was fond of saying, "Your ba gua is not my ba gua. You are this tall," as he would hold his hand far above his head. "Well, I am only this tall," he would continue, while indicating his own short stature. Large ba gua boxers will naturally rely more on power techniques, while smaller fighters will use timing and positioning and rely on crafty techniques. Powerful ba gua fighters will use more hard techniques in which their power will meet their opponents' force head-on to simply crush the oncoming power. Smaller ba gua practitioners will tend to give before force and come back to where there is no force in front of them—the ideology of softness and the ultimate use of angles. The highest-level ba gua boxers of all sizes will switch between hard and soft techniques, sometimes in milliseconds.

Ba gua zhang techniques are sometimes classified by their change patterns. These patterns correspond to the eight trigrams of the Chinese *Book of Changes,* the *Yi Jing.*

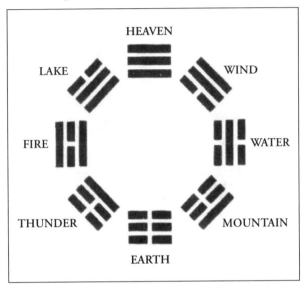

Heaven techniques tend to be hard and move forcefully upward and/or outward. The most simple of these techniques is Great Roc Spreads Its Wings, in which the ba gua boxer simply walks into the opponent with his arms outstretched, blocking the attack with one arm, while attacking the opponent with a cutting palm strike of the opposite hand.

Great Roc Spreads Its Wings

Earth techniques can be light and fluffy—like stepping past a technique while just barely touching the attacker—or have heavy, downward movements. They also include movements that draw in an opponent. Driving a kick (or a whole opponent) downward is an earth techniques. Drawing an opponent to you or past you are also Earth techniques.

An Earth Palm strike. The energy that powers it is drawn in and down.

Double Yin Palm strike

Wind techniques demonstrate the amorphous-to-solid quality of the wind. We can't touch the wind, but it can knock us down. Techniques that spin in past an attack and then attack the opponent from the inside are wind techniques. Some wind techniques flow past the attack to the outside and then roll into the opponent at one of his or her weak angles.

Toe in and deflect the blow.

Turn and strike with the buttocks.

Toe out and deflect the blow.

Step behind and cut downward.

Thunder techniques have the quality of a shock wave. They are *yang* explosions followed by a series of *yin* reverberations. All techniques that use the shaking energy known as Fa Li fall under this category. The vibrating, multiple-fist techniques of ba gua are also thunder techniques.

Fa Li Palm strike

Thunder Fist

Fire techniques cling to an opponent and coil around them. These techniques coil in past an opponent's defenses before ending in either an explosive strike or a bone-crunching throw. There are multiple ways in which this effect is accomplished.

Coiling around an attack, and then coiling the opponent to the floor.

Water techniques move in wave patterns. They tend to draw opponents in and then pound down on top of them or roll across their midsections. These techniques often drive an opponent into the ground in the same manner that a big wave can pound a surfer who is caught underneath it into the sea bottom.

Wave attack of the Sixth Palm Change of the Cheng Style Eight Basic Palms.

Wave attack of the Sixth Palm Change of the Cheng Style Eight Basic Palms.

Completion of the Sixth Palm Change wave attack.

Mountain techniques use the energy of the compressed stillness in a center that is ready to explode into light rays that shoot off in all directions—in other words, the energy of a volcano. Mountain techniques draw the opponent into a still moment, then explode to send the opponent flying away from the ba gua boxer.

The opponent is draw in as a punch is deflected.

The boxer starts to explode up-ward into knee strike.

The boxer continues to explode upward and outward, thrusting and kicking simultaneously.

The energy of **Lake techniques** is inconsistent yet it doesn't recreate the energy patterns of any of the previous seven patterns. Lake techniques can go anywhere in random sequences and often are seen put to use in multiple-opponent defense patterns.

Multi-directional Lake energy used against multiple opponents.

To become a ba gua fighter, a practitioner must first learn the martial techniques of the forms through many hours of repeated two-person drills and two-person sets. When a practitioner becomes familiar with the form applications, he or she must take the techniques that work best for him or her and begin to use them in Rou Shou practice. Once the practitioner learns how to apply these techniques with a little power, and against an opponent who is actively resisting during Rou Shou, it is time for him or her to try out the techniques in light, controlled contact sparing, during which he or she can learn to use the techniques at a fast pace and at different ranges. Before the ba gua boxer can be sure that he or she can apply the techniques in an actual combat situation, he or she must practice these techniques in some form of medium- to full-contact sparing. Only by being hit with some power can the ba gua boxer learn which techniques he or she can remember and apply after being hit—these are the only techniques that are useful for actual combat. Medium- and heavy-contact sparing practices are not for everyone, which is why a limited number of ba gua practitioners progress to becoming actual ba gua boxers. That said, practitioners of all levels of ba gua zhang derive many benefits from their practices. Basic training in the art improves a practitioner's general health and endurance, while the meditative aspects of the art clear the mind and calm the emotions. The *Yi Jing* correlations of the art teach about the phenomenon of change and how to move through the changes of life. The movements of ba gua are their own performance art, but one can only learn to fight by fighting.

The range of fighting techniques in the art of ba gua zhang is vast; a few more examples are illustrated below.

A deflection and a palm strike

Bear Stretches Its Paw

Controlling the head to set up a throw.

Side step and strike with the knee.

An elbow strike from the Fifth Palm Change of the Cheng Style Eight Basic Palms.

A ba gua roundhouse kick.

A short thrust, called Unicorn Hands Over the Book.

Step around and strike with the elbow.

5

The Exotic Weapons of Ba Gua Zhang

Although the great challenge-match fighters of ba gua zhang won their victories with their bare hands, the ba gua fighters of the Boxer Rebellion and the famous ba gua bodyguards, imperial guards, and cargo guards never went to work empty-handed. The whirling and circling movements of the art of ba gua zhang lend themselves well to the use of a wide array of weapons. The weapons techniques of ba gua zhang are highlighted by the unique and exotic weapons used by the leading masters of the art.

The **Deer Horn Knife** was the personal weapon of ba gua zhang founder Dong Hai Chuan. This is a paired weapon, which means you always hold one in each hand. In ancient times, the Deer Horn Knife was often called the Meridian Knife because the weapon represented the philosophy of the unity of the opposites of *yin* and *yang,* day and night, and sun and moon. The weapon is also called the Ba Gua Mandarin Duck Knives, because the knives are always used together and are therefore likened to an affectionate couple that goes everywhere together, like duck couples do. The name Deer Horn Knife is also popular—the top part of the weapon looks somewhat like a deer's antlers.

The Deer Horn Knife

Traditionally, the Deer Horn Knife is described using five animal shapes: the deer horn, which is the top part of the knife; the snake body, which is the side of the knife that curls like a snake; the fish tail, which is the bottom part of the knife; the bear back, which is located in the middle part of the knife; and the phoenix eye, which is the hole where your hand holds the weapon. The Deer Horn Knife has four points and nine edges, making a total of thirteen attacking surfaces.

The Deer Horn Knife is unique because it is the combination of a sword and a hooked knife. It is a powerful short weapon that is easy to carry—Dong Hai Chuan never left the palace without his pair of knives. Although Dong taught martial arts in the palace, his main job was that of a tax collector for Prince Su Wang. Dong's martial arts were considered so powerful that he was often sent alone or with only one assistant to collect taxes from the prince's unruly subjects, who lived on the far side of the Great Wall. Once he stepped beyond the wall, the authority of the central government was always in question, and the people who lived beyond the wall were not always inclined to pay taxes on grain that they had slaved to grow to a Mandarin lord living far away in the capital. The imperial guards were not there to help him, and Dong had only his skills, his wits, and his Deer Horn Knives with which to extract his lord's taxes from these uncooperative subjects. After acquiring the monies, Dong then had to be able to protect the collected taxes on the long journey home. There are many stories of Dong defeating entire gangs of bandits and groups of disgruntled taxpayers with his Deer Horn Knives. The whirling, twisting, and circling movements of Dong's ba gua techniques made his Deer Horn Knives seem like relentless razor-edged propellers that parried, trapped, and sliced everything within their range. The uniqueness of the weapon combined with the skill of the founder of the art have made the Deer Horn Knife the trademark weapon of ba gua zhang.

Ba Gua Deer Horn Knives

Dong Hai Chuan's first inner-door disciple, Yin Fu, was known for his use of the **Ba Gua Zhang Needles.** Each needle consists of nine or ten inches of thin cylindrical steel with points on both ends. There is a ring in the middle that is attached to the needle with a swivel joint, allowing the needle to spin in circles when the ring is worn on the ba gua boxer's middle finger.

The Ba Gua Needle was originally a naval weapon used by swimmers. The design allowed for minimum water displacement, so the needle allowed the sailor to swim as he normally did, while still having a means to defend himself both in and out of the water. The needles adapted quite readily to the techniques of ba gua zhang—the points augmented all of the thrusting techniques of the art, while the shaft could be used to enhance blocking and deflecting techniques, and the spinning feature of the weapon allowed it to also be used in locking techniques.

Ba Gua Needles

The needles were the perfect weapons for Yin Fu, as his style of ba gua zhang included a lot of striking and contained a wide array of thrusting techniques. The weapons are also very easy to conceal and are not likely to be noticed before they are brought into play. As with all paired weapons, in most techniques, one of the needles is used to block or deflect an attack while the other needle is used to launch a counterattack. Yin Fu made use of his Ba Gua Needles when he settled the dispute between the Eastern Granaries and the Western Granaries in Beijing. The blinding speed and cold efficiency of Yin Fu's needle-enhanced thrusting and locking techniques brought Yin much of the fame that led to his employment in the imperial palace. To this day, adherents of Yin's style of ba gua zhang usually practice some variation of his needle techniques.

Ba Gua Needles

After Yin Fu went on to open his own school and guard service, the top student in Dong's ba gua school was the wrestling champion and eyeglass maker, Cheng Ting Hua. Cheng's favorite weapon was the **Elbow Knives.** This is another paired weapon, which consists of two large knives with blades of a foot long or longer. The knives are single-edged and held in the backhand position with the blunt edges of the blades lying along the forearms. When the forearms move, the sharp edges of the knives slice along the pattern formed by the forearms' movement. This adapts perfectly to the whirling and slashing arm movements of Cheng Style ba gua zhang.

Ba Gua Elbow Knives

The Elbow Knives were originally used by foot soldiers who faced mounted opponents. The soldiers would roll under their opponents' horses, slashing the horses' bellies as they rolled by, thereby evening the playing field.

Cheng Ting Hua used his Elbow Knives to bring a lot of death and destruction to the German troops who were pillaging his neighborhood during that fateful encounter in 1900. The whirling slashes and darting thrusts of his Elbow Knives dispatched a dozen of his assailants and increased Cheng's fame, even in death. Although more people practice Cheng's style of ba gua zhang than any other style, few of its adherents continue the tradition of Cheng Ting Hua's Elbow Knives.

Li Cun Yi was known as "Single Saber Li" thanks to his use of the **Ba Gua Broadsword.** Li was a large man, which certainly helped him wield his weapon of choice, as the ba gua variation of the broadsword is almost twice the size of the standard Chinese broadsword. With almost four feet of cutting edge, this single-edged sword could cut a wide, bloody swath through an army of opponents. The wielder of the broadsword could increase the power of the sword by placing a hand on the blunt edge and pushing with it; when used in conjunction with the continuous twisting, coiling, and circling movements of ba gua, this allowed the swordsman to create a cocoon of edged steel around himself.

Ba Gua Broadsword

Li Cun Yi created such havoc on the battlefield with his broadsword that armed troops would often run away from him. During the Boxer Rebellion, Li sliced and diced many foreign troops and chopped up a few missionaries along the way. It was a time when all "foreign devils" were alike and the only good one was a dead one. During his Boxer Rebellion exploits, Li Cun Yi stained a number of his shirts with blood all the way up the sleeves to the shoulders. To the end of his days, Li wore these shirts with pride. The Ba Gua Broadsword continues to be one of the more popular weapons of the art.

Li Cun Yi's friend Zhang Zhao Dong was unique among ba gua practitioners for his preference of a **leather bullwhip** as his weapon of choice. It was known as his "red cross whip," because he was often able to place a bloody X on the chest of his opponent as soon as the encounter began. On one occasion, Zhang took his whip with him out to a ship that was holding young Chinese girls who were to be taken to the brothels of San Francisco. Using his whip, Zhang defeated the entire crew of the ship; he brought the girls ashore and sent them home. In another well-known incident, Zhang angered an entire street gang by not letting them disrupt the performance of one of his favorite plays. After he beat a handful of the gang members at the theater, Zhang was challenged to meet the entire gang at an abandoned temple. The thirty gang members were further insulted when Zhang arrived to confront them with only two friends in tow. With the help of his ba gua–trained friends, who took care of any thugs who managed to get inside the range of his whip, Zhang was able to drop most of the gang members in their tracks by lashing a bloody X into their chests as soon as they moved toward him. The gang was quickly subdued and never seen on the streets of Tianjin again. Zhang was not known to have passed on his "red cross whip" techniques to any of his students.

Dong Hai Chuan's youngest inner-door disciple, Liang Zhen Pu, was known to practice with the **Rooster Knives.** These unique weapons have blades that run down the forearms and extend beyond the hands. They can be rotated in the hands to place either the long or short ends of the blades in front, leaving longer or shorter blocking surfaces along the forearms, depending on the needs of the practitioner. A unique feature of the Rooster Knife is a small claw in the center of the side of the

Ba Gua Rooster Knives

blade. Like all paired weapons, in most techniques, one Rooster Knife is used to block or deflect while the other one is used to attack.

Like most Chinese martial arts, ba gua zhang also uses the standard Chinese straight sword, or Jian. The circling and coiling movements of ba gua zhang provide a perfect format for the soft finesse of the techniques of this most popular weapon. Some styles of ba gua use an oversized straight sword, much like the oversized ba gua broadsword. Most styles of ba gua zhang have their own versions of a straight sword set. The most popular of these sets, and the one most practiced worldwide, is the Cheng Style sword set taught by Grandmaster Liu Jing Ru.

Deer Horn Knives Set

When martial artists think of ba gua weapons, the first one that comes to mind is always the Deer Horn Knife. Not only is this weapon completely unique to the art of ba gua zhang, but it was also the personal weapon of the founder of the art. For these reasons, if a ba gua zhang school only teaches one weapon, it will almost always be the Deer Horn Knife. For these same reasons, we have de-cided to use the Deer Horn Knife to illustrate the unique

Ba Gua Straight Sword

method in which ba gua zhang adapts its movements to weapons training. The form presented in this chapter is one of the Deer Horn Knife sets taught by Cheng Style Grandmaster Liu Jing Ru.

Deer Horn Knife practice uses the same principles as ba gua zhang empty-hand techniques. However, because of the endless flow of the techniques and the skill level needed to handle the weapons, the classical Deer Horn Knife form is only taught to students after they have spent years practicing ba gua zhang empty-hand forms.

When you hold a Deer Horn Knife, don't bend your wrists—you need to be able to transfer the power from your body in an uninterrupted flow through the arms and wrists to the hands. Use the same coiling motions used in empty-hand forms to make the knives turn in different positions and angles; knife strikes are merely exten-sions of palm strikes. When using the weapon, you should apply all of the aspects of ba gua zhang palm techniques: the coordination between the waist and hip move-ments; the coiling of the arms, hands, and body; the nonstop footwork; and the use of internal power. In other words, proper knife work has the following elements: the knives follow the body, the stepping patterns dictate changes in direction, and the proper postures and movements are maintained, with the attacking points and surfaces of the knives clearly visible at all times. In general, correct use of the Deer Horn Knives in combat depends on your mastery of the empty-hand techniques of ba gua zhang; it's your understanding of the empty-hand components of the art that will dictate how well you guide the weapons and how well you extend your internal energy past your hands into the various attacking points of the weapons. Weapon practice should advance the level of your ba gua zhang practice and demonstrate perfect harmony between the empty-hand methods and the knife techniques.

We are happy to introduce this classical form of Cheng Style Ba Gua Zhang Deer Horn Knife that was developed by Cheng Ting Hua and is taught today by living legend Grandmaster Liu Jing Ru. It is based on the Cascading Palms empty-hand set and contains forty-two postures with martial arts form names. The form names, which are usually made up of four Chinese characters, are a traditional way to help students remember the sequence of the movements. Most of them describe the outside appearance of the motions, facts of life, or images of animal movements. This is part of the culture of Chinese martial arts and the culture of Chinese language arts, and it's worth spending a little time studying the names and trying to figure out why they were given to certain postures and movements.

Grandmaster Liu Jing Ru's Deer Horn Knives

Classical Cheng Style Deer Horn Knives

BY GRANDMASTER LIU JING RU

1. Opening; Look at the Sun, Look at the Moon
2. Fishermen Cast the Net
3. Step Back and Hook the Knife
4. Green Dragon Stretches Its Claws
5. Close the Door and Cover the Knife
6. Conceal the Flowers under the Leaves
7. Green Dragon Stretches Its Claws
8. Step Up and Raise the Hem
9. Pick Up the Helmet from behind the Head
10. Swallow Skims the Water
11. Sweep the Rider from His Saddle
12. Conceal the Flowers under the Leaves
13. Green Dragon Stretches Its Claws
14. White Snake Turns Its Body and Spits Out Its Tongue
15. Double Snakes Spit Out Their Tongues
16. Steal the Peach under the Leaf
17. Yin Yang Fish
18. Wiseman Points Out the Direction
19. Wind Sweeps the Lotus
20. Looking for the Snake in the Grass
21. The Sun and the Moon Walk Together
22. Push the Boat along the River
23. Lion Holds the Ball
24. Dull Sickle Cuts Grass
25. Cutting through Hua Mountain
26. Double Swallow Stretches Its Wings
27. Young Swallow Flying
28. Cow Turns Its Horns
29. Slicing Knives
30. Sweep Away Thousands of Soldiers
31. Pointing to Heaven and Plunging to Earth
32. Dead Roots around the Tree
33. Open the Window to Look at the Moon

34. Golden Wind Sweeps the Land
35. Jade Belt around the Waist
36. Lift Up the Knee and Knife
37. Python Overturns Its Body
38. Anaconda Overturns Its Body
39. Golden Snake Coils around the Tree
40. Three Basins Drop to the Ground
41. Look at the Sun, Look at the Moon
42. Closing

Posture 1: Opening; Look at the Sun, Look at the Moon

Start in a natural stance, holding the Deer Horn Knives at your sides (Figure 5-1). Step forward with the left foot, but leave most of your body weight on the right foot. As you step forward, bring the knives in front of you; your palms should face upward and the fish tails, or the ends of the knives, fold together and overlap (Figure 5-2). Turn your palms inward so that they face each other, and lower the knives back to your sides (Figure 5-3). Step forward with the right foot, and rotate the knives upward so that your palms are facing out and the knives are a bit higher than your head. The knives should be close together to show the shape of the deer horn (Figure 5-4). In combat, these two upward-facing knives are for blocking the attack of either short or long weapons.

| Figure 5-1 | Figure 5-2 |

Figure 5-3

Figure 5-4

Posture 2: Fishermen Cast the Net

As you bring the left leg closer to the right leg, rotate the left hand in an inward-hook motion (Figure 5-5). Step forward with the left foot into a bow stance; as you do this, thrust the right knife forward, with your palm up, and cut downward with the left knife, bringing it to the side of your left thigh, with your palm facing downward (Figure 5-6).

Figure 5-5

Figure 5-6

Posture 3: Step Back and Hook the Knife

Take a step backward with the right foot, and simultaneously rotate both hands in inward circles (Figure 5-7). As you bring the left foot close to the right foot to form a low empty stance, bring the right hand up, with the palm facing outward, and move the left hand down, with the palm facing backward (Figure 5-8). This is the Deer Horn Knives hook that is used to block and deflect other weapons in application.

Figure 5-7   Figure 5-8

Posture 4: Green Dragon Stretches Its Claws

Pull both knives out so that they're parallel to each other, then step the left foot forward into a standard ba gua zhang stance, with both knives extending outward past the left leg (the left arm extends while the right elbow bends). Walk in a circle (Figure 5-9).

Figure 5-9

Posture 5: Close the Door and Cover the Knife

Take a toe-in step with the right foot, and keeping your body weight on the left foot, coil your body and your left arm inward. The right palm faces downward to put the knife in a flat position (Figure 5-10). Shift your weight onto the right foot and take a toe-out step with the left foot; coil your body and your left arm outward, with the knife cut flat, palm facing downward (Figure 5-11).

Figure 5-10

Figure 5-11

Posture 6: Conceal the Flowers under the Leaves

Take a toe-in step with the right foot (to make a stance like a letter A) and twist your body to the left. The right knife goes underneath the left armpit; the palms of both hands face inward (Figure 5-12).

Figure 5-12

Posture 7: Green Dragon Stretches Its Claws

Turn and twist the body from the waist to the right. At the same time, the right palm faces upward, both palms face each other, and the right palm passes under the left arm to become to the front palm (Figure 5-13). Then, as you start to take a toe-out step with the right foot to walk in a circle, turn both palms over at once (Figure 5-14).

Figure 5-13

Figure 5-14

Posture 8: Step Up and Raise the Hem

Take a toe-out step with the left foot as you coil the left arm and palm inward and upward, As you cut upward with the left arm, move the right arm back to the right side of the body, with the palm facing backward (Figure 5-15).

Figure 5-15

Posture 9: Pick Up the Helmet from behind the Head

Take a toe-in step with the right foot; both palms coil to face each other and the right palm thrusts forward under the left palm. Your body weight is on your left foot (Figure 5-16). Shift your weight onto your right foot and twist your waist to the left, bringing the right palm behind your head and the left palm under your right armpit (Figure 5-17). Twist the waist as much as possible to the left side without moving your feet, and thrust the right palm forward (Figure 5-18).

Figure 5-16   Figure 5-17   Figure 5-18

Posture 10: Swallow Skims the Water

Take a step out to the left with your left foot and drop your center of gravity to form a crouching stance. The right palm drops low in front and the left palm coils upward, with the palm facing backward (Figure 5-19).

Figure 5-19

Posture 11: Sweep the Rider from His Saddle

Rise up slightly from the crouching stance, turning and coiling the body to the right as the right palm hooks a circle around the right side of the body (Figure 5-20). Then, repeat the same motion on the left side (Figure 5-21). Repeat it once more on the right side (Figure 5-22), and yet again on the left side, this time ending with the palm in a slightly higher position (Figure 5-23). This sequence uses the waist's power to twist from one side to the other; the movements can all be done at the same speed (fast or slow) or at different speeds.

Figure 5-20

Figure 5-21

Figure 5-22

Figure 5-23

Posture 12: Conceal the Flowers under the Leaves

Take a toe-in step with the right foot to make a letter A stance and twist the body to the left. Bring the right knife underneath the left armpit, with the palm facing inward (figure 5-24).

Figure 5-24

Posture 13: Green Dragon Stretches Its Claws

Turn and twist the body to the right as you pass the right arm under the left arm toward the center of the circle. The palms face each other (Figure 5-25). Walk in a circle.

Figure 5-25

Posture 14: White Snake Turns Its Body and Spits Out Its Tongue

Continue circle walking. When the left foot steps forward, bend the right elbow and rotate the waist (Figure 5-26). Then, as the right foot steps forward, rotate the right palm upward and thrust forward (Figure 5-27). Take a toe-in step with the left foot and bend the right elbow (Figure 5-28); shift your weight onto the left foot immediately, and pivot on the left foot to make a 180-degree turn to form a front stance. The right palm will be extended slightly forward (Figure 5-29). All movements in this posture must be connected with very smooth footwork.

Figure 5-26

Figure 5-27

Figure 5-28

Figure 5-29

Posture 15: Double Snakes Spit Out Their Tongues

As you take a toe-in step with the left foot, simultaneously turn over both palms so that they face each other and quickly thrust the left palm forward (Figure 5-30). Pivot on the left foot 180 degrees and bend the right elbow, bringing the right palm in front (Figure 5-31). Thrust the right palm forward (Figure 5-32). Rotate and shift your body weight into a half horse stance to the left; at the same time, curl the left arm slightly inward and immediately thrust it outward to the left in a fast motion (Figure 5-33). Repeat this movement on the right side, rotating and shifting your body weight into a half horse stance to the right and curling your right arm slightly inward before thrusting it outward to the right in a fast motion (Figure 5-34). This posture requires you to use the waist to quickly direct the motions.

Figure 5-30

Figure 5-31

Figure 5-32

Figure 5-33

Figure 5-34

Posture 16: Steal the Peach under the Leaf

Bring the left foot closer to the right foot and rotate the left palm inward (Figure 5-35). The left foot steps to the left side, and the left knife cuts outward so that the left palm faces backward (Figure 5-36). Bring the right foot to the left foot. The right palm faces upward, the left elbow is bent, and the left palm faces downward over the right forearm (Figure 5-37).

Figure 5-35   Figure 5-36   Figure 5-37

Posture 17: Yin and Yang Fish

Take a toe-in step with the left foot and fold the right forearm over the left forearm (Figure 5-38). The right foot then steps toe-out, coils, and pushes the left palm (which also coils) in front of the right shoulder (palm facing outward). The right palm coils down to the lower back, with palm facing outward (figure 5-39). Walk in a tight, small circle, then expand out into a bigger circle.

Figure 5-38

Figure 5-39

Posture 18: Wiseman Points Out the Direction

Take a toe-out step with the left foot, and turn the left palm upward, cutting out flat (Figure 5-40). Take a deep toe-in step with the right foot to make the body turn to face the center of the circle, and thrust the right palm forward toward the center of the circle (Figure 5-41).

Figure 5-40

Figure 5-41

Posture 19: Wind Sweeps the Lotus

As the left foot steps forward and to the left at a 45-degree angle, both palms sweep downward to the right and rotate upward to the left. As they cut upward, both palms begin to face toward each other (Figure 5-42). As the right foot steps forward, both palms cut upward higher (Figure 5-43). As the left foot steps forward with a toe-in step, which changes the angle to 45 degrees to the right, both palms cutting upward higher still (Figure 5-44). Then, as you take a step forward with the right leg, both palms sweep downward to the left and rotate upward to the right, cutting upward (Figure 5-45). Repeat this motion on the right side, then repeat it once more on the left side (Figures 5-46 to 5-50). This posture walks a zigzagging line. Every direction requires three steps; the third step is a slightly toe-in step, used to change direction.

Figure 5-42　　　　　　　Figure 5-43　　　　　　　Figure 5-44

Figure 5-45　　　　　　　Figure 5-46　　　　　　　Figure 5-47

Figure 5-48   Figure 5-49   Figure 5-50

Posture 20: Looking for the Snake in the Grass

Take a deep toe-in step with the right foot and fold the right arm over the left (Figure 5-51). Shift your weight onto your right foot and turn your body 180 degrees into an empty stance; you should be facing the center of the circle with both palms cutting to the sides (Figure 5-52).

Figure 5-51   Figure 5-52

Posture 21: The Sun and the Moon Walk Together

Step forward with the left foot and shift your weight onto it. Push both palms out directly in front of you (Figure 5-53).

Figure 5-53

Posture 22: Push the Boat along the River

Take a step back with the right foot and pull both arms inward and to the right side of the body so that the palms face each other (Figure 5-54). The left foot steps out at a 45-degree angle as the right palm turns over; both palms face upward (Figure 5-55). As you step forward with the right foot, push the palms out a little farther (Figure 5-56). The right foot steps toe-in to make a direction change and both palms rotate (Figure 5-57). Repeat the same three steps, walking on the right side (Figures 5-58, 5-59, and 5-60). These walking steps should be along the line of the circle.

| Figure 5-54 | Figure 5-55 | Figure 5-56 |

Figure 5-57

Figure 5-58

Figure 5-59

Figure 5-60

Posture 23: Lion Holds the Ball

The left foot steps forward and both palms rotate upward, with the right palm above the head and the left palm thrusting toward the center of the circle. Continue walking in a circle (Figure 5-61).

Figure 5-61

Posture 24: Dull Sickle Cuts Grass

As the right foot steps forward, the right palm turns over and cuts toward the center. At the same time, the left palm draws in closer to the body until the palms of both hands face each other (Figure 5-62). Then, the left foot advances toe-in and the left palm cuts to the center (Figure 5-63).

Figure 5-62   Figure 5-63

Posture 25: Cutting through Hua Mountain

Take a wide toe-out step with the right foot toward the center of the circle. The right palm circles upward and then cuts downward to the center of the circle (Figure 5-64). Take a toe-in step with the left foot as the left palm cuts downward

(Figure 5-65). Bring the right foot behind the left foot, stepping back into a cross stance; at the same time, thrust the right palm upward, crossing it over the left palm (Figure 5-66).

Figure 5-64   Figure 5-65   Figure 5-66

Posture 26: Double Swallow Stretches Its Wings

Both feet pivot and turn the body 180 degrees to form a horse stance as the arms open, thrusting to both sides (Figure 5-67).

Figure 5-67

Posture 27: Young Swallow Flying

Take a deep toe-in step with the left foot and cross your arms, with the left palm on top and facing outward (Figure 5-68). As you step forward with the right foot, uncross your arms and open up; the right palm faces upward and the left palm faces downward (Figure 5-69). As you step forward with the left foot, both palms face each other and then cross through the center and open up (Figure 5-70). Repeat the entire sequence twice, first on the right side, then on the left side. Each complete set actually has three steps; the first toe-in step is used for changing direction. You can change the direction actively depending on how deep you make the first toe-in step (Figures 5-71 to 5-76).

Figure 5-68

Figure 5-69

Figure 5-70

Figure 5-71

Figure 5-72

Figure 5-73

Figure 5-74   Figure 5-75   Figure 5-76

Posture 28: Cow Turns Its Horns

As you take a toe-out step with the right foot, turn over both palms. The right palm is positioned above the head and the palms face each other. Walk the circle (Figure 5-77).

Figure 5-77

Posture 29: Slicing the Cloud

This is another posture that uses three steps to complete one segment, which then repeats three times. The right foot steps forward first; the right elbow is bent and the wrist is turned outward. As the left foot steps forward, the right palm slices so that the palm is facing downward. The right foot steps toe-in to change the direction

(Figures 5-78 to 5-80). Repeat these steps twice more, first on the left side (Figures 5-81 to 5-83), then on the right side (Figures 5-84 to 5-86).

Figure 5-78

Figure 5-79

Figure 5-80

Figure 5-81

Figure 5-82

Figure 5-83

Figure 5-84

Figure 5-85

Figure 5-86

Posture 30: Sweep Away Thousands of Soldiers

The right palm crosses over the top of the left arm (Figure 5-87). The left foot steps forward and both palms sweep to the left side (Figure 5-88). The right foot steps forward and the left palm crosses over the top of the right arm (Figure 5-89). Both palms sweep to the right side (Figure 5-90).

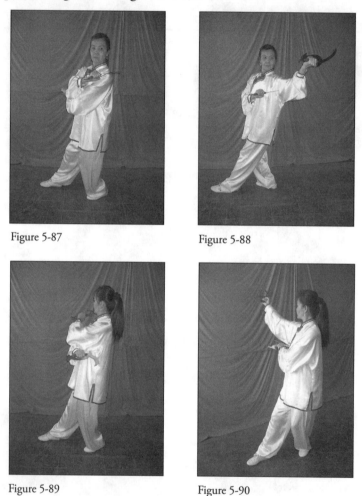

Figure 5-87

Figure 5-88

Figure 5-89

Figure 5-90

Posture 31: Pointing to Heaven and Plunging to Earth

The left foot steps toe-out and the body leans forward as the left palm coils (pointing up) and the right palm coils underneath the left armpit (Figure 5-91). Take a tight toe-in step with the right foot and shift your weight onto it; the body coils into an upright position, with the right palm up and the left palm in front of the right side of the body; both palms face backward (Figure 5-92). Lower your center of gravity and turn the left palm outward as you drop down on the right side of the body (Figure 5-93).

Figure 5-91 Figure 5-92 Figure 5-93

Posture 32: Dead Roots around the Tree

Cross your arms in front of the *dan tian* area, with the right palm over the left palm (Figure 5-94). The left foot steps out to form a crouching stance with both arms extended to the sides (Figure 5-95). The right foot takes a deep toe-in step to prepare the body to turn, and both palms cross over each other again (Figure 5-96). The left foot steps out to again form a crouching stance, with the body turned 180 degrees (Figure 5-97).

Figure 5-94

Figure 5-95

Figure 5-97

Figure 5-96

Posture 33: Open the Window to Look at the Moon

Pull the left leg back to step behind the right leg while pulling both palms to the right side of the body; the palms are flat and face each other (Figure 5-98). The left foot steps forward and the right foot steps behind the left foot into a cross stance as both palms push forward (Figure 5-99).

Figure 5-98

Figure 5-99

Posture 34: Golden Wind Sweeps the Land

The feet pivot to make the body turn 180 degrees, and the right foot steps out to form a crouching stance; both palms are open and face downward (Figure 100).

Figure 5-100

Posture 35: Jade Belt around the Waist

Rise from the crouching stance and step toe-in with the right foot, crossing the arms in front with the right palm on top (Figure 5-101). Take a toe-in step with the left foot, and cross the left palm over the right (Figure 5-102). Then, cut outward with both palms to the left side of the body and toward the center of the circle (Figure 5-103).

Figure 5-101   Figure 5-102   Figure 5-103

Posture 36: Lift Up the Knees and Knife

Take a step out with right foot and turn the body to the right; the right palm crosses over the left palm (Figure 5-104). Take a step forward with the left foot and shift your weight onto it (Figure 5-105). Lift the right knee and strike with the knives toward the center of the circle, keeping the left elbow bent (Figure 5-106).

Figure 5-104　　　　　Figure 5-105　　　　　Figure 5-106

Posture 37: Python Overturns Its Body

Step to the right side with a right toe-out step and lean forward; the body coils and turns to the right. The right palm coils and rotates upward along the back, and the left palm goes under the right armpit, coils, and rotates palm up (Figure 5-107). Take a left toe-in step as the body and arms continue to coil and rotate (Figure 5-108). Open the arms, extending the right arm behind the head and the left arm in front of the body (Figure 5-109).

Figure 5-107　　　　　Figure 5-108　　　　　Figure 5-109

Posture 38: Anaconda Overturns Its Body

Take a toe-out step to the left side with the left foot and lean forward; the body coils and turns to the left. The left palm coils and rotates upward, and the right palm goes under the left armpit, coils, and rotates palm up (Figure 5-110). Take a toe-in step with the right foot as the body and arms continue to coil and rotate (Figure 5-111). Open the arms, with the left palm behind the head and the right palm in front of the body (Figure 5-112). Execute an extended toe kick with the left foot—extend the leg forward, toes pointed, using the power from the waist and the hips—and open both arms, palms up, in opposite directions (Figure 5-113).

Figure 5-110   Figure 5-111   Figure 5-112

Figure 5-113

Posture 39: Golden Snake Coils around the Tree

The left foot steps toe-out and the left palm coils upward to about shoulder height (Figure 5-114). The right foot takes a forward toe-in step as the right palm thrusts forward under the left elbow; at the same time, the left palm turns over to face downward (Figure 5-115). Twist the body to the left and bring the right palm forward from behind the head (Figure 5-116). The right foot takes a toe-in step, and the right palm comes down and crosses over the left arm (Figure 5-117). Use the left toe-out and right toe-in steps to walk in a small circle (Figures 5-118 to 5-119).

Figure 5-114

Figure 5-115

Figure 5-116

Figure 5-117

Figure 5-118

Figure 5-119

Posture 40: Three Basins Drop to the Ground

When you walk to face the same direction and location from where you started the form, the left foot steps out into a crouching stance, with the palms facing downward (Figure 5-120).

Figure 5-120

Posture 41: Look at the Sun, Look at the Moon

Pull the left foot in and step forward, bringing both knives to the front to block with both palms facing upward (Figure 5-121). As you lower both palms to your sides, step forward with the right foot (Figure 5-122). Bring both knives back up and together, with the palms facing downward (Figure 5-123).

Figure 5-121   Figure 5-122   Figure 5-123

Posture 42: Closing

Step back with the right foot while lowering both palms to the sides (Figure 5-124). The left foot steps back to bring the feet together, which returns you to the opening position (Figure 5-125).

Figure 5-124

Figure 5-125

Deer Horn Knife Fighting Applications

The fighting applications of Deer Horn Knife techniques are vast and varied. Most employ one knife to block, parry, or deflect an attack, while the other knife counterattacks, but some techniques use both knives for defense, whereas a few techniques use both knives for the attack. Deer Horn Knives were especially useful when defending against multiple attackers. Below is a sample of the many fighting techniques that can be applied with Ba Gua Deer Horn Knives.

The Deer Horn Knives versus a long staff.

Deer Horn Knives defend against a saber.

Deer Horn Knives defend against a
straight sword.

A counterattack against a staff.

Using the knives to deflect the sword and
attack the throat.

Deer Horn Knives against a broad sword.

Deer Horn Knives against a pair
of daggers.

Deer Horn Knives block a
staff attack.

6

The Ba Gua Zhang Classics:
The Thirty-Six Songs and The Forty-Eight Methods

The Thirty-Six Songs are about how to practice ba gua zhang. The Forty-Eight Methods are about how to train fighting techniques and strategies. Both are Dong Hai Chuan's classic works that have been handed down orally. These "songs" and "methods" were presented in technical terms within a lyric-poem format that the second-generation practitioners kept and passed on secretly to their inner-door disciples. The third-generation masters of ba gua zhang, Li Zi Ming and Jin Shu Hui, released these works to the public so that practitioners could have access to the only classical written guidance on learning and using the art of ba gua zhang.

The "secrets" of the practice of ba gua zhang's have been clearly detailed in these songs and methods, including proper breathing techniques, stepping patterns, and strategies for fighting, as well as how to activate the internal energy of the body, how to use the palms, and how to power a strike. The Chinese characters are provided with their translations as references.

The Thirty-Six Songs (三十六歌):
Lyric Poem Formats for Ba Gua Zhang Training

Song One

歌一: 空胸拔顶下塌腰，扭步掰膝抓地牢.
沉肩坠肘伸前掌，二目须冲虎口瞧.

The chest relaxes, the crown of the head lifts up, and the waist sinks,
The toes point inward with the steps, the knees are close to each other.
The shoulders sink, the elbows drop, and the front palm extends forward,
The eyes look through the space between the thumb and the index finger.

Song One discusses the proper alignment in ba gua zhang posture. When you practice circle walking in ba gua zhang, you should keep the chin tucked slightly inward to put the crown of the head in the proper position. The chest should be relaxed in order to breathe naturally with the qi that flows from the lower abdominal area.

172

Keeping the spine straight connects the upper back to the neck in a natural, straight way.

The lead arm and palm position are maintained by extending from the shoulder blade; this position makes the shoulder joints flexible and keeps the shoulders dropped. The elbow is slightly bent and dropped; the palm is open and the wrist is slightly bent to make the entire arm and palm extend forward.

The eyes should look between the thumb and index finger of the bent wrist, which is at about the same height as the shoulder. A calm mind and a deeper level of concentration develop during the practice of ba gua. The circle walking footwork in ba gua zhang is the most important training. To simply walk around a circle, you need to step forward with the foot that is away from the center of the circle by turning the toes slightly inward to make a circular motion; the foot that is closest to the center of the circle should step straight forward. Keeping the knees close together and slightly inward toward each other trains the flexibility of the knee joints as well as protects you if an opponent tries to step into the centerline in between your legs.

Song Two

歌二：后肘先叠肘掩心，掌再翻塌向前跟．
　　　跟到前肘合抱力，前后两掌一团神．

The rear elbow is folded and in line with the stomach,
The palm turns downward and extends forward.
The rear palm is below the elbow of the lead arm,
Both palms coordinate in harmony to become to one whole power.

Song Two discusses how to form the position of the palms in a basic ba gua zhang posture. The arms in ba gua zhang practice are almost in one line with the lead hand and rear hand positions. The basic palm position should be learned correctly early on in order to reinforce good habits for further practice. The lead arm extends forward with the elbow dropped, and the rear arm folds with the elbow in front of the stomach. Both palms open with the power of the *yin-yang* harmony toward the center of the circle. The lead and rear arm positions change when the direction changes in circle walking—the arm that is closer to the center of the circle becomes the lead arm. Most of the time, the center of the circle is aimed at the position of the opponent, so for training, the lead palm in this basic ba gua zhang position is always toward the center of the circle. When both palms are face the center of the circle, the head, shoulders, elbows, waist, hips, knees, and feet have to coil and twist to face the center of the circle in order to ignite the whole power of the entire body. In fighting applications, the lead and rear palms always change for effective use in both defense and offense.

Song Three

歌三: 步弯脚直向前伸，形如推磨一般真.
　　　屈膝随胯腰扭足，腿到三面不摇身.

Walking with curved step and straight foot,
Pushing the millstone is the same motion.
Twisting the waist, hips, knees, and feet,
With steady steps, watch the surroundings.

Song Three is about the stepping pattern. Circle walking requires you to keep the step of inner foot straight and the step of the outer foot curved. This motion is exactly like that of Chinese farmers back in the old days pushing millstones to grind grain into flour. If one looked carefully, he or she would see that their feet were walking in a circular pattern; their knees, hips, and waists were using twisting and circular motions; and their hands pushed the handles of the millstones to make them go around. The lower part of the body in ba gua zhang circle walking should be very steady and stable. The speed of walking and the angles of the toes (inward or outward) depend on the needs of each situation and on the changes of direction taken by the practitioner.

Song Four

歌四: 一式单鞭不为奇，左右循环乃为宜.
　　　左换右兮右换左，抽向到步自合机.

Single-sided skill in practice is not unique,
Dual-side practices are a good way to train.
Change from left to right and right to left,
Coil the body inward and step backward to find an opening.

Song Four discusses how ba gua zhang trains the body to develop abilities on both the left and right sides. This is also complementary training to the old traditional form practice of tai ji quan, in which the major postures of "ward off, roll back, press, push, and single whip," were only practiced on one side. Both sides are evenly trained in ba gua zhang, a practice that definitely benefits both the health and the skill-level of the practitioner. Only techniques practiced on both sides will be able to change quickly, freely, and naturally to deal with whatever an opponent throws our way.

Song Five

歌五： 步即转兮手亦随，后掌穿出前掌回.
去来来去无二致，要如弩箭离弦飞.

Turn the foot and hand simultaneously,
The rear hand withdraws when the lead hand thrusts.
Attack and retreat without wondering,
Like the bow is bent and the arrow is shot.

Song Five discusses the importance of the coordination between the hands and feet in ba gua zhang. The hands and feet, and the upper body and lower body movements, in ba gua zhang are highly coordinated. If the hands reach the opponent slower than the feet do, the power generated may not be strong enough to damage the opponent, because the power is not connected to the feet and to all parts of the body—the hands are then like the branches on a tree without roots. If the footwork is quicker than the hands, you risk leaving too many open spaces, thereby giving your opponent an advantage. The feet and hands must move at the same time. Both hands also need to coordinate with each other—if the lead hand is thrusting forward, the rear hand is pulling backward simultaneously. The upper body coordinates with the lower body, and the mind is focused at the same time, like bending a bow and shooting an arrow.

Song Six

歌六： 穿时直掌穿肘行，后肩改做前肩成.
莫要距离莫犹豫，脚如裆兮是准绳.

Thrusting the palm right below the elbow,
The front shoulder becomes the back one.
Don't leave a space and don't hesitate,
Step in, between their feet.

Song Six tells how to apply a thrusting palm, one of ba gua's most efficient hand techniques. A famous saying among martial artists and ba gua zhang practitioners in the old days was, "Three thrusting palms make fear even in brave men." The rear palm thrusts forward toward the opponent, traveling closely underneath the elbow of the lead arm; the power of the thrust comes from the same side of the body as the foot that steps forward when that palm is thrust. The shoulders are also a source of power and connected to the body. The thrusting palm changes push one hand forward at a time, then the other. When you apply the thrusting palm, the foot that goes forward with the palm should insert the step between the two feet of the opponent to control them—there is no need to leave a space.

Song Seven

歌七: 胸欲空兮气欲沉，背紧肩垂臂前伸.
气到丹田缩谷道，直拔颠顶贯精神.

When the chest is relaxed, the Qi will sink,
Round the back, drop the shoulders, and extend the arms.
When the Qi reaches the Dan Tian, the hips are tucked under to help the Qi
*   circulate,*
The Qi will flow and the spirit will lift up.

Song Seven discusses the methods of internal posture and energy exercise in ba gua zhang. Ba gua zhang is an internal martial art—practice is not only done externally, but also internally to develop more energy through proper postures and breathing. Making the qi really sink into the *dan tian* area to promote the circulation of this microcosmic orbit is a lifelong practice. Always breath low in the abdomen, relax the chest and waist area, open the upper back and shoulder blade area, extend the arms, and keep the spine straight and the tailbone tucked slightly inward to store energy and promote blood circulation. This basic internal posture should be kept during all practices—it's not just for stance practice. The standing posture is for starting to learn ba gua and checking to make sure the internal principles have been understood and that they are practiced within the circle walking and palm changes exercises. Since ba gua zhang is not a standing art, but a highly skilled combat art, one needs to practice the walking and fighting applications in a powerful and flowing manner. A healthy body and strong energy flow also affect the health of the mind and spirit, a combination of which develops great willpower and physical power.

Song Eight

歌八：走时周身莫动摇，全凭膝下两相交．
低盘虽讲平膝胯，中盘也要下腿腰．

Do not sway the body when walking,
All depends on the interchange below the knees.
The lowest postures keep the knee and hip level,
The middle posture also sinks the waist and legs down.

Song Eight refers to the three basins of training in ba gua zhang. Circle walking is the signature and unique technique of ba gua zhang. So, this training is the main thing used to develop strong, rooted legs and stable footwork. When you walk, you basically keep the upper body light and stable, as the lower limbs do most of the work. Choose a level at which to walk the circle and keep it steady—don't bounce up and down as you walk. There are three different levels of stances: in the upper level, the knees bend slightly; in the middle level, the knees bend more and you sink down more; in the lower level, the knees are bent and the body sinks down so that the knees are in line with the hips. The latter position is the most advanced level of training. For most people, starting with the upper level and reaching the middle level is a practical training goal.

Song Nine

歌九：抿唇闭口舌顶腭，呼吸全凭鼻孔过．
力用极处哼哈泄，混元一气此为得．

Closed mouth, tongue touching the roof of the mouth.
Inhale and exhale completely through the nose.
Use the "Hen" and "Haa" sounds when releasing the power,
The whole body's energy rises.

Song Nine is about the breathing method used in the internal martial arts. Ba gua zhang requires cultivating qi in the whole body. To cultivate energy, one has to practice breathing correctly. Use the natural *dan tian* breath, and inhale deeply and evenly through the nose, never opening the mouth. The longer you train, the more qi will gather in your *dan tian*. The whole body will benefit from this kind of inner power. The energy flows from the *dan tian* to the rest of the body, bringing you an improved circulation of qi and blood that prevents, or even heals, diseases, granting greater long-term health. When you release power, you might use the sounds "Hen" and "Haa" as you exhale through the nose and mouth to help release the energy. Whole-body power is something internal martial artists talk about a lot and train for incessantly.

Song Ten

歌十: 掌形虎口要撑圆，中指无名裂缝开.
先戳后打使腕骨，松膀长腰跟步钻.

Stretch the palm and make the Hu Kou round,
Separate the middle finger and ring finger.
Strike with palm first, then with the wrist bone,
Relax the shoulders, sink the waist, and use half steps.

Song Ten discusses the shape of the palm and its use. The opening and rounding of the "Hu Kou," a space between the thumb and the index finger, is a signature of original style ba gua zhang. Opening the Hu Kou, and leaving a natural space between the middle finger and the ring finger, will allow the energy to easily reach the fingertips for use in palm strikes. The palm strikes are usually directed straight toward an opponent first, but it's the heel of the palm that strikes. At the same time, the front foot steps into the centerline between the legs of the opponent, and the rear foot takes a half step, following the front step, while you drop the shoulders and waist (or Kua) to connect the whole-body power to the heel of the palm.

Song Eleven

歌十一: 上步合膝倒步掰，换掌换步矮身骸.
进退退进随机势，只需腰腿巧安排.

Advance with knees close and retreat with knees open,
Lower the body when changing palms and steps.
Advance or retreat according to the situation,
The key is in the skills of the waist and legs.

Song Eleven is about the quick changing of direction that makes ba gua zhang unique among martial arts. When you change direction, you take a toe-in step (a *Kou Bu*) and the knees are close together; then, you take a toe-out step (a *Bai Bu*) with the other foot and the knees are open. (You also lower your center of gravity for stability when changing directions.) It doesn't matter if the steps are for advancing or retreating, or if they're done fast or slow—they all have to be done in accordance with the situation to make a correct decision. Therefore, the coordination of the waist, the hips, and the legs is very important; all movement is governed by this coordination. Classical Chinese martial arts writings state that "seventy-percent footwork and thirty-percent hand work" is needed for a good offense or defense.

Song Twelve

歌十二：此掌与人大不同，进步抬前乃有功.
　　　　退步还先退后足，跨步尽外要离中.

This palm technique is quite different from others,
Advance with a step of the front foot first.
Retreat by starting to move with the rear foot,
Step around the opponent's center.

Song Twelve is about the advancing and retreating stepping patterns of ba gua zhang. Ba gua zhang's defining feature is its footwork, which emphasizes the long Mud Tread Step as well as the half step, or so-called "following step," which is used for speed and power. When stepping forward, move the front foot first, which saves time in getting closer to the opponent; the rear foot follows immediately with a half step to be able to employ the whole body's internal power in a palm strike. When you need to step back, the rear foot goes back first, followed by the front foot. Another special technique in ba gua zhang involves stepping around an opponent to void an attack, while drawing his power into an empty space, which causes him to lose his balance. Step around to the side of an opponent to find a weak angle to strike.

Song Thirteen

歌十三：此拳与人大不同，手未动兮膀先攻.
　　　　未从前伸先后缩，吸足再吐力独丰.

This palm technique is quite different from others,
Shoulders move ahead of the striking palm.
Backward first, then extended,
Compress then release for special power.

Song Thirteen refers to the power release used in palm strikes. The second difference between ba gua zhang and other martial arts is that the shoulders move before the palms do when palm-striking. The shoulders are the connection between the body and the palms. Direct the intent to the shoulders, loosen the joints around the shoulder blades and the ends of the arms to store the power, and then send the power from the shoulders into the arms and palms. Gathering power and exploding forward with the strike requires a very quick action, which is also a part of special internal power training.

Song Fourteen

歌十四：此拳与人大不同，前掌后掌力相通.
　　　　欲使梢兮先动跟，招招如是不得松.

This palm technique is quite different from others,
Front and rear palms connect in power release.
The root moves first and moves out to the fingertips,
Every technique uses the same method.

Song Fourteen is about energy discharge. The third difference between ba gua zhang and other martial arts is that ba gua uses energy discharge from the roots for greater power. The roots for palm strikes are the feet and shoulders. In every different kind of palm strike, though the palm angles and shapes are slightly different, the training methods are the same.

Song Fifteen

歌十五：此掌与人大不同，未击西时先声东.
　　　　指上打下人莫测，卷珠倒流更神通.

This palm technique is quite different from others,
Make a sound to the east before attacking to the west.
Point high when striking low,
A great skill is to roll pearls upward.

Song Fifteen is about combat strategies. The fourth difference between ba gua zhang and other martial arts is the technique of redirecting the opponent's attention and using the strategy of change to launch an effective attack. For example, you might make a sound like you're about to attack the east side of the opponent when the actual attack is to the west side, or point to a high position, then attack the lower part of the body instead. "Roll pearls upward" means that the striking power comes from the ground and travels up (and internally): it is rooted in the feet, directed by the waist, and expressed in the palms.

Song Sixteen

歌十六：天下精术怕三穿，不走门外是枉然.
　　　　他走外兮我走内，伸手而得不费难.

Three Thrusting Palms is a powerful technique,
It wastes time if you don't walk around the opponent.
If he walks to the outside and I walk to the inside,
It's easy to defeat him.

Song Sixteen is about Three Thrusting Palms, one of the important palm techniques in ba gua zhang. It uses constant palm strikes to attack the opponent's eyes, nose, and face in order to break his concentration and make him confused and disoriented. To be able to use this technique well, one needs to pay attention to positioning, which involves stepping around the side of the opponent. In other words, you're always attacking from the side, not face to face. Whenever you find yourself in a face-to-face position, it probably means it's time for you to quickly change the palm and step to the side—don't let the opponent break into your centerline.

Song Seventeen

歌十七：掌使一面不为功，至少仍需两面通.
　　　　一横一直三角手，使人如在自怀中.

It's not skillful enough to use the palm in one dimension in combat,
At least two dimensions have to be managed.
One crossing and one straight from a triangle hands position,
It will easily control a person like embracing them.

Song Seventeen discusses the triangular position and the practice of changing palms. Not many of the powerful techniques in ba gua zhang combat can only be done from one side or one dimension. The changing of the left and right is a necessity. The position of the hands and feet should be triangular, with one hand across the body and the other hand extended straight forward. The stepping pattern also can be triangular in nature for endless repeating and changing of techniques. Willpower and an undefeated attitude are qualities a person can use to control an opponent.

Song Eighteen

歌十八： 高欲低兮矮欲扬，斜身绕步不须忙.
斜翻倒翻腰着力，翻到极处力要刚.

Attack a taller person low and a shorter person high,
Stay calm and step around the opponent.
Using the waist turning or overturning the body,
Strong force comes when rotation reaches its utmost.

Song Eighteen provides a few basic combat strategies. If the opponent is taller than you, attack a lower target; if he is shorter than you, take advantage of it and attack a higher target like the face. Always use ba gua zhang's circular stepping to go around the opponent. If you circle correctly, the opponent will think that you're at his side, when you are actually attacking his center, or he'll think that you've escaped, only to find that you are attacking him from the side. When turning the body, use the waist to turn; when you reach the point at which you cannot turn any more, release hard force.

Song Nineteen

歌十九： 人道掌法胜在刚，郭老曾言柔内藏.
个中也有人知味，刚柔相济是所长.

It's said that the palm method wins over power and hardness,
Master Guo used to mention that softness is hidden power.
This secret has been known by some people,
The combination of soft and hard is most advantageous.

Song Nineteen is about the theory of soft and hard techniques in ba gua zhang. Normally, people think that the winner of a match or fight must have strong and hard power, but Master Guo Ji Yuan, who was a martial arts uncle of Dong Hai Chuan, used to say that combining the soft power with the hard force makes a greater power. Basically, this is the soft-and-hard power combination and changing in the power practices of ba gua zhang.

Song Twenty

歌二十： 刚在先之柔后藏，柔在先兮刚后张.
他人之柔腰与手，我则吸腰步法扬.

Hard power comes first, with softness hidden inside,
Soft power appears first, with hard force following.
Others think soft power is about the waist and hands,
My stepping is additional.

Song Twenty is a further exploration of the soft and hard aspects of ba gua zhang. In ba gua zhang combat, soft and hard power is always combined and changes frequently. Before we use the hard force, we should have soft power hidden inside; if we apply the soft power, the hard force will follow immediately. When an opponent uses hard power, you should use soft power to neutralize or reverse his efforts and to use a different power than your opponent. Some other martial arts think soft power is all about the waist and hands, but ba gua zhang's specialty is using stepping as an additional technique to foster this kind of power.

Song Twenty-One

歌二十一： 用到极处需转身，脱身化形不留痕.
如何变化端在步，出入进退腰先伸.

When in the extreme, the body has to turn,
Moving freely without leaving a trace.
All changes depend on footwork,
The waist moves first in advance or retreat.

Song Twenty-One is about turning the body. The "extreme" refers to the changing point in between two postures. Using a turn or changing direction are common ways to connect one posture to another. Moving freely and quickly is ba gua zhang's essence—it's hard to catch the movements of a good ba gua zhang fighter. These free and quick changes and movements all use the waist.

Song Twenty-Two

歌二十二：转掌之神颈骨传，转项扭项手当先.
　　　　　变时缩颈发时伸，要如神龙首尾连.

The spirit is transmitted from the neck bone,
The hands move right before turning the neck.
Extend the neck for the release of power and relax it for change,
Like a spiritual dragon linking its head and tail together.

Song Twenty-Two is about spirit ("Shen" in Mandarin) in ba gua zhang. Keeping the spine straight is an important point and required in the training of the internal martial arts. The spine connects to the hip in the lower body and neck in the upper body; its posture and health affect the image of one's spirit. Hold the neck straight and the energy will be transmitted naturally from the bottom of the feet, through the legs, hips, and spinal column, and up to the head to show one's great spirit. If you don't hold the neck and spine straight, the basic proper posture is impossible to achieve, as are overall health and martial skills. When you need to turn or change, the eyes should follow the movements of the hands and the hands should follow the movements of the eyes, but the neck is never crooked and your centerline is never changed. When releasing power, the neck is compressed first, as with other parts of the body, to gather the energy. Then expanding the neck is also like expanding every other part of the body to release power. In this way, the move is like a dragon linking its head and tail energetically.

Song Twenty-Three

歌二十三：打人凭手膀为根，膀在肩端不会伸.
　　　　　欲要进时进前步，若进后步枉劳伸.

The shoulder is the root when striking with the palm,
But the shoulder's reach has its limitations.
Step the front foot first when advancing,
It's a waste, if the back foot moves first.

Song Twenty-Three again addresses the coordination of the hands and the feet when attacking. In ba gua zhang palm striking, the shoulder is the root of the palm. But the shoulder can only reach so far. Using the footwork to be able to reach an opponent faster and from a longer range is the key strategy in ba gua zhang combat. Move the front foot first when advancing—it is a total waste of time to step with the back foot first if you wanted to advance.

Song Twenty-Four

歌二十四：力是发自筋与骨，骨中出硬筋相随．
　　　　　足跟大筋通脑脊，发招跟步力能摧．

Power is released from the tendons and bones,
The hardness comes from the bones and softness through the tendons.
The big tendon of the heel connects to spine and head,
A half step gives extra power.

Song Twenty-Four discusses the source of *Fa Li*, the great energy used in ba gua and the technique used to discharge it. Combat requires power. This power is different from a human being's natural power or from any stiff, uncoordinated power. This internal power is developed by combining hard and soft powers. The hardness of the power comes from the bones, and the softness of power comes from the tendons and ligaments. The power discharge must start from the heel, pass through the thigh, hips, waist, and spine, and come out of the palms and fingers. This verse also reminds us that taking, a half step will provide extra force.

Song Twenty-Five

歌二十五：眼到手到腰腿到，心真神真力又真．
　　　　　三真四到合一处，防己有余能胜人．

The eyes, hands, waist, and legs reach simultaneously,
With real heart, real spirit, and real force.
Combination of three reals and four reaches,
Will defend one's self and defeat others.

Song Twenty-Five is about intent. The three reals and four reaches are inherent in the basic training of ba gua zhang. The eyes are watching while the hands sense the opponent; at the same time, the practitioner uses the waist and legs to move the whole body to do whatever is needed. These four reaches also have separate purposes and functions: the eyes can see the strong and weak sides of the opponent, the hands can sense the substantial and insubstantial aspects of the opponent, the waist can stabilize the practitioner's center, the legs can initiate the power release. The three reals are also the three harmonies: the harmony of the heart and the intent, the harmony of the intent and the qi, and the harmony of the qi and the power. All these together become internal power.

Song Twenty-Six

歌二十六：力要刚兮劲要柔，刚柔偏重功难收.
　　　　　过刚必折真物理，优柔太盛等于休.

Force should be hard and soft,
Overly hard or overly soft creates imbalance.
Something too hard is easily broken,
Something too soft is powerless.

Song Twenty-Six discusses the balancing of the soft and hard powers. Normally, strong power is great for attacks and soft force is good for neutralization. However, force, like steel, can still be broken if it's too hard, and if it's too soft, like thread, then it is inefficient, as it cannot even be straightened. This is a principle that appears in physics as well as in internal martial arts.

Song Twenty-Seven

歌二十七：刚柔相济是何言，刚柔相辅总无难.
　　　　　刚柔当用乾坤手，掀天揭地海波澜.

Soft and hard complement each other,
Balanced Yin and Yang overcomes difficulties.
Softness and hardness are present within the Heaven and Earth Palms,
It would be like lifting the sky and turning the earth.

Song Twenty-Seven addresses specifically the soft and hard palm techniques. Soft and hard have to be balanced. Power release and neutralization, advance and retreat, defense and offense, quick and slow, toe in and toe out—all techniques have *yin* and *yang* in them and keep changing all the time. Heaven is *yang* and Earth is *yin*; in these techniques, both palms turn and move in opposite positions, make projections, and draw in the combined *yin-yang* power of ba gua zhang.

Song Twenty-Eight

歌二十八：人刚我柔是正方，我刚人柔法亦良．
　　　　　刚柔相济腰求胜，解此纠纷步法强．

It's a good method when I am soft when he uses hard force,
It's also a good method when I use the hard force and he is soft.
When soft and hard meet, the body method makes the victor,
Footwork solves the dispute.

Song Twenty-Eight addresses the relationship between soft and hard when using power strikes and stepping patterns. If the opponent uses hard force to attack, neutralize the oncoming power and avoid direct force. If you use power to attack, the opponent can use the skill of neutralization, too, if he is also a good fighter. In this case, whoever can use the waist better may win the fight. If both are equally skillful in the use of all the techniques and body methods, whoever has better footwork may win, because superior positioning wins the engagement, and proper footwork gives you superior positioning.

Song Twenty-Nine

歌二十九：步法动时腰先提，收缩合宜显神奇．
　　　　　足欲动时腰不动，跟苍迈去误时机．

Move the waist and hips slightly right before moving the step,
Proper retraction and release would appear magical.
Move the foot without moving the waist and hip,
The opportunity would disappear in a stiff step.

Song Twenty-Nine discusses the importance of waist and leg positioning in circle walking. When walking, always use the waist and hip to move the leg forward, as they are the center part of the body and govern the lower limbs. The *Kua,* where the joints between the legs and hips connect, does a slight retraction to move the leg, so the looser your hip joint, the quicker and longer the step you will be able to take. This method of walking makes your stepping lighter, more agile, and more active. Waist movement also helps keep you stable and better able to control your center of gravity. Walking without using the waist and hips will only lead to stiff movements and lost opportunities in combat.

Song Thirty

歌三十: 转身变法步莫长，擦地而行莫要慌.
看准来势方伸手，巧女穿针稳如刚.

Don't overextend the step when turning and changing the palm,
Don't lift the foot too high above the ground.
Observation first, then response,
Like a fair lady threading a needle.

Song Thirty instructs that when changing directions while walking and turning the body, you need to take a small step instead of a big step. A tighter step takes less time, uses a quicker motion, and offers better stability than a bigger step, and you need to not lift the foot too high off the ground to complete one. All you need to have is a calm mind. When responding to an attack, first you have to quickly and clearly observe the situation, then use good techniques in response to your assessment. It's like a fair lady threading a needle: She needs a calm mind to deal with a hard, tiny needle and a soft thread. With her steady hand and good eyes, she will accurately put the thread through the eye of the needle.

Song Thirty-One

歌三十一: 人持利器我不慌，飞剑遥遥到身旁.
看他来路哼哈避，邪不胜正语颇良.

Be calm when you dealing with weapons,
Even if his sword is getting close to you.
You can use "Hun" and "Haa" sounds for defense,
Evil never overcomes Virtue.

Song Thirty-One is talking about having courage when using empty hands against weapons. The most important thing in combat is one's courage—skill comes second. When someone comes at you with a weapon, you need courage to deal with the situation: courage keeps you calm, the calmness keeps you relaxed, the relaxation keeps your vision clear, the good vision keeps your movements quick and light, and the speed and agility keep you out of your opponent's reach. Then, you can use the sounds "Hun" and "Haa" to shock your opponent and get a chance to fight back.

Song Thirty-Two

歌三十二： 短兵相接似难防，哪怕锋利是鱼肠．
伸手来取囊中物，指山打磨妙中藏．

Defense in close distance seems difficult,
It's worse if a fish-intestine sword is present.
It's actually as easy as taking things out of one's pocket,
The secret is distraction.

Song Thirty-Two also addresses empty-hand combat versus an armed opponent. A short-range confrontation with an armed opponent is very difficult to defend against. In this kind of situation, again, don't be nervous. Taking over or knocking down the weapon is as easy as taking something out of someone's pocket. Use a strategy to distract him and misdirect him to provide an opportunity to attack and succeed. The "fish-intestine sword" was an extremely sharp sword from the Spring and Autumn Period in Chinese history. In the Wu state, Prince Wu had an assassin smuggle a sword into the king's court by hiding it inside the belly of a fish. When Prince Wu presented the fish to King Liao, he thrust the sword into him and took over the king's position. The type of sword used was named "fish-intestine" after this tragedy.

Song Thirty-Three

歌三十三： 人众我寡力难挡，巧破千钧莫要慌．
一手不劳凭指力，梨牛犹怕反弓张．

It is difficult to defend against many attackers,
Smart strategies are most needed.
Finger force can be used instead of a full hand,
Even a bull fears its horn turned.

Song Thirty-Three warns that it's very hard to fight against multiple opponents no matter how skilled you are. In this situation, calm and courage are needed. Use intelligent strategies to find any possible advantage. Think of it this way: a scale is very small, but it can weigh one thousand pounds by turning its pivot. A bull is big and strong, but it can be thrown down by turning its horn.

Song Thirty-Four

歌三十四：伸手不见掌前伸，又无松油照彼身.
收缩眼皮努睛看，底盘掌使显神奇.

It's too dark to see the palms,
No fire can be used to see the body.
The eyes focus and stare carefully,
Low posture made the miracle.

Song Thirty-Four is about fighting in the dark. In ancient times, people often used pine-tree oil lamps to provide light for nighttime fights. If you don't have anything that can help provide light, drop into a lower stance to fight. This will help you see the opponent clearly, using only light from the stars and the moon, by helping your eyes focus on him or her.

Song Thirty-Five

歌三十五：冰天雪地雨泞滑，前脚横使且莫差.
翻身切忌螺丝转，高低紧避乃为佳.

On those snowy, icy, and rainy days,
When stepping forward, the foot should have the toes pointed inward.
Don't pivot the foot on the ground,
Avoid bumpy and uneven surfaces.

Song Thirty-Five is about fighting in the snow and rain. How do you walk and fight on those snowy, icy, and rainy days? When you step forward, always use the toe-in step (*Kou Bu*), and keep the knees close together to increase stability. When you need to change positions or turn, do not use either the ball of the foot or the heel of foot to pivot because it's easy to fall down on slippery ground. Always use the toe-in and toe-out steps when putting the foot down flat. Try to avoid fighting on bumpy or uneven ground.

Song Thirty-Six

歌三十六： 用时最要是精神，精神焕发耳目真.
任凭他人飞燕手，蚁鸣我听虎龙吟.

It is important to have a strong spirit in combat,
Brilliant spirit makes the senses of the eyes and ears more intensified,
Even if the opponent's hands are as fast as a bird,
I can hear the ants singing as loud as the roaring of tigers and dragons.

The final song discusses the importance of spirit. A martial spirit is equally important, whether you're training for better health or for combat. If no spirit shows in one's practice, it's a waste of time, or at the very least, a low quality of martial arts training that has no harmony of spirit and motion. The spirit directly reflects through the eyes and ears. A good, positive spirit makes the eyes clearer and the ears more sensitive. No matter how fast your opponent is, you'll be faster, because you are more sensitive than him, allowing you to make good decisions when responding to any type of attack.

The Forty-Eight Methods: The Secret Rhymed Formula Methods of Ba Gua Zhang's Fighting Applications

1. Body Method (身法诀)

手法步法要相随，手到步落力必微。
手脚具到腰欠力， 去时迟慢难抽回。

Hands and footwork must be coordinated,
Not enough power if the steps are slower than the hands.
Without waist power, you only have hands and feet,
Then it's difficult to quickly advance and retreat.

Ba gua zhang's power is an internal, whole-body power. Eyes, hands, body, and footwork are highly coordinated and rooted in the feet. If the hands have thrust toward the opponent but the feet have not yet followed, the power from the hands is limited to a local area and has just the strength of the arms backing it up. Even if both hands and feet are used together, but the waist is not used, this still means that power only comes from the limbs, not the whole body. The waist is the center of the body that creates the harmony between the upper body and lower body; without its central control, it's hard to move quickly when advancing and retreating or when changing directions.

2. Observation Method (相法决)

对御群敌相法先，未曾进步退当然。
退步审势知变化，以逸待劳四两牵。

Observe the opponents first,
Stay back instead of advancing.
Step back to know the situation,
Small force can deflect much greater power.

No matter how many opponents you face, the most important thing you can do is observe them quickly in order to figure out their strong and weak points before they know yours. Good fighters always know when to advance and how to retreat for defense or change the situation to their advantage. This is the same strategy as "four ounces deflect a thousand pounds" found in tai ji quan.

3. Stepping Method (步法决)

为从动梢先动根，手快不如半步跟。
出入进退只半步， 制手避招而安神。

Move the root before moving the fingertips,
Fast hands are not faster than the half step.
Use a half step for advancing and retreating,
Control the opponent and calmly evade them.

If you want to do a palm strike, you should move your feet and waist before moving your hands and arms. Regardless of how fast your hands are they can never be as fast and effective as a half step forward or backward in close-distance fighting. A half step can change the situation dramatically because it is so quick compared to a full step. When you use the full step going forward or backward, you have to readjust body weight and position. The half step does not require you to change the body weight ratio completely. In addition, the heel of the rear foot adds more power to the body when you attack. So, ba gua zhang fighters should not stop training half-step techniques until they can naturally apply them in sparring practice and in fighting.

4. Walking Method (迈法诀)

功夫本从弯步来，两手变化随步开。
高挑低搂横掩臂，推拖带领不离怀。

Skills come from the circle walking,
Hands change when steps change.
Block high, brush low, and elbow strike,
Push, lift, carry, and roll to follow one's bend.

All skills of ba gua zhang are developed and derived from circle walking. When you walk in the circle, the palm techniques always follow the stepping changes—hands follow the feet. All the forms that you practice impart many ba gua zhang techniques and training skills. The importance of practicing palm changes is that they help you develop all kinds of skills, which will eventually become your natural movements that prepare you for fighting.

5. Cascade Step Method (连步法诀)

连步必三费功夫，使手要简自然无。
搭手转身是空手，机会临巧是江湖。

Linking step takes longer than a simple step,
All techniques have to be simple, natural, and efficient.
Turn the body and make the attacker fall into emptiness,
Taking the opportunity is a real "Jiang Hu" skill.

The "linking step" refers to taking more than three steps at a time when practicing stepping patterns. This is an excellent way to move quickly, but it doesn't fit all situations. If you can simply use one step instead of three or more, you may defeat the opponent with a simple technique and simple stepping pattern. (That said, you have to also gain the ability to use combination techniques and not limit your mind and action to the efficient use of simple techniques.) For example, when dealing with an attack, if you can simply turn your body to the side to make your opponent fall into emptiness, you are demonstrating "Jiang Hu," just as a highly skilled kung fu master would do. Jiang Hu refers to the area in China that contained the Shaolin Temple, Chen Village, and other rural settlements that were known for their martial arts skills. The martial skills of this area were so famous that the term "Jiang Hu" came to denote the highest level of martial arts skills.

6. Prohibiting Double-Weighted Step Method (囫步法诀)

囫步不要两相齐，前虚后实差相宜。
若要站齐前后倾，亦且腰短少灵机。

Never stop walking with the feet together,
The back foot takes most of the body weight.
Standing on both feet in one line is double weighted,
Standing double-weighted makes the waist stiff and it's hard to move away.

The stepping patterns of ba gua zhang keep the practitioner in motion most of time; however, there is a tiny pause whenever you use palm strikes or change positions and strategies. During this very short pause, you must make sure that the back foot is supporting most of your body weight (there should be no more than thirty percent of your weight on the front foot). In this way, you'll be able to take a very quick step forward or backward. Keep in mind that there is no double-weighted footwork in ba gua, because from a double-weighted position, it is very difficult to control your balance or properly twist your waist.

7. Yin and Yang Hands Method (手法诀)

偏沉则随双重滞，外硬里软拈枪式。
横推里勾身为主，只有吸手腰腹随。

Single-weighted alive and double-weighted stiff,
Hard on the outside and soft on the inside.
Palm pushing outward or hooking inward,
The waist is indeed always moving.

Like the footwork, the hands in ba gua zhang require a certain balance—one substantial and the other insubstantial. Hard power comes from the surface of the palm, and soft power comes from the inner side of the circle. The body is like a long spear and the hands are like the head of the spear—the head moves to open a door so that the body and its power can get in. If the attack comes diagonally, push it away; if the attack comes in a straight line, coil the palm and hook it away. All of these palm movements can only be done with the waist and body moving as one piece.

8. Internal Power Method (力法诀)

人说冷弹脆硬快，我说冷快是一般。
脆硬细分无二致，发动全凭心力合。

People say cold, springing, crisp, hard, and rapid are powers,
I say cold and springing powers are ordinary.
Crisp and hard powers are almost the same,
Power discharge is from harmony of mind and force.

Many martial arts consider cold (sudden), springing, crisp, hard, and rapid powers to be good ones. Ba gua zhang players think that springing power comes from the combination of cold and rapid powers and that the powers of crisp and hard both have each other in them and are, therefore, virtually the same. In ba gua zhang, even a single palm strike will release internal power. The intent and concentration of the mind, or willpower, is also a power, which comes from internal energy stored in the *dan tian*. It's rooted in the feet; comes up through the legs; is directed by the waist; travels through the back, shoulders, and arms; and releases through the palms. This single, whole-body power includes all five powers mentioned above.

9. Power Storing Method (存力法诀)

只会使力不会存，力过就如箭出弦。
不但无功却有害，轻输重折且失身。

Only knowing power release and not knowing power storing,
Power is gone just like an arrow leaving the bow.
This is harmful and worse than just useless,
It leads to defeat or damage of the body.

When releasing power, you shouldn't release all of it, but keep a very small amount in reserve. This is one of the principles of internal power—power can be restored quickly and one should be able to continue to use that power in a very short time period. If you release all of your power at once in one strike, you won't have any power left to defend yourself. In internal martial arts, breaking an opponent's balance, neutralizing an opponent's strikes, and borrowing an opponent's power to use it against him are all methods of using power. The strong power release, known as Fa Jin, should be really forceful and leave no chance for the opponent to come back.

10. Power Continuation Method (续力法决)

力着他人根已断，若再续力彼难逃。
此时唯有冲前步，长膀长腰一齐交。

When the opponent's root is broken,
Put more pressure on him to not let him escape.
Steeping forward is needed,
Expanded arms and waist are applied.

When the opponent's root is broken, his balance is off, or his foot is moved by force, you should take this opportunity to continue using the same technique that you have been using to finish him off or stop his escape. Use a forward step to get even closer to the opponent—expanding the arms and sinking the waist for power is particularly effective. When you notice that your opponent's balance has been upset, you do not need to change your strategy to capitalize on the opportunity. If you change the strategy at this moment or try to apply different palm techniques, you give the opponent a chance to adjust his position and restore his power and balance.

11. Higher Skill Method (降人法诀)

快打慢兮不足夸，强制弱兮不为佳。
最好比人高一招，顾盼中定不空发。

Depending on faster speed is not good enough,
Heavier weight is not the only solution.
It's better to have exceptionally great skills,
With center equilibrium and nothing missing.

Ba gua zhang trains highly skilled fighters who do not have to rely on being faster or heavier than their opponents to win. Practitioners who understand internal power, the techniques of the palm strikes, and the various strategies of ba gua zhang can deal with all types of situations, even disadvantages in speed, height, and weight. Acquiring general skills and a few special skills requires hard, long-term training and practice. Some practitioners train one or two special techniques extensively; these are the techniques that they always use, which are often chosen because they have worked well for the practitioners in previous combat situations. But special skills are secondary: all practitioners must train and perfect the principles of internal martial arts such as center equilibrium, neutralization, and power release.

12. Winning Method (决胜法诀)

彼力千钧如快梭，避强用顺快步挪。
千人只有三五近，稍伸手脚不难遮。

When a powerful and fast attack comes towards me,
I avoid the oncoming force and step around.
Only three or five opponents can get close to me, even if there are a thousand,
It's not difficult to defeat them using the palms and legs.

No matter how powerful and fast the attack is you must stay calm to be able to see it coming and avoid being hit. Step to the side of an opponent to make the attack miss its target and his power will fall into an empty space, which will upset his balance. When dealing with multiple opponents, Dong would not make major changes to his strategy; he would stick to his usual method of dealing with the various changes as they came toward him. He would use his palm strikes, stepping techniques, and changes of direction to defend against any attack, and even if there were many opponents around him, only three to five of them could get close to him at a time.

13. Application Method (用法诀)

高打矮兮矮打高，斜打胖兮不须摇。
若遇瘦长凭搂带，年迈无力上下瞧。

Hit low on the tall man, strike high on the short man,
Use angle attacks on the fat man.
Throw or pull the thin man down,
Simply glare at the old man.

These are the basic methods for dealing with different types of opponents. When the opponent is taller than you, hit him low and use a lower stance so that he cannot use his greater height and longer reach effectively against you. Attack the head and face of a shorter opponent to stop the lower-level attacks he may try on you. Attack a heavier person on his sides and back, as he will be slow at turning and changing position. On a thinner person, use your power to control him and throw or pull him down. If you face an older or weaker person, simply glare at them (looking confident and intense) to scare them. No matter how your opponent looks, you should use the same combination of stepping, turning, twisting, and changing directions.

14. Compressing the Joints for Blocking Method (封闭法诀)

手讲三关脚伸屈，一手三关脚直遇。
肩腕膝胯肘可用，缩颈空胸步带躯。

Three joints on the arms and legs,
Palms coordinate with the steps.
Shoulders, waist, knees, hips, and elbows are useful,
Body moves to follow the steps.

The three joints of the arms—the shoulders, elbows, and wrists—should always work together. The three joints of the legs are the hips, knees, and ankles; they should also always work simultaneously. These joints all can be used for attacking, but none are efficient if their movements aren't properly coordinated with the steps. Remember, the feet always lead any motion. Be careful not to overextend the arms or legs, as this give your opponent a chance to attack.

15. Analyzing the Opponent Method (接拳法诀)

五花八门乱如麻，长拳短打混相加。
你越快兮我越慢，我若发时鬼神夸。

Many are the styles and variations in the martial arts.
Mix long fists and short strikes.
The quicker you are, the slower I am.
Release power that is undefeatable.

There are so many different styles and variations in the Chinese martial arts, and they all have their strong points. When you fight against opponents with styles different from yours, you must keep calm and analyze them out quickly. Don't blindly attack. When you see the opportunity open up, attack, and release the entire body's power efficiently. Use a combination of long and short strikes to effectively neutralize your opponent.

16. Dissolving Joint Locks *(Qin Na)* Method (摘解发诀)

拿法莫夸技，两手拿一力固奇。
任他神拿怕过项，穿鼻刺目势难敌。

Don't envy joint-lock skills,
When both hands grab one, power is stuck.
Push over the head to dissolve the joint lock,
Thrusting palms to the nose and eyes are more powerful.

Ba gua zhang does not emphasize joint-locking or grabbing techniques. Only use these occasionally. When you grab someone, your hands are stuck, too. Also, joint locks and grabs are relatively easy to escape if you know what you're doing—you can simply push the hand that has grabbed your waist over your head or use your twisting power to limit your opponent's range of motion, forcing him to release your hands. When struggling out of a grab or lock, you should follow up with palm strikes to the nose and eyes—if you haven't completely dissolved your opponent's clinch, these will help you to do so.

17. Double-Handed Method (接单补双法诀)

莫说两手仗坚兵，一来一往是其能。
闲住左手右无用，双手齐来更无功。

Attacker comes with a weapon in his hands,
The skill is making one come and one go.
If either hand is blocked, the other one will be useless,
Easy to evade if both hands come toward me.

These lines explain how to defend against short weapons with empty hands. If the opponent has one weapon, take control of one of his hands—either the hand with weapon or the empty one—to make his motion as limited as a single-hand movement. If both hands hold the weapons, you need only use the steps to evade a direct attack.

18. Confusing the Opponent Method (指山打磨法诀)

他人来手我不然，侧身还击彼自还。
他若还时我入手，他若峰时三手连

When his hand comes, my hand is waiting,
If I turn my body, he will withdraw.
My hand enters when his hand withdraws,
Three thrusting palms before he attacks again.

When an opponent attacks with a punch or palm strike, quickly step to the side or turn your body to avoid it. This may confuse him momentarily and make him pause. He will, however, surely strike again. When he pulls his arm back for the next attack, step forward to get closer to him and deliver palm strikes continuously, without giving him time to breath.

19. Moving Shadow Method (脱身化影法诀)

他不来时我叫来，他要来时我化开。
不须手避凭身法，步步不离两胯哉。

I tempt him to come when he doesn't,
I move away when he comes.
Using the body to move, no need to use the hands,
Every step should be controlled by the hips and waist.

These lines describe a unique characteristic of ba gua zhang's footwork when used in fighting applications. This strategy becomes especially important when both parties have equally great techniques. As an opponent waits for you to attack first, tempt him to make the first move, for example, by making an opening in your defense as a trap or faking an injury. When he takes the bait and attacks, step away from the attack. Use the hips and waist to control the steps during this maneuver—no need to use the palms. The idea is not to lose your opponent or make risky moves, but simply to wait and follow his moves, while watching for offensive opportunities.

20. Turning the Body Method (背后转身法诀)

伸手要小步要大，开步半胯贴身抓。
胯步落地蹲身转，他要转时我鹰拿。

Less extension in the hands with bigger steps,
Small steps when making a tight turn,
Turn by lowering the center of gravity,
Dragon Claw Palm stops his turning.

Ba gua zhang practitioners always try to step behind their opponents to attack. When doing palm strikes, do not extend the arms and palms too far—use the steps to get within striking range. After you've slipped behind an opponent, you only need to take a small step to finish him. Remember to lower your of center of gravity and sink your hips to make the turn smooth. When he starts to turn or follow your turn, you'll already be behind him and can use the Dragon Claw Palm to strike.

21. Striking, Pounding, Chopping, and Bumping Method (盖 砸 劈 撞 法诀)

盖来还盖我要先，砸右换步左手粘。
劈来叠肘桩横立，撞来乾坤手摇圈。

He strikes, I will strike first,
His right hand pounds, my left hand sticks to him.
His chopping comes, my elbow bends,
He bumps, my Yin-Yang Palm will twist him.

If the opponent strikes, you can strike at the same time, but you have to be faster than him. If the pounding comes from his right hand, step to the side and use your left hand to deflect the punch. The left hand sticks to his arm so that you can then enter through his defense, by stepping in as he withdraws his punch, and strike him. When he chops to your head, raise one of your arms and a bent elbow to dissolve his force with a springing power; the other hand pounds his body. If he bumps you, use both hands to twist him with your waist power.

22. Half Circle Method (半圈手法诀)

他人手法多直线，跨上半步等如闲。
即或指直打斜法，再跨半步不相干。

Most people attack in a straight line,
Walk a half step to his side and wait patiently.
Point straight forward for oblique punching,
It's still all right to walk another half step to his side.

When opponents attack, they usually punch in a straight line; you need only take a half step to the side to avoid this strong attack. Even if it looks like the opponent is throwing a straight punch but he actually lands it obliquely, you can still take another half step to the side first. These half steps make a half circle that can be used for walking away or changing from a passive position to an offensive position.

23. Full Circle Method (整圈手法诀)

四面敌人我在中，穿花打柳任西东。
八方凭势风云变，不守呆势不守空。

I am in the center and surrounded by the opponents,
Moving like a butterfly fluttering among flowers.
No matter how the wind and thunder change in eight directions,
I remain calm and stick with my strategies.

When you are under attack from all directions, your steps must be nimble and quick. You must change directions very often to deal with multiple attackers. The movement should be like a butterfly fluttering among the flowers, which is very hard to track. It is the way to confuse your opponents and make them forget their strategies. At the same time, maintain your calm and stick to your strategy of mixing real and false attacks.

24. Heart and Eyes Method (心眼法诀)

心如大将眼如法， 见景生能制他。
最忌心痴眼不准，手忙脚乱费周折。

The mind is the general and the eyes are the weapons,
It's possible to conquer him with awareness.
If mind and eyes do not perform at their best,
This leads to the confusion of all movements.

To be a good fighter, you must have a highly focused mind, and your eyes have to be sharp enough to observe the ever-changing situations of combat. The mind directs the qi, the eyes tell the hands and feet where to go, and the mind and eyes coordinate with each other to decide on the best strategy and lead the direction of the action. Otherwise, any action is blind and confused.

25. Glaring Method (定眼法诀)

四面刀枪乱如麻，又当昏夜月无华。
矮身定睛招路广，步步弯行自赢他。

Attacks come from all directions,
As well as in the dark, without moonlight.
Lower the center of gravity and observe carefully,
Using curled steps to achieve victory.

This method addresses the problem of fighting more than one opponent in the dark. When visibility is low, you need to lower your center of gravity by dropping into a lower stance and observe with a wide eye to deal with the changing situation. You can also use curved steps, like *Bai Bu* and *Kou Bu,* to puzzle opponents and go around them with quick steps and changes of direction.

26. Fighting with Weapons Method (接器法诀)

长短单双器固精，算来不如两手灵。
铁掌练来兵一样，伸手偏找肱腕行。

Long, short, single, and double weapons are perfect,
The hands techniques are even more valuable.
Iron palms are as perfect as a weapon,
They can cut the wrists and arms.

Weapons were important in ancient times. But palms skills may ultimately be more valuable in training and fighting. When an opponent with a weapon comes toward you, step to the side and forward, and immediately use your palm to strike his wrist or arm. The palms have to be trained to be like iron; when they strike an opponent's wrists or arms with whole-body power, they will cut the opponent's blood vessels to make him lose control of his weapon.

27. Protect the Body Method (保身法诀)

以强制弱不足夸，弱能胜强方是法。
任他离弦箭快硬，左右磨身保无差。

No surprise that the strong beat the weak,
It's a real skill if the weak can defeat the strong.
No matter how powerful and fast the opponent is,
Turning and rubbing the body to left, and go around to the right.

A high-level internal martial artist is often not the bigger or heavier person in a fight. He is, however, the one with the exceptional skills to defeat bigger and stronger opponents. One technique used by ba gua fighters is called the "turning and rubbing" technique, in which you stay close to your opponent's body and relentlessly move the steps and the turns to the side of (or behind) him, even if he is fast and uses a lot force. Constantly change and turn to protect yourself until you find a better angle to attack.

28. Confusing the Opponent Method (乱人法诀)

心乱先从眼上乱，千招不如掌一穿。
对准鼻梁连环使，跨步制人左右还。

To be able to confuse his mind, first confuse his vision,
Thousands of techniques are no better than one thrusting palm.
Palm thrust to the nose continuously,
Alternate the steps around both sides.

One efficient way to break the concentration of an opponent is by "confusing" his vision. Blurred vision directly puts the mind in an "I have no idea" state. To do so, continuously thrust your palms into his nose, eyes, and face. At the same time, use footwork to step to his left and right side alternately, making it even harder for him to focus on you.

29. Opening and Closing Method (开合法诀)

欲合先开是一般，见开防合不二传。
诈败佯输知卷土，　指东打西意中含。

It is common to open before closing,
It is important to see the opening and prevent the closing.
A comeback will be staged after a failed attack,
Understand pointing to the east and then striking to the west.

Almost all types of techniques include opening and closing stages. Pay attention to the opponent when they open (i.e., prepare to release force)—if you can see the opening, you will be able to take the correct action to prevent the opponent's power release. It is, however, important to be careful when an opponent has failed to deliver his attack, as he will undoubtedly come back with another attack. Lastly, it is also important to figure out his strategy of "pointing to the east and striking to the west," which means identifying the types of feints and distractions he is apt to use so that you don't repeatedly fall for them.

30. Center Method (定南法诀)

任他千手千眼快，守住中身是枉然。
不到要时不伸手，伸手即要发手还。

No matter how fast his thousands of hands and eyes,
I stay with my center and protect my center.
No need to extend my hand when it is not necessary,
The hands will be returned after they extend.

When an opponent is attacking with countless strikes at countless different angles, you need only keep yourself centered and protect your center to weather the attack. Keep your hands close to your body. When you get the chance to strike, your hands should reach the opponent quickly and land the strike as accurately as possible. After striking, retract the hand back toward your body as quickly as possible.

31. Approaching Method (求进法诀)

封闭固是护身招，躲过他人自逍遥。
切记远出尺步外，开门绕道法不牢。

Blocking is a skill of protecting,
To avoid attacks with a casual attitude.
When the distance is more than inches away,
Skills are useless and power will not be effective.

Blocking is always an important skill to learn. Superior ba gua zhang skills allow you to block in a casual and effortless manner and step away from the opponent. But always remember that your distance from your opponent should be "neither too close nor too far." You have to be close enough to block the attack—if you step too far away from the opponent, you won't be able to control him, and your skills will be useless.

32. Six-Direction Method (六路法诀)

他人六路是空言，我之掌法六路观。
动步即能八方顾，瞻前顾后自无难。

Six-direction method is in many other martial arts,
My palm method reflects the principle of six directions.
Moving a step will observe eight directions,
Look forward and pay attention to the back at the same time.

All kinds of Chinese martial arts emphasize the six directions of combat (front, back, left, right, upper, and lower). The eight directions of ba gua are the four cardinal directions of east, west, north, and south, and the four diagonal directions of southeast, southwest, northeast, and northwest. Circle walking is a practical method in which to observe the six directions and eight directions; you can see all of the directions as you walk in a circle.

33. Accuracy Method (不二法诀)

法不准兮不妄发，发不中时第二发。
任他鬼神多灵妙，不勾魂兮亦裂牙。

Do not shoot an arrow without a target,
Shoot again if the target is missed.
Even if he moves like a ghost,
I catch the evil spirit in no time.

It is necessary to be accurate when striking. If you're uncertain that you will land a strike, it is better to wait than to throw a blind or useless strike. Otherwise, you not only end with a failed strike, but also leave yourself open to your opponent. If you do strike and miss, however, you should strike again and constantly, giving your opponent no time to catch his breath.

34. Preventing a Slip Method (防滑法诀)

冰天雪地步难牢，前横后直记心梢。
动步需用小开步，切记挺身去打高。

Walking in the ice and snow is difficult,
Use inward toes when you step forward.
Small steps are necessary for rotation,
Straight up the body to reach high is prohibited.

When fighting on a snowy day or on icy ground, keeping your balance becomes the key to winning. Just remember this: a toe-in step of the front foot is required when you walk forward; the back foot should be straight to deal with the slippery ground. When you turn or change direction, a small step is a smart step to use. If you straighten the body to try to strike high, you will be in danger of falling, because your center of gravity goes up and you may lose control of your lower body and slip. So, strike low when fighting on slippery surfaces.

35. Stabilizing Step Method (稳步法诀)

步不稳兮身必摇，脚踏实地胜千招。
进屈足趾退悬踵，不扣步兮莫回瞧。

The body will sway if the steps are not stable,
Stable stepping is better than learning a thousand strikes.
Go forward with the toes and backward by lifting the heel,
Do not turn around without a toe inward step.

Footwork is the most important thing in ba gua zhang. Unstable footwork lends its instability to the body. Learning a lot of strikes without learning proper footwork merely gives you punches without the body power or proper positioning to back them up. This is only focusing on a minor part of the technique and forgetting about the main aspect of the art. The key to walking is stepping forward with the toes extended, landing on the ball of the foot first, and stepping backward with the heel lifted, again landing on the ball of the foot first. It's not logical to turn around if you don't use a toe-in step. In other words, don't look back without taking a *Kou Bu* step.

36. Small Step Method (小步法诀)

回身转步必须小，步大身摇不灵巧。
欲要转身迈半步，人难擒兮人不晓。

Use a small step when turning the body,
No balance and no agility if the step is too big.
Always turning with a half step,
It is difficult to be caught and followed.

Ba gua zhang practitioners use small, tight steps for turning and changing directions. Big steps sometimes limit agility. Often, small steps are the easiest method of getting closer to the opponent's body when you are already in close range. Mobility training includes the use of half steps as small steps for quick changes when going forward or backward or for stepping to the left or right side.

37. Levels of Posture Method (掌法诀)

掌法虽有上中下，上下不过是掌架。
圆转自如惟中盘，高下全以此变化。

Palm posture positions are upper, middle, and lower.
The upper or the lower are just different frames.
The middle posture guarantees the ease of rotation,
In which the change is easy to the high and the low.

Almost all the Chinese martial arts have upper, middle, and lower postures; these three different levels are created by lowering the center of gravity and bending the knees. When training and practicing, keep in mind that the lower the posture you train in, the faster your conditioning and skills will improve. This is because the lower postures require more energy than the higher postures. In fighting, however, the middle posture is recommended, because power comes from the middle part of the body. It's important to make this part of the body totally free and loose and able to easily transfer energy from the feet, through the waist and hips, and upward. Also, the rotation of the waist and hips is important for whole-body movement. Only when you are in a middle posture can you easily switch into upper and lower postures.

38. Prohibiting Forward Bending Method (忌俯法诀)

低头如同眼不开，亦且身易往前载。
低头猫腰中枢死，全掌全步使不来。

Bending the head is like closing the eyes,
This leads the body into falling forward.
Bent forward at the head and the waist,
Body and palm power cannot be fully used.

Every type of martial arts training prohibits looking down by bending the neck. This position causes the whole body to lean forward and lose its center of balance, thereby making it difficult to look straight ahead. If you can't see in front of you, you may as well just close your eyes and try to fight blind. Bending the neck and the waist restricts the energy flow from the *dan tian* area to the whole body, which affects the body's control of the limbs and eliminates the source of their power. A bent-over posture is definitely not the position that a good fighter would naturally arrange himself in or that a healthy person would normally adopt for daily life.

39. Prohibiting Backward Bending Method (忌仰法诀)

紧背空胸静中求，挺胸坦腹悔难收。
叠肚吸腰来不及，最怕转身不自由。

Maintain silent stillness, with the chest relaxed and back open,
Incorrectly pushing the chest and belly outward brings regret.
Sinking the belly not soon enough,
The fear is created when the body cannot rotate freely.

Bending backward, or arching the chest and back too much, adversely affects the transfer of energy and power. The correct posture involves relaxing the chest and waist, spreading the shoulder blades, and calming the mind—all basic parts of internal martial arts training. If the Pushing the chest and belly outward is as bad as bending forward in terms of how it affects energy flow and power. When practicing ba gua zhang, the correct posture should be maintained at all times. If you don't do this, and you try to sink down and relax the chest as an attack starts, it will be too late to deal with the situation. What's even worse is you won't have the freedom of movement to be able to change and turn fast enough to protect yourself.

40. Straight Body Method (正身法诀)

全身力量在中枢，自身斜歪力不周。
别看弯步身必正，发手如箭不停留。

Power lies in the middle of the body,
Power is not right if it is not centered.
The steps are curved but the body remains straight,
Shoot the arrow without stopping.

The primary principle in internal martial arts is keeping the body centered. The power release comes from the waist (which is the center part of the body) and from keeping the spine straight. If the body is not centered, the energy channels are not connected well, making it difficult to train for full-body power. When walking in a circle or using toe-in or toe-out steps, the feet and steps are curved, but the body remains straight. You can only strike like an archer who constantly shoots arrows fast and accurately by staying in motion while staying centered.

41. Body Supplement Method (辅身法诀)

身如君王腰腿臣，君正臣强可制人。
进退躲闪凭身法，若无腰腿不生神。

The body is like the king and the limbs are like ministers,
A powerful king and strong ministers can conquer their enemies,
Advancing, retreating, and moving around all depend on body methods,
No spirit and no power without the waist and legs.

"The body is like the king and the limbs are like ministers," is an ancient phrase that describes the relationship between the body and the arms and legs. Coordination and movement all depend on how the body moves. Without the legs and waist strongly supporting the power of the palms, victory cannot be achieved.

42. Twisting Body Method (扭身法诀)

人来制我已贴身，此时手脚不赢人。
左右吸腰用扭法，化险为夷把人擒。

If the opponent approaches me closely,
When my hands and feet cannot protect me,
I twist my body to either side accordingly,
Changing the danger into safety and capturing him.

Twisting the body is another specialty of ba gua zhang. For instance, when your opponent throws a punch and you don't have enough time to either step to his side or use another palm strike, you can twist your body (with your chest sinking inward) to avoid this danger and find another opportunity to attack.

43. Step Around Method (跨步侧身法诀)

穿梭直入势难停，先发制人显他能。
若遇此手接连退，不如跨步侧身灵。

A direct forceful attack is difficult to stop,
The first attack has its advantage.
Retreating instantly in a fight,
Will never be as good as taking a side step and turning the body.

If your opponent strikes first and continuously attacks with thrusting palms, you cannot just retreat (i.e., walk backwards to defend yourself). Instead, you should use a side step, and turn your body to the side to avoid the attack.

44. Swimming Body Method (左右甩身法诀)

闪躲东方西又来，摇身一变甩身开。
左右连环皆如此，前推后搂腰安排。

I come from the west after I evade in the east,
Turn the body to make the situation change.
Do the same on both sides, connected like rings of a chain,
Pushing and pulling are coordinated by the waist.

When dealing with several attackers at the same time, use toe-in and toe-out steps to turn the body around and walk in a stepping pattern that resembles a figure-eight or the rings of a chain. In this way, you will be able confuse your opponents and find opportunities to use your power to push and pull them. Remember that the power to do this comes from the waist.

45. Sinking Body Method (跨步沉身法诀)

身高架大路上三，举手招封势所难。
跨步沉身使就下，入我机关用法宽。

Meeting a tall and big opponent,
It is difficult to reach his height and fight.
Bending the legs and sinking the body downward,
Draw him into your range.

When fighting a taller, larger opponent, there is no advantage in trying to rise up to reach him. All you need to do is sink your center of gravity to make him follow you. Then you are free to use high, middle, and low postures against him, and he is left only with the choices of middle or low postures. In this way, a disadvantage becomes an advantage in a fight.

46. Joint Lock *(Qin Na)* Method (忌拿法诀)

八卦之手不讲拿，我拿人兮我亦差。
设若人多更不便，直出直入最甚夸。

Ba gua zhang does not emphasize joint-locking or grabbing,
My skill is not superior if I grab a person.
Grabbing is not appropriate to deal with multiple opponents,
It is best to employ a direct attack and directly withdraw.

Whether in training or fighting, ba gua zhang never emphasizes joint-locking and grabbing techniques, even though many of the movements and postures contain potential joint-locking applications. When you grab someone or apply a joint-locking technique, your hands are also tied up—your palm skills are useless if your hands are occupied by grabbing someone else's hands. Also, when you are dealing with multiple opponents, grabs or joint-locks can only can applied to one person at a time, leaving you vulnerable to attack from the others. It is much better to use direct attacks, quick withdrawals, and correct timing.

47. Prohibiting Stop Walking Method (忌站法诀)

浑元一气走天涯，八卦真理是我家。
步步不离脚变化，站住即为落地花。

Walk without any limitations on mixing Yin and Yang into one force,
The principles of ba gua zhang are true guidance.
Every technique depends upon changing steps.
Standing still is like a flower on the ground.

The skills of ba gua zhang are developed by spending a very long time practicing circle walking and developing *yin-yang* power. Endless walking is the foundation that both practical training and fighting techniques are based on. If you stand still, or don't move enough, you are vulnerable, just like a flower on the ground, which can easily be trampled. Nonstop walking practice cultivates qi, making a long, healthy life more possible.

48. Ultimate Method (太上法诀)

力要足活招要准，即或使空三不紊。
招套招兮无穷尽，精神法术在乎纯。

Power must be full and technique must be accurate,
Even a missed technique cannot affect the heart and body.
Strokes within strokes and no limit,
Spiritual methods make pure and proficient palms.

Striving for pure, high-level skills in ba gua zhang takes hard work. Those considered to have high skills have full-body power, accurate techniques, and highly controlled, calm minds. When a high-level practitioner misses one strike in combat, it does not affect his or her mood or abilities. Instead, a miss inspires the fighter to fight better and to extend him or herself further. Constant strokes within strokes and circles within circles are the signatures of well-refined martial skills in ba gua zhang. Highly skilled ba gua zhang practitioners do not choose certain limited ways in which to practice their techniques; they use all the principles of the art to perfect pure and superior skills. They also must have a deep understanding of ba gua zhang theory.

7

The Daoist Roots of Ba Gua Zhang

Ba gua zhang's relationship to meditation is unique among martial arts. Other martial arts that have a meditative component began as fighting arts. Then, at some point in their history, a practitioner realized that by adding meditation to his daily training, he could help remove fear and its resulting hesitation from his fighting. Often, the meditation aspect of the art would grow from this seed. Ba gua zhang, on the other hand, is the only martial art in which the founder took a meditation art and adapted it into a fighting art. One might say that from the view of a Daoist monk, Dong Hai Chuan took a sacred meditation practice and devolved it into a fighting art.

The ancient Daoists attempted to be practical in their viewpoints. They saw that people primarily do four things: lie down, sit up, stand up, and move about. Therefore, the ancient Daoists created lying, sitting, standing, and moving meditative practices. Apparently, these Daoists looked to their predecessors—the shaman founders of Chinese culture—for some of the patterns of their moving meditations. Some of the oldest texts relating to the study of the Dao have chronicled a few of the dance patterns of the legendary Yu, mythical father of Chinese shamanism. The patterns of many of these shamanistic practices were circles and spirals.

Most ba gua zhang practitioners agree that Dong Hai Chuan's art was founded on a practice of Daoist circle walking meditation, and many of them believe that Dong was learned in this circle walking art himself. There are, of course, a few enthusiasts of the art who cling to the belief that Dong learned an earlier martial art, which had been developed from a Daoist circle walking practice. Few ba gua schools can agree on which Daoist circle walking meditation Dong Hai Chuan learned and from which era of Daoism that practice came.

The most noted scholar among modern ba gua zhang experts, Professor Kang Ge Wu of Beijing, teaches that the Daoist circle walking practice that the art of ba gua zhang was founded on was developed by the Longmen, or Dragon Gate Sect, of Daoism. The legendary origins of the Dragon Gate Sect trace back to Daoist Master Qui Chuji, who retired to seven years of study and meditation at a place in Shaanxi, called Dragon Gate, in the early thirteenth century. The actual, practicing sect existed during the late Ming dynasty, but its established lineage didn't start until the early Qing dynasty. Master Wang Changyu was the abbot of Baiyun Guan (White Cloud Temple) in Beijing, when the lineage of the Dragon Gate Sect began with him in 1656. Wang developed an ideology that combined the roots of his Daoist training with an ethical code that conformed to the Confucian ethics of the ruling dynasty. This led to great success and White Cloud Temple became a major training center and ordination site for all kinds of Daoist schools. The Dragon Gate Sect promoted a standardization of religious rules and eventually claimed supremacy over the Daoist priesthood in Northern China—as the Celestial Masters Sect did in the south. To this day, White Cloud Temple remains the leading Daoist temple in Northern China.

The authors at White Cloud Temple.

From its earliest beginnings, the Dragon Gate Sect had a circle walking meditation practice called "Rotating in Worship of Heaven." The monks credited their legendary founder, Qui Chu Ji, with the creation of this practice, which they performed every morning and every evening. In this practice, the members of the sect created a moving *yin-yang* symbol by walking in a circle and making an S curve through the middle of the circle to change direction. They had separate chants for morning and evening, which accompanied their circle walking. Through this practice, they hoped to achieve stillness in motion.

American ba gua zhang expert Jerry Alan Johnson has written that he believes the circle walking roots of ba gua zhang were derived from a practice of the Daoist monks in Southern China. This practice was called "Natural Supreme Empty Palm," and in it, the monks faced the center of the circle while walking around the circumference. Their meditation during this practice was, "Starting from nothing, 'Wu Ji,' we begin gathering energy to evolve into a harmony of yin and yang, 'Tai Ji'."

B. P. Chan taught his students his own variation of ba gua meditation. His meditation set consisted of walking in four static postures and practicing four movements that traveled along the circumference line of the circle. Chan called this set "The Eight Inner Palms," and he used it to create calm concentration and increased awareness in his students. Within this set, students maintained a basic "be here now" mindset, focusing on their current inner and outer environments while avoiding fantasies or thoughts of the past or future. Chan never made any attempt to explain the origins of this practice.

B. K. Frantzis began studying the meditative aspects of ba gua zhang with his first teachers but felt that he discovered the highest levels of the art with his last ba gua master, Liu Hung Chieh. The last half of Liu's life was almost entirely focused on his meditation practices. Liu learned some form of ba gua meditation from one of his earliest teachers, Zhu Wen Bao, who was a pupil of Dong Hai Chuan's student Liang Zhai Wen. Liu Hung Chieh credited the ba gua meditation practices of Zhu for allowing Liu to easily absorb the meditation techniques of the Tien Tai sect of Buddhism later in his life. In the mid-1930s Liu studied with the sect for a few years, after which the Tien Tai sect declared Liu Hung Chieh to be a "formally recognized

B. K. Frantzis and B. P. Chan (Tai Chi Farm, 1993)

enlightened being." Liu was enlightened enough to recognize that it was time for new teachers and promptly left for the mountains of southwest China, where he spent the next decade studying with the various Daoist masters whom he encountered there.

While traveling to the Daoist temples and hermitages in the Wu Dang and Emei mountains, Liu believed that he discovered the specific Daoist circle walking practices that Dong Hai Chuan had learned. Liu learned these from a group of practitioners who walked in a circle and changed direction in a manner similar to the walking and basic changing of direction in Dong's ba gua zhang. The meditative goal of these practices was to "make heaven and earth reside within one's own body." The idea being that when the practitioner's inner world joined with that of the outside world, the person had achieved "Becoming One with the Dao." This practice claims an oral lineage, which stretches back three thousand years to the foundations of Chinese culture. From the time that he learned them until his death forty years later, the ba gua zhang practices of Liu Hung Chieh were based on what he learned from the Daoists in the southwestern mountains of China. Although he was not a member of the Dragon Gate Sect, throughout the later years of his life Liu Hung Chieh performed his daily meditation practices at White Cloud Temple. His disciple B. K. Frantzis also practiced daily at White Cloud Temple while training in Beijing.

The ba gua meditation practices taught by B. K. Frantzis begin with the Daoist Water Style method of removing blockages from one's energy systems. Many schools of Daoist practice contain some variation of this practice. Terminology and levels of refinement vary, but at their base, all the Daoist "water" methods serve to relax, release, and dissolve and/or float away energy blockages, as opposed to the later Neo-Daoist "fire" methods, which burn, blast, and blow away the blockages. This dichotomy of methods of energy blockage removal of course bears no relationship to the use of pure water and fire energies in the practices of Daoist internal alchemy. From Liu Hung Chieh, Frantzis learned a very extensive and highly refined version of the Daoist water method of energy blockage removal—and how to apply this method to his ba gua zhang meditation practices.

To remove energy blockages, one must first feel energy. Energy is, in fact, less dense than flesh, and therefore, a person must learn to first feel their body in order to later feel energy. B. K. Frantzis was introduced to this concept early on in his internal martial arts studies. On a misty spring morning in 1968, in a park in the Taiwanese city of Tai Zhong, ba gua master Wang Shu Jin was instructing a young American, who was on break from college in Tokyo. Wang casually instructed the young collegiate karate champion, "Please move his liver a little to the left." As the American student stared at the rotund Chinese master in complete confusion, Wang eyed the young man in perplexity. Suddenly a light appeared in the master's eyes and Wang surmised, "I understand. You can't even feel your liver." A very young B. K. Frantzis replied, "I'm supposed to feel my liver?" At this point, the portly pontiff of ba gua zhang on the island of Taiwan walked over to the young karate champion, grasped his wrist in two steel-claw fingers, picked up his arm, looked at it disdainfully, and reproachfully announced to the youngster, "I don't know whose body this is, but obviously, it isn't yours. I hope you got a good price for it!" He then disgustedly threw Frantzis' arm back against the young man's body and marched off to attend to another student. Wang believed that only those who could feel their entire bodies were truly alive and that anyone who is physically unaware is one of the walking dead. It was also Wang Shu Jin's somewhat harsh opinion that the walking dead should get out of the way of the living. This incident with Wang Shu Jin marked the start of B. K. Frantzis' journey to wake his nervous system and be able to feel his body both inside and outside.

The primary practice of awakening the nervous system is often called "What's Alive and What's Dead?" A practitioner begins by directing his consciousness to the top of his head or to the top of his qi field (if he can feel this area). One's qi field projects outward from all around his or her body and often is referred to as one's "aura." Qi is a person's life-force energy. When a person is feeling strong and healthy, her qi field may project a couple of feet around her body. On the other hand, when a person is feeling weak and unwell, her energy or qi field may only rise a few inches from her skin.

Students must learn to feel their bodies by awakening their nervous systems. At the same time, they must do their best to shut off visualizations of their bodies. Once the nervous system has been awakened, a practitioner can simultaneously visualize his body and still be able to feel it, but if he engages in visualization during the first few months of this practice, his mind will only make mental pictures of his body and he will never learn to really feel it.

After feeling whatever they can of the top of the qi field, the practitioner's awareness drops to the top of her head, where she tries to feel the hair, scalp, skull, the plates of the skull, and the sutures of the skull where the plates come together. Students must simply list what they can feel and what they can't feel. They must also recognize the simple fact that there are no perfect human beings. We are so far from perfect that if there ever are any perfect humans, we probably won't recognize each other as the same species. Trying to be perfect can lead to insanity, and striving for perfection in energy work and meditation can render a practitioner crazier than a bedbug. In meditation and energy work practices, it is essential to recognize when you're doing your best and simply be satisfied with that. Perfection is not an option. This is reflected in most practitioners' first experience in feeling the top of their heads—they usually only feel the scalp out of all the parts listed above. This is quite normal for beginners. After taking inventory of the top of the head, the practitioner then simply moves down his or her body a bit and feels along a cross section, trying to sense skin, bone, connective tissue, organs and/or glands in the region, fluids moving through their various fluid systems, and the empty spaces or cavities of the body. They simply list what they can feel (What's Alive) and what they can't feel (What's Dead).

With this focus, the practitioner continues down his or her body in consecutive cross sections, like visiting fifteen or twenty floors of a building. At each level, he or she simply lists what is alive and what is dead and continues downward to the bottom of the qi field below the feet. In the first stage of this exercise, and in the following practice of blockage detection and removal, it usually takes a minimum of twenty minutes to actually feel one's way completely through the body. As your practice hours build up, and more body parts move from the Dead column to the Alive column, your nervous system will awaken and become sensitive. At this point, you can allow your visualization skills to return and join with the feeling of your now-awakened nervous system. What's Alive and What's Dead practice allows you to monitor your own body and adjust your health practices and lifestyle accordingly. It is also a great help in manipulating small muscle groups and connective tissue for greater movement and power in martial arts practice.

Wu Tang P.C.A. members in seated meditation.

When in the course of his or her regular What's Alive and What's Dead practice the practitioner finds sensations of congestion and constriction arising and impeding the ability to feel the body, he or she has found an energy blockage. This is the starting point of feeling the body's energy. The practitioner then focuses in on the sensation of the blockage until it seems to form a solid shape. She applies her intent to this shape and begins the dissolving process in which the edges of the shape transform from a solid to a liquid and finally to a vapor, which floats outward to the edges of the practitioner's qi field. The feeling of this process is somewhat akin to squeezing your fist tightly until the knuckles turn white, then relaxing the muscles of the hand—without actually moving the fingers or releasing the position of the fist—and feeling the relaxation radiate from the center of your fist to the edges. Few blockages are dissolved away in one sitting. Many of the blockages you'll encounter took a long time to form, and it will take a long time to make them dissolve. It is essential that the practitioner recognize when she has dissolved all that she can of a particular blockage and then moves on accordingly, continuing to feel her way down her body and pausing to work on dissolving any other blockages that might arise.

Energy blockages are caused by shocks to a person's energy fields; the blockage consists of the congealed energy of a particular field. Most of the blockages that you detect early on are in the body and the qi field. When the vapor that dissolves off of these blockages reaches the edges of the qi field, it reenters the qi system as usable qi and helps to energize the practitioner. This process is like breaking up a logjam and then using the logs. At the center of each blockage resides the shock that created the blockage. This shock is manifested as either a physical or emotional sensation, which will be released when the blockage is finally dissolved completely. Anything that shocks a person—jolts them inside and freezes their nervous system—will create an energy blockage. Any overwhelming physical or emotional sensation received at a critical time can create such a blockage. Physical shocks can come from either pain or pleasure; emotional shocks can arise from joy or from fear, sorrow, and anger. A surprise party could create a blockage of joy as large as one caused by the pain of a surprise slap in the face. An equal amount of effort is needed to dissolve away both types of blockages.

When the sensation of the shock that created the blockage is released, it must be recognized and then let go. To either repress the sensation or hang on to it and feel it over and over will immediately recreate the blockage and you'll have to do the work of dissolving it all over again. Some practitioners repress and refuse to feel these sensations, while others mistake the heat, cold, shaking, electric, pressure release, nerve impulse, and emotional sensations for some sort of power and hold on to them. Either of these practices can completely stagnate one's progress in the dissolving practices. At its core, dissolving energy blockages is somewhat akin to relieving one's bowels. Children who refuse to let the waste out become physically ill, and children who won't flush the waste away be-

Wu Tang P.C.A. members meditating while walking in a circle.

cause they made it and therefore want to play with it, have psychological problems. Not recognizing and releasing the central shocks that created the energy blockages is akin to this childhood dilemma, and will leave one in an ill state.

When a practitioner has been dissolving energy blockages for a while, he often begins to sense a difference in the texture of some of these blockages. Whereas the average blockage used to feel rough, like a block of sugar or a rock, some of the new blockages begin to feel very smooth, like a ripe grape. Beginning to feel these blockages means that the practitioner's sense of feeling is becoming refined. He also notices that when he dissolves these smooth blockages, instead of wearing away at them unevenly like water wears away sugar cubes and rocks, he is able to wear them down in even layers, like he's peeling onions. These smooth, subtle blockages are attached to a person's energy layers, such as the emotional energy field and the thinking energy field, which extend beyond the range of the qi field. Because these energy fields extend way beyond the normal range of a person's consciousness, when the edges of these blockages are dissolved to a vapor, the vapor then implodes into the center of the blockage instead of floating out to the edges of the person's qi field. The shock at the center of these subtle blockages is almost always an emotional sensation. The process of dissolving these subtle blockages, causing the vapor to implode inward is called "inner dissolving," whereas the process of dissolving the rougher, denser blockages and letting the vapor float out to the edges of the qi field is called "outer dissolving." Once a practitioner can begin to sense these subtle, smooth blockages, all of his dissolving practices will use both the inner- and outer-dissolving processes; he can apply whichever process the encountered blockage seems to require.

These initial dissolving processes are usually practiced while either standing or sitting. Standing can be done in the martial posture of one's choice or in a basic double-weighted stance with the feet parallel, the knees slightly bent, and the spine straight and erect. Sitting can be in the classic cross-legged meditation pose or in the Daoist chair-sitting posture, known as the "emperor's posture," because legend states that this was the posture in which the emperors of China conducted court. In this posture, the practitioner sits on the edge of a chair, with the feet parallel and shoulder-width apart, the spine straight, and the hands on the knees. Breathing during these practices is always diaphragmatic and flows unbroken through the nose. Never breathe with your chest or hold your breath.

After about ten months to a year of practicing the outer and inner dissolving processes, the practitioner might notice that she has reached stabilization within the practice. This means that for the past few weeks her practice has been the same. All the little blockages that could be eradicated have been gone for a while, and she seems to remove the same amount from each of the big blockages during each practice session.

Remember that there is no such thing as perfection in this exercise, so stabilization is as good as it gets. If there exists a point of zero energy blockages, it is beyond what human life can experience.

When stabilization is achieved, it is time for the practitioner to begin the more advanced dissolving practices. The most common of these is the creation of a continuous dissolving ground wire in one's secondary consciousness. The first step in this process is for the practitioner to speed up her dissolving until she can sweep down her body in five second scans and dissolve everything—blockages that were formerly taking twenty minutes or more to work on. When this is achieved she begins to make a continuous loop of five-second scans by looping her consciousness up the back of her qi field after each downward scan, which in turn sets up the next five-second downward scan. When this continuous loop has been developed, the practitioner begins to practice drawing this loop into her secondary consciousness, thereby freeing her primary consciousness for other thoughts. The secondary consciousness is that part of the brain that allows you to sing along with an advertising jingle in the back of your mind while carrying on a conversation using your primary consciousness. One of the simplest ways to practice dissolving in the secondary consciousness is to occupy the primary consciousness with conversation while practicing dissolving. When the continuous dissolving loop in the secondary consciousness becomes second nature, it provides a dissolving ground wire, which becomes a safety device for all and any energy gathering, distribution, and discharge practices in which the primary consciousness might engage.

When practitioners have reached stabilization, they are also ready to begin practicing the specific method of dissolving energy blockages within their ba gua zhang practice. This, of course, involves dissolving blockages while walking in a circle.

First, while walking in the posture of his choice, the practitioner dissolves from the top of his qi field to his lower *dan tian,* a point a few inches below the navel. This is done with the slower-speed dissolving of the initial practices. Next, he walks and dissolves from the bottom of his qi field up to the lower *dan tian.* Then, walking in an arms-extended posture, he dissolves from the sides of his qi field inward to the lower *dan tian.* He begins to reverse the process and walk the circle as he dissolves upward from the lower *dan tian* to the top of the qi field. Next, he walks and dissolves from the lower *dan tian* downward to the bottom of the qi field.

The second stage of this process is finished when the practitioner learns to walk and dissolve from the lower *dan tian* outward to the sides of the qi field. The third stage begins with slow inward sweeps, dissolving from all the edges of the qi field inward to the lower *dan tian*. Then the flow is reversed, and the practitioner does slow outward sweeps, dissolving from the lower *dan tian* to the edges of the qi field.

Each stage of this process should be practiced for many hours—until it becomes comfortable and easy—before moving on to the next stage. When the ba gua practitioner can comfortably dissolve from the edges of the qi field to the lower *dan tian* and back again, he or she begins to speed up the process and use quick dissolving techniques, such as those used in the five-second loops. He or she then practices pulling these fast dissolving pulses into the secondary consciousness. When a practitioner can dissolve in quick, comfortable pulses within the secondary consciousness, he or she begins to pattern these dissolving pulses to the movements of all of his or her ba gua zhang practices. Each inward movement, shortening of the tissues, and compression of the joints carries an inward dissolving pulse, and each outward movement, lengthening of the tissues, and expansion of the joints carries an outward dissolving pulse. This becomes the continuous energy dissolving practice of ba gua zhang.

When a practitioner of Daoist Water Style energy blockage removal has cleared much of the congestion from the energy passages, he begins to draw energy into his body from outside his own energy systems. One of the more common methods of doing this in ba gua zhang is called the "energy gathering walk." As a practitioner walks the circumference of her circle, she coils her arms up from her sides and brings her hands over her head. She then brings her hands down in front of her, first crossing her wrists at the level of the third eye, then bringing each hand out, palm down, to the opposite shoulder. The wrists cross again at the solar plexus (palms still down), and the hands roll over each other and come to rest, palms up, at the lower *dan tian*. The fingers then turn outward and toward the back, and the arms begin another upward and outward coil to above the head. Practitioners simply walk the circle using the basic Mud Tread Step and don't attempt to coordinate the arm movements to the walk. The object is with each arm circle to feel yourself taking a bite of energy out of the sky, washing this energy down through the body, and placing any remaining energy in the lower *dan tian,* which is an energy bank. This basic ba gua method of gathering and storing qi requires an awakened nervous system—first developed through the "What's Alive and What's Dead" meditation practice—which is never in danger of being overfilled or being impeded by blockages because of the dissolving pulses or loops present in the secondary consciousness of the practitioner.

When students of ba gua zhang learn and practice the meditation methods of their art, they gain an understanding of the Daoist foundations of ba gua zhang that cannot be learned in any other manner.

8

A Moving *Yi Jing (I Ching)*

By its very name, the art of ba gua zhang, or Eight Trigram Palm, proclaims its relationship to the Chinese *Book of Changes,* the *Yi Jing* (known as the *I Ching* in the old Wade-Giles system of Romanizing the Chinese language). The *Yi Jing* maps out the phenomenon of change using a binary system consisting of solid lines to represent the *yang,* or heaven/male principle, and broken lines to represent the principle of *yin,* the earth/female aspect of duality. The foundations of Chinese philosophy teach that from emptiness, or *Wu Ji,* was born the duality of *yin* and *yang,* or *tai ji,* and that everything else is made up of combinations of *yin* and *yang.* The *Yi Jing* dissects this concept further by showing that when *yin* and *yang* are represented in sets of three lines, only eight combinations are possible. These eight patterns of three broken or solid lines each are the trigrams of the *Yi Jing* and represent the eight basic patterns of change. When combined into groups of six lines each, there are sixty-four possible patterns—the sixty-four hexagrams of the *Yi Jing.* This progression represents the potential of an ever-outward expansion of the combinations of *yin* and *yang,* following the original mathematical progression. The overall system is a method of charting the flow and relationships of change.

The *Yi Jing* is one of the foundations of Chinese culture; its origins stretch back four thousand years to the very beginning of the culture of the "Middle Kingdom." The legendary founder of Chinese culture, Fu Xi, is credited with discovering the original eight trigrams and recognizing their relationship to the phenomenon of change. A common tale states that he saw the original trigrams on the markings of the shell of an old turtle. His work was recorded in two early books, the *Yi,* or Change Book, of the Xia dynasty (2005 BC to 1766 BC) and the *Yi* of the Shang dynasty (1766 BC to 1122 BC). Unfortunately, all but fragments of these books were lost. During the Zhou dynasty (1122 BC to 221 BC), King Wen, following the work of Fu Xi, arranged the sixty-four hexagrams and wrote his Decisions on the hexagrams. His son the Duke of Zhou added the *Yao Texts,* and the renowned sage of the Zhou dynasty, Confucius, wrote his commentaries on the text and added the sequence of the hexagrams. After the sages of the Zhou dynasty added their work to the original ideas of Fu Xi, the *Yi of Zhou* became known (and revered) as the *Yi Jing*, or *Book of Changes*. All schools of Chinese thought respect the *Yi Jing* as one of the founding blocks of their ideology.

The trigrams of the *Yi Jing* are expressed in either the Pre-Heaven pattern of Fu Xi or the Post-Heaven version of King Wen. Most schools of ba gua zhang work with the Fu Xi Pre-Heaven pattern.

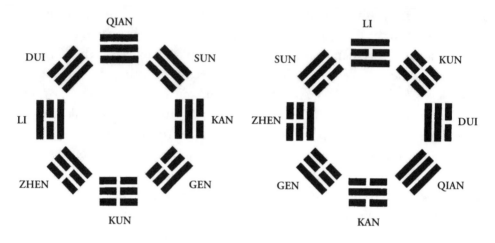

Pre-Heaven Trigram Arrangement   Post-Heaven Trigram Arrangement

Naturally, the different schools of ba gua zhang have different methods of expressing their relationship to the *Yi Jing*. Some schools have eight different hand positions, which represent the eight trigrams. As the left and right hands work in unison, they create the hexagrams. In other schools, the low, middle, and high sections of the body represent the bottom, middle, and top lines of the trigrams. When students of these schools practice a posture that represents a trigram, their bodies follow the pattern of the trigram, such as having a *yin* lower body and a *yin* middle body but a *yang* upper body when practicing a Mountain Trigram posture. Still other schools train with the ideology that each trigram relates to a part of the body, usually four external body parts and four internal organs. When they practice movements in their forms, which correspond to certain trigrams, they feel their movements and energy come from the corresponding organs and/or body parts. There are schools of ba gua zhang that practice the eight-section form, usually called Eight Palm Changes, as eight animal actions. Each animal represents a trigram and exhibits an energy that corresponds to that trigram. In these schools, the Heaven Trigram is usually related to the lion, and the Earth Trigram relates to the unicorn. Some styles of ba gua zhang have students practice walking the circle while holding eight

Ba gua zhang's Eight Steady Postures with their corresponding *Yi Jing* trigrams.

different static postures. Each of these postures corresponds to a trigram; the practice of a posture helps the practitioner to feel the energy of the corresponding trigram.

Some ba gua schools have eight palm changes, which represent the eight trigrams, and each of these palm changes contains eight techniques. These techniques are separate from the circular palm changes and taught in sixty-four straight-line drills, which then correspond with the sixty-four hexagrams of the *Yi Jing*. There are a few styles of ba gua zhang that practice eight sets of eight palm changes. Each set corresponds to a trigram, and each palm change within each set also corresponds to a trigram. Matching a palm change trigram to the trigram of its set creates a hexagram.

When Liu Hung Chieh found the Daoist circle walking practice that he felt was the forerunner of ba gua zhang, he discovered a system of circular movement, which, at its ultimate, became a physical and energetic manifestation of the *Yi Jing*. Liu Hung Chieh taught this system to his American disciple, B. K. Frantzis, who introduced this Moving Yi Jing system to the West.

B. K. Frantzis and Liu Hung Chieh

After doing the practices that strengthened their bodies, opened their energy channels, and gathered energy supplies, the Daoists of China's southwest mountains who taught Liu Hung Chieh the Moving Yi Jing would begin developing the energy-change patterns that are symbolized by the trigrams of the *Yi Jing*. The founding ideology of this system is that these energy-change patterns are *the* eight basic patterns of all change. Changes become more complex when the eight basic patterns are combined, creating the hexagram patterns or the patterns of the mathematical progression that moves outward from the hexagrams.

The founders of this system realized that a simple method of creating change was to walk around a circle and then change direction. They then developed eight methods of changing direction while walking around a circle, which manifests the eight basic change patterns that are represented by the eight trigrams of the *Yi Jing*. Over time, they came to realize that different physical-movement patterns could be used to express the same pattern of change, but that the same energy-change pattern was always inside the corresponding trigram movement. The eight basic energy-change patterns, sometimes referred to as energy-change matrixes, are:

Heaven Trigram

Heaven—This pure *yang,* all-male energy moves upward and outward while being effortless, endless, and emotionless. It is the creative foundation of the other energy-change patterns and is often compared to the energy of adolescent male sexuality. This energy-change pattern corresponds to the physical patterns of the various single palm changes in ba gua zhang.

Earth Trigram

Earth—This pure *yin,* all-female energy sinks downward, soft and heavy, while drawing inward. It is a receptive energy, which nurtures the energy of Heaven and brings manifestation from the creative potential of pure *yang*. This energy-change pattern can be compared to the sexuality of an ancient earth-mother symbol, such as the Venus of Willendorf. The Earth energy-change pattern corresponds to the physicality of the various double palm changes within the vast variety of ba gua zhang styles.

The other six energy-change patterns are combinations of Heaven and Earth energies. It is therefore imperative that ba gua zhang practitioners understand the first two energy-change patterns before attempting to comprehend the other six patterns.

Wind Trigram

Wind—Like its namesake, the Wind energy-change pattern constantly changes from amorphous to solid and back to amorphous. You can't touch the wind, but it can knock you down. When manifested physically, this energy-change pattern allows a ba gua boxer to seem to disappear and then suddenly crash into their opponent with the power of a tornado. Wind energy makes one seem to be everywhere at once, but nowhere that they can be touched. With Wind energy, one turns around their central core.

Thunder Trigram

Thunder—This is the energy of a shock wave. It is a *yang* explosion followed by a series of *yin* reverberations. The energy-change pattern of Thunder is the sudden shock that comes out of nowhere. When applied martially, Thunder energy is the quick, multiple-striking technique that drives reverberating energy deep into an opponent's organs. When used therapeutically, Thunder energy is the vibrating massage that relieves tension and congestion within a patient.

Fire Trigram

Fire—This energy-change pattern clings, coils, and spirals. It is *yang* and firm on the edges, but soft and *yin* at its center. This is the energy of a flame that coils around your Christmas tree, clings to your curtains as it spirals up them, and then circles into your ceiling. In all of its applications, martial and otherwise, this is the energy that sticks to another person and coils around him.

Water Trigram

Water—This is the pattern of a pounding wave. This pattern is soft and *yin* on the edges, but at its center is a solid *yang* mass, much like how the cap and undertow of a wave can be frothy, but at its center is a solid mass of heavy water. The Water energy-change pattern is considered to be the dark and destructive aspects of the water element. It is manifested physically by using the *yin* aspects of the body's opening and closing movements.

Mountain Trigram

Mountain—Mountains radiate stillness, but the Mountain change pattern is a compressed stillness in the center that has the potential to explode outward, emitting light energy in every direction simultaneously. This is akin to the internal pressures of a volcano, which give it its explosive abilities. In this change, one coils his or her energy inward to a momentarily still place and then allows it to explode outward. When doing this, one's body seems to shrink and then grow.

Lake Trigram

Lake—The ancient ideogram for this trigram literally meant "a depression in the earth which holds water and makes people happy." The first Westerners to translate this thought this meant that lakes are fun to sit by, boat in, swim in, and so on, which is why they make people happy. Actually, the ancient Chinese had little time for these leisure activities and the depression in the earth that held water and made them happy was probably a marsh. They could grow rice there and then have something to eat. This energy is the positive aspects of water. It is a subtle energy-change pattern that is not consistent, and yet it never recreates any of the previous energy-change patterns. The Lake energy-change pattern is the form of formlessness. This pattern is difficult to understand and even more difficult to manifest, as it has many different forms. Its physical manifestations often look erratic and undisciplined.

These eight energy-change patterns, or matrixes of change, are developed with the practice of their corresponding palm changes. Experienced ba gua zhang practitioners, who have solid foundations in their physical styles and have awakened their nervous systems and opened their energy channels, begin to feel these energy patterns as they practice their palm changes. By focusing the attention and applying the mind's intent to the feelings of these energy-change patterns, a practitioner can strengthen these feelings, making them a bit less subtle and a bit more concrete.

When a practitioner can feel an energy-change matrix quite clearly while practicing the corresponding palm change, he begins to practice developing the energy-change pattern within seated meditation. First, the practitioner will practice a palm change until the feeling of the corresponding energy-change pattern is strong and revved up within him. Then, he will suddenly sit in a meditation posture and try to maintain the feeling of the energy-change pattern. When the feeling fades, he stands up and again begins to practice the corresponding palm change until the energy is strong again. He again tries to sit with the feeling of the energy change. After practicing this process for a reasonable length of time, trying each of the eight palm changes, a practitioner can simply sit and bring up the feeling of an energy-change matrix, as well as bring up the same pattern by practicing the corresponding palm change. At this point, the energy-change matrixes have become fully developed and can be combined or separated from their corresponding palm changes.

Ba gua zhang practitioners must then test the development of these energy-change patterns by trying to manifest them in a manner that can be ascertained by someone else. The standard method of starting this testing process is to practice either basic Soft Hands or simple Push Hands with another ba gua practitioner who is somewhat familiar with the concept of the eight energy-change patterns. Each practitioner in turn attempts to manifest an energy-change pattern within his or her technique and then checks with the training partner to see if he or she felt what the practitioner was attempting to manifest (i.e., up and out, in and down, clinging and coiling, stillness to light, and so on). When a ba gua practitioner becomes familiar with working the energy-change patterns within their Push Hands and Soft Hands practices, she then begins to move her energy-change practices into her sparring techniques. At that level, she works on recognizing an opponent's oncoming energy-change pattern and transposing it into a more favorable situation through the application of her own energy-change pattern. Once mastered, this technique can be applied to any confrontational aspect of the ba gua practitioner's life.

When the eight basic energy-change patterns have been fully developed, the ba gua zhang practitioner can begin to combine these energy-change patterns with palm changes other than the corresponding ones. By combining the Water energy with the Earth palm change, the Heaven energy-change matrix with the Fire palm change, or any of the other sixty-two possible combinations, practitioners can create physical and energetic manifestations of the sixty-four hexagrams of the *Yi Jing*. Sometimes, this practice is learned as sixty-four specific movement patterns. It can also be practiced by simply inserting an energy-change pattern into the required physical palm change and letting the energy lead the physical movement. These practices help students of the *Yi Jing* to understand the classic on physical and energetic levels as well as on an intellectual basis.

This practice of a Moving Yi Jing is usually learned in conjunction with the Daoist teachings of the eight energy layers of all sentient beings, known as the Eight Energy Bodies. These layers or Energy Bodies are:

1. **The Physical Energy Body.** This is the energy within the flesh that makes it alive.
2. **The Qi Energy Body.** This is the life-force energy that travels through channels in the flesh, is stored in the lower *dan tian,* and emanates from the body to form the qi field.
3. **The Emotional Energy Body.** This is the source of all emotions. It

stretches from a person's center outward to the level of the stars that can be seen with the naked eye. It is interesting to note that a being's emotional outbursts can ripple energy fields in all directions outward to the edges of their Emotional Body. From this point, each of the energy bodies stretches farther away from its origins at the being's center.

4.   **The Thinking Energy Body.** This is where thoughts coalesce before they are intellectualized. It is the source of all true meditation.

5.   **The Psychic Energy Body.** This is the energy from which all psychic abilities emanate. Beings with strong connections to this energy body often balance that with frail connections to their first three energy bodies.

6.   **The Causal Energy Body.** This is where the seed of every cause that creates an effect is born. It's where and how one makes things happen. A being that could completely control this energy body would be a true magician, but would probably have a weaker connection to his or her first three energy bodies than even the psychic.

7.   **The Body of Individuality.** This is where everything that differentiates a being from everything else is formed.

8.   **The Body of Dao.** This is the energy layer that connects a being to everything else in existence.

The goal of Daoist meditators within this system is to access and feel all eight of their energy bodies and then to bind them into one coherent being. For the ba gua practitioner, each of the eight energy-change patterns corresponds to one of the energy bodies: the Heaven change corresponds to the Physical Energy Body, the Earth change to the Qi Energy Body, the Wind change to the Emotional Energy Body, the Thunder change to the Thinking Energy Body, the Fire change to the Psychic Energy Body, the Water change to the Causal Energy Body, the Mountain change to the Body of Individuality, and the Lake change to the Body of Dao.

The energy-change patterns can be used in meditation as gateways to accessing their corresponding energy bodies. This means that if a practitioner wants a better connection with his or her body physical body, he or she can work on it by practicing the Heaven palm change and its corresponding, pure *yang* energy-change matrix. If a ba gua student is trying to be in better touch with his or her emotions, he or she can work on the Wind palm change, with its amorphous-to-solid energy-change pattern.

This gives ba gua zhang practitioners a method with which to work on changes in their lives. For example, if a practitioner has a relationship problem, which has him in a constant state of emotional turmoil, and he needs to acquire some clear, emotionless thought, he must begin with the fact that to get out of something you must first get deeply into it. The practitioner will begin to walk the circle and periodically perform the Wind palm change and feel its connection to his Emotional Energy Body. As he does this, his emotional intensity will increase. When this intensity is at a boiling point, the practitioner suddenly changes his technique to a Thunder palm change; as he performs the movements and feels the shock-wave energy, he'll most likely forge a connection with his Thinking Energy Body and begin to get his much-needed clear thoughts. He can continue to practice the Thunder palm change as his mind works out his problem. This process could be reversed for the practitioner who is caught in a thinking loop and needs better emotional clarity.

When you are able to somewhat manipulate change in your life in this manner, it is essential that you are familiar with the patterns of the flow of change. The best way to accomplish this is to study the names and sequences of the sixty-four hexagrams of the Yi Jing. It is said that the Dao of Yi, or the Way of Change, is contained in the names and sequences of the hexagrams. By repeatedly reading and meditating on the names and sequences of the hexagrams, you will develop a feel for the flow of change. The sequences are short, and all sixty-four of them can easily be read in a half-hour to forty-five minutes. After some study of this flow of change, ba gua practitioners recognize the larger wave patterns of the upper cannon and the smaller waves of change recorded in the lower cannon of the Yi Jing. Practitioners begin to recognize where in the flow pattern they currently reside and understand that they can manipulate change in the direction of the flow (though not in cross currents to the general flow of change). It is a matter of literally understanding the old adage of being smart enough to know what you can change and wise enough to know what you can't change.

As ba gua zhang practitioners become familiar with the flow of change, they begin to recognize the stillness behind this flow. This is known as the constant behind the phenomenon of change. Some say that this constant is simply the fact that you can count on things to constantly change, so there is consistency of change. On a meditative level, this manifests as a still place where change stops. Ba gua practitioners learn to recognize the moments where change pauses and to rest and rejuvenate within these still places before their next roller-coaster ride on the phenomenon of change.

Today, most practitioners of ba gua zhang are not likely to have to use their skills in life-threatening, close-quarter combat situations. And although the practices that have developed their martial skills will have also improved their physical and mental health and perhaps helped to increase their longevity, they might have been able to accomplish all this with other practices. The unique quality of the art of ba gua zhang, which makes it a skill of unparalleled usefulness in the modern age, is its application as a Moving Yi Jing and its ability to help practitioners understand the phenomenon of change.

Acknowledgments

This book is dedicated to the memory of the late Master B. P. Chan, who was my first ba gua zhang teacher and the one who introduced the art to me. I am especially thankful for the many years of ba gua training with internal martial arts master B. K. Frantzis, who introduced me to the depths of the art as a meditation, energy, and life practice as well as a premier combat art. Without Master Frantzis' awe-inspiring demonstrations of his skills, I might not have realized the deep potentials held within the art of ba gua zhang. I would also like to thank Jiang Jian Ye, a master of myriad styles, for so generously teaching us the Old Eight Palms of Dong Hai Chuan.

We are eternally grateful to the most knowledgeable and respected grandmaster in all of Cheng Style ba gua zhang, Liu Jing Ru, who not only introduced to us to the classical methods and teachings of the Cheng Style through his traditional and professional teachings in Beijing, but also continues to inspire us with his youthful demeanor, energetic presence, and positive attitude on life.

We cannot thank enough Sifu Jamie Dibdin of Wu Tang P.C.A. in Frankfurt, Germany for the years of dedicated support and for our many successful ba gua zhang workshops in his school. We will also never forget the time spent in Chris Chappell's Real Taoism Studio in London and the great ba gua zhang workshops made possible there through Chris' dedication to promoting the events. We're also grateful to the president of Healing Tao U.S.A. University, Michael Winn, for his years of support and for sponsoring our retreats in his summer programs.

A very special thank you must go out to ultra-talented artist Joshua Vogel, who drew the nineteen illustrations of the ba gua zhang masters that appear in this book. Josh is also a dedicated martial artist and skilled ba gua zhang practitioner and tournament fighter. I would like to thank my friend, ba gua master John Painter, for supplying the quote from the genius of the London School of Economics, Richard Henry Tawney, which appears at the beginning of the history chapter. I would also like to thank John for the many insights into the art of ba gua zhang he's provided over the years.

The countless students who have practiced ba gua zhang over the past thirty years at Wu Tang Physical Culture Association are greatly appreciated for their discipline and support. We also want to thank those who contributed their time to assist with the photos of the martial applications in this book: Jamie Dibdin, Moritz Dornauf,

William Shackman, Steve Nardi, Jonathan Molenar, Dion Workman, Asako Kitaori, and Jia Qi.

We want to thank our publishing mentor, Jesse O'Brian, for his years of support and guidance. We are extremely grateful to our editor, Anastasia McGhee, for all of her patience and work on our project, and we are also thankful for the beautiful design work of the talented Susan Quasha.

Most of the credit for seeing this book come into existence must go to my co-author and partner, Tina Chunna Zhang—without her dedication, hard work, and persistence, this work would never have seen the light of day.

—FRANK ALLEN, JULY 2006

About the Authors

Frank Allen

Frank Allen has studied and practiced the internal energy arts since 1973. He was an early student of Master B. P. Chan, from whom he learned the internal martial arts of ba gua zhang, xing yi quan, and tai ji quan, as well as the healing art of qi gong. Frank began studying with Master B. K. Frantzis in 1976, and over the next two-and-a-half decades he studied Frantzis' Internal Arts, including ba gua zhang, tai ji quan, xing yi quan nei gong, and Daoist meditation. He has also studied the internal martial arts with Master Jiang Jian Yee. Currently, Frank travels annually to Beijing, where he studies Cheng Style ba gua zhang with Grandmaster Liu Jing Ru and Northern Wu Style tai ji quan with Grandmaster Li Bing Ci. In 2007 Allen became the formal disciple of Cheng Style Ba Gua Grandmaster Liu Jing Ru. Since 1984 Allen has been the disciple of Western boxing master Verne "The Bulldog" Williams.

Frank was the first person certified to teach the ba gua of B. K. Frantzis and has been certified to teach ba gua and tai ji quan by Jiang Jian Ye.

In 1979 Allen founded The Wu Tang Physical Culture Association of New York City, which has a brother branch in Frankfurt, Germany. Over the years, the Wu Tang P.C.A. has produced many tournament champions and a core of competent instructors.

With Tina Chunna Zhang, Frank Allen is the co-author of *Classical Northern Wu Style Tai Ji Quan: The Fighting Art of the Manchurian Palace Guard,* and he has authored or co-authored over thirty articles for major martial arts and Daoist-related periodicals in the U.S. He and the Wu Tang P.C.A. video production crew have produced twelve instructional videos covering the subjects of ba gua zhang, tai ji quan, xing yi quan, Daoist philosophy, meditation, and the Fighting for Health system.

Allen teaches workshops around the U.S. and in Europe in addition to teaching his regular classes in New York City. He has been the internal martial arts instructor of Healing Tao U.S.A. University Summer Retreats since 1999, and in 2005 he started a joint Healing Tao U.S.A.–Wu Tang P.C.A. Ba Gua Zhang Instructor Certification Program.

For more information about Frank Allen, please visit the web site http://www.wutang-pca.com.

Tina Chunna Zhang

Tina Chunna Zhang has been interested in Chinese martial arts and dance since her childhood days in Beijing, China; she moved to the U.S. in the 1980s. She has studied and trained with the most skillful and experienced internal martial arts masters in China. She is a disciple of Northern Wu Style Tai Ji Quan Master Li Bing Ci, the president of the Beijing Wu Style Tai Ji Quan Research Center. She is also the formal disciple of Classical Cheng Style Ba Gua Zhang Grandmaster Lui Jing Ru.

Zhang has won two gold medals in women's sparring in Chinese martial arts tournaments. In the U.S., she is a nationally ranked medalist in both tai ji quan and ba gua zhang forms, weapons, and Push Hands. She was the U.S. National Champion in Women's Wu Style Tai Ji Quan in 2005. Tina is also the co-author of *Classical Northern Wu Style Tai Ji Quan: The Fighting Art of the Manchurian Palace Guard,* and the founder of the Earth Energy Qi Gong for Women program, which is taught in classes at the Wu Tang P.C.A. and in workshops and retreats around the world.

Serving as a cultural bridge between the East and West, and as a professional tai ji quan and ba gua zhang instructor and personal trainer, Tina Zhang has helped many people with their physical and emotional health through her training methods. She actively teaches tai ji quan, ba gua zhang, and qi gong classes, and retreats in New York, as well as workshops in Europe.

For more information about Tina Chunna Zhang, please visit the web sites http//:www.wutangpca.com and http://www.earthqigong.com.